Stitches In Time

A Collection
by Elizabeth Donaldson

Copyright © 2012 by Elizabeth Donaldson
First Edition – September 2012

ISBN
978-1-4602-0383-5 (Paperback)

All rights reserved.

No part of this publication may be reproduced in any form, or by any means, electronic or mechanical, including photocopying, recording, or any information browsing, storage, or retrieval system, without permission in writing from the publisher.

Published by:

FriesenPress
Suite 300 – 852 Fort Street
Victoria, BC, Canada V8W 1H8

www.friesenpress.com

Distributed to the trade by The Ingram Book Company

Table of Contents

Foreword _____ 1

Early life in Box Alder _____ 5

    First Memories   8
    Saturday's Child   26
    School Days And Teachers   36
    Teachers at Box Alder School   48
    Christmas   52
    The Two Churches In Box Alder   57
    High School Years   69
    My First Teaching Job   76

Nostalgia _____ 97

    Christmas Concert Time   98
    The Kitchen Stove   103
    As Time Goes By   106
    Corsets   111
    The Shadow Of A Doubt (Fiction Based On Truth)   115
    Warmth   120

Family & All That Kind Of Thing _____ 127

    Branches On The Family Tree   129
    Family Matters–Our Life In Burriss   140
    Chickens, Geese, Turkeys And Quail   165

Raising Cattle In Burriss _____ 173

    Hockey   180

    Fire At Donaldsons March 31, 1973   186

    The Old White Chev   190

My Mother _____ 197

    Prairie River   198

    Rainycrest- The Second Time Around   205

    Summer–July 1992   211

    My Mother's Hands–Summer 1989.   213

    August, 2000   215

    Walking—1990   217

    A Little Romance   219

    Homeless- February 2000   222

    The Call–January 2001   225

Selected Poetry _____ 229

    Poems   231

    The Millionaire   232

    If You Could Know   233

    Violets   234

    First Snowshoe   235

    Lavallee Lounge   237

    The Wanderer   238

    The Tower   239

    Chores   240

    My Crooked Eye   241

    Late Spring   242

    Lines For To Day   243

    November Promise   245

    Memory   246

If Wishes Came True	248
The Sisters	249
Things My Mother Taught Me	250
Swimming	252
LESSONS	253
TO A 4H C ALF	254
The Gift	256
Cosmetic Surgery	257
Treasures	258
The Morning After	259
The Tamaracks	261
Weeds	262
I Remember –	263

Time's Passages And Thoughts _ _ _ _ _ _ _ _ _ _ _ _ 265

The Remnants	266
Food	272
Burriss School Destroyed By Fire	285
Making Connections	289
None So Deaf	299
One Day At A Time.	305
Closing	314

Dedication

This book is lovingly dedicated to my grandchildren and great-grandchildren.

Acknowledgements

The items on the cover of the book are all very familiar to me. The buffet was part of a set of the nicest furniture that my parents owned. My son Brian has restored it and it is in his home in Thunder Bay. The wall clock hung in the home of my grandparents and had been a wedding present for them in 1898. My brother Eric had it repaired and after many years passed it on to my daughter Emily Mosbeck. My mother's sewing basket has been passed on to Leanne Donaldson. The quilt was sewn by me in my quilting phase. Leanne designed the cover of this book.

I thank all my family for the interest shown and for their support and technical help of this project and for being patient and understanding of my absorption with it in the past months. They have all been involved in the process but none of them has read the complete book. I think I can safely assure them that it will be a onetime venture.

I also thank my extended family and my friends who have shown such interest and confidence in this project.

Foreword

*I*t may now be safe to admit that I have always wanted to write a book. It seems that plots were forever boiling in the back of my mind, ready to be put on paper as the great Canadian novel. However, at a certain stage in life you realize it is not going to happen, just as you realize you are never going to see the pyramids along the Nile. When I was given the wonderful opportunity to be the editor of two local history books I found that writing about other people's lives might go hand in hand with writing about my own. Each person's life holds certain defining moments that set the path for future actions. Work on these books was such a moment for me and sharpened my desire and need to write.

I viewed the list of writings that I had done, some during the work on the history book, some before and much after the completion of that, and began to wonder what to do with it. Should I copy it just for family or go a step further? I have led an ordinary life but realize that everyone has a story. I greatly enjoy biographies and autobiographies and am especially interested in the early and formative years of people and maybe others also like this kind of reading. My writing might add to others that have been written about local history. I have found the books by local authors extremely interesting and valuable in documenting stories and experiences of a different time.

How do I describe the writings that I have gathered together? There may be many things that they are, but most certainly more that they are not. There are elements of the autobiographical in what I have written, but that is not the whole focus of my work and sometimes I go off on a tangent and just write about things that cross my mind.

This book is not totally about the distant past although I have expressed some of my memories and thoughts of "those dear, dead days beyond recall." Someone once said 'that we write not to be understood but to understand', and one's past sometimes determines how we react to issues in the future. William Faulkner wrote, "I never know what I think about something until I read what I have written," and that might explain writings such as "Food" or "The Remnants."

My writing is not in chronological order and does not follow any set pattern. This book is not a poetry book although I have included some of my thoughts in poems. I have found that a certain line or phrase will keep running through my head and will not go away until I sit down and actually put something on paper.

My mother has been a great influence on my life and though I have written about her, this book is not totally about her. I wrote of her in her later years and some may find similarities in a situation with an aging parent. It was one of the joys of my life, with my sister Marion, over twenty years ago to put together and see to printing the small book of our mother's writing that many have enjoyed.

My family might be described as my greatest defining moment and the most meaningful. Sometimes when telling of an aspect, often humorous, of our family life, someone would say to me, "You should write a book" so while this book tells some of that, it is not wholly about my family.

I have titled my book STITCHES IN TIME, because it is not whole and complete, but rather like a patchwork quilt with bits and pieces of my thoughts, stitched together in no particular fashion, with threads of fact and some fantasy or fiction. Like an old fashioned crazy quilt it is made up of old and worn patches of revived memories, but also with some new bits to brighten and strengthen the completed article.

Some may question why I have included certain "patches" or may say that I have left out whole sections, but I have put the pieces together in the fashion that seems right to me at this time. Some of my recollections of growing up and living in the Rainy River District may stir memories of your own and you may desire to piece your own quilt. You do not have to be famous to write of your thoughts or memories. Remember, everyone has a story.

Early life in Box Alder

"I consider it the best part of an education to have been born and brought up in the country."
A B Alcott

- First Memories
- Saturday's Child
- School Days and Teachers
- Christmas
- The Two Churches in Box Alder
- High School Days
- My First Teaching Job

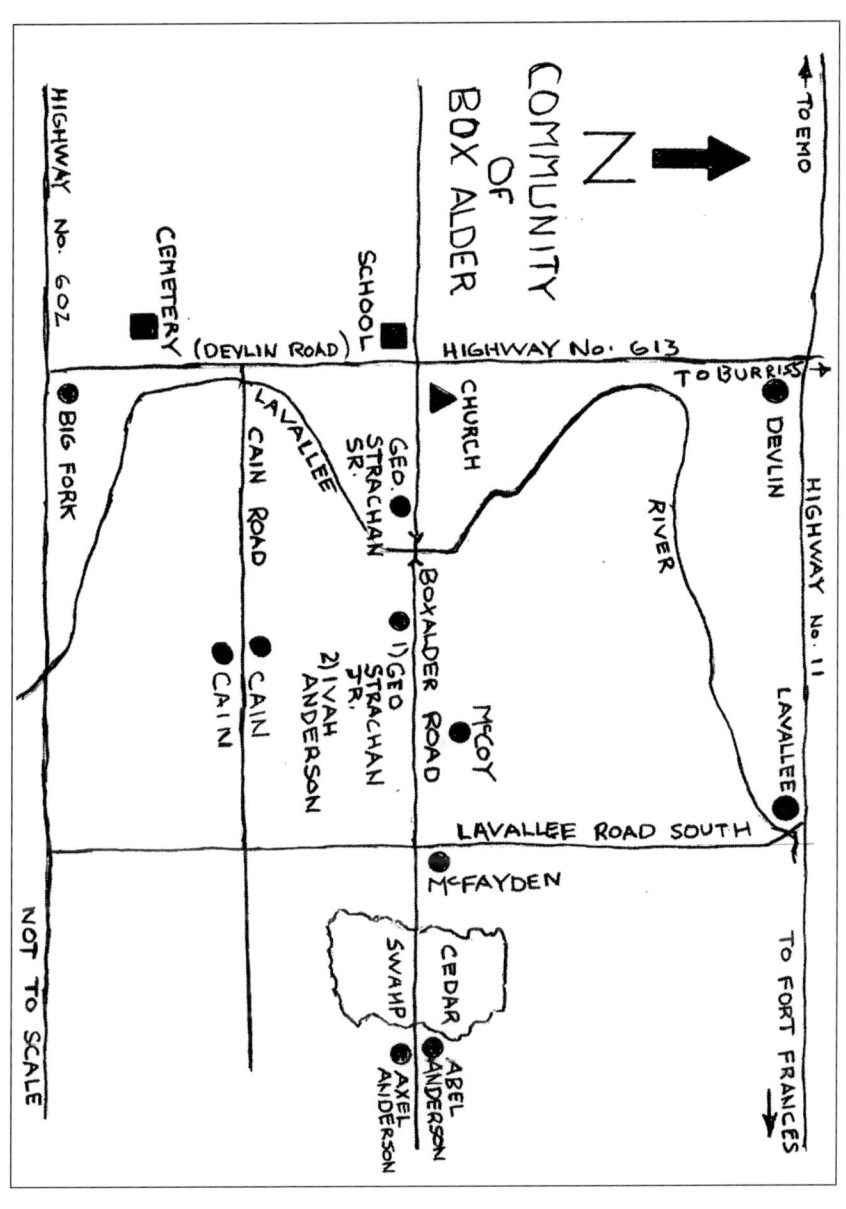

Map of Box Alder

First Memories

I lie looking up through the golden-green light filtered by the giant leaves and sturdy ruby stalks. I am drowsy, and faintly from far away, I can hear my mother's voice. It does not occur to me to answer as I am still under the spell of sleep. At last I rouse and pull myself to my feet to see my mother coming toward me. She takes me in her arms, half laughing half scolding, as she says that she has been looking for me and here I am asleep in the rhubarb patch.

I was about four years old and that is perhaps the earliest conscious memory I have of the mother who nurtured my siblings and me so lovingly. We were still living east of McFayden's corner through the sinister cedar swamp that is in all our memories. I do have memories of living at that old place and of Eric and me following Uncle Tom as he plowed with King and Riley, the Anderson horses that were quite spirited.

Grandma Anderson lived a little further up the road from our house but on the opposite side. We had a path where we could cut across the field to get to her house. Tom, Emma and Helen lived with Grandma in the big house that our grandfather Abel had built for his family before he died in 1926. Uncle Carl was also part of our lives but he was not home very often as he worked in the bush camps. Emma was a very pretty girl and I have snatches of memories of her. Helen had brown eyes and hair and a sweet smile. She lay on the leather couch one day when Doctor Young came, walking past the sand cherry bushes where I was playing, to see her. Helen had diabetes and died in 1938 so I would be past three years old. Uncle Tom preferred to walk to LaVallee from Box Alder for the groceries and the mail rather than hitch up the horses. I recall him coming up the road with a huge loaded packsack. Mom would have a chair ready for him and he would wearily swing the pack over onto the chair.

Grandma was a little Swedish lady who spoke quite broken English. She called me "Liz-abet." I don't recall her ever holding or hugging or caressing us in any way but we loved her and seemed to know that she loved us. She made strong coffee and a delicious brown toffee that was boiled and poured into tin pie pans. When it had cooled enough Grandmas would whack it against the edge of the sideboard and it would shatter into lovely shards and pieces ready to be sucked and chewed.

We had heard stories of our grandfather Abel. He had come from Sweden and was a talented carpenter, millwright and blacksmith and was able to turn his hand to many things. He apparently was quite rough and ready in his younger days and we heard tales of drinking and fights in barrooms. He was said to have a knife scar across his stomach from such a fight. Uncle Tom told these stories of the "Pa" that he idolized. I formed a picture of a stern, perhaps harsh man who became ill, but built the house in the country for his family to make a living on the farm before he died.

Many years later I revised my opinion when Cousin Bill Anderson gave me a letter written by Abel to Anna before their marriage in 1903. A large black trunk held certain family papers and photographs including this letter. It was written in Swedish in excellent handwriting with flourishes on the capitals. Abel was living in Unity, Wisconsin and Anna in Minneapolis. With the help of a Swedish-English dictionary I translated the letter as best I could. There was no mistaking that it was a love letter and he was laying out plans for their wedding. His first wife had died and he had one small son Carl. (Karl in the letter). Anna is called "My Darling Friend" and he makes plans for selling his farm and perhaps taking a trip back to Sweden after the marriage. He wrote, "So it seems that everything is going the way I had planned and soon you, my friend, and I will meet and I can take you in my arms and hold you close to me. And I hope that we don't have to part for a long time. Yes, I long for you more than you imagine. I must close now with many hundred kisses to you, my friend."

It thrilled me to see this letter and it changed my vision of the stern, cranky old man I had held in my mind. Now I could see the darkly handsome and ardent young suitor who had enough romance in his makeup to write such a touching letter showing consideration and the desire to please his "darling friend." I felt better knowing that Grandma had had romance in her life and was glad that she had saved this letter.

I can see that house in my mind, the kitchen and the pantry with the shelves lined with newspaper. There was a big cook stove and the table, covered with oilcloth, always held a jar full of teaspoons ready for stirring cream and sugar into that strong black coffee. The living room had a heater and severe oak furniture, a sofa and chair with black leather cushions, and a library table. Big portraits in wooden frames hung on the walls. Grandma's bedroom was off the living room. It was stark and plain and clean with a crocheted spread on the bed. Her dresser had a container that held the big bone hairpins that were a lovely amber colour. Grandma's dark hair was very long, braided, and done up in a big bun securely anchored by these pins.

There were no frills or softening touches in my grandmother's house but in my mind it was a wonderful home. To go upstairs you had to pass, on the landing, an enormous stuffed moose head with huge antlers. Its glass eyes seemed to drill into mine and I would plaster myself against the wall as far from this thing as I could get and go up the remaining stairs. The four rooms upstairs were neat and immaculate with heavy dark furniture.

I find it odd now that I can remember my grandmother's house quite plainly, but do not have clear a picture in my mind of the little house that my father had built where we lived. We must have spent a great deal of time at my grandmother's house. I remember the most about my brother Eric but I had an older brother Alan and a younger sister Marion.

Axel Anderson Sawing Wood with Eric. Elizabeth is in background.

Farther east lived a bachelor named Charlie Matthews whose shack was on the north side of the road. One day several cars were seen on the road. This was not a common occurrence and we heard from the adults that Charlie had shot himself. This meant little to Eric and me, for we were about four and six but we were very curious. With Eric as the instigator we went up the road to see what was going on. There were several men there and one asked gruffly, "What are you kids doing here?" They gave us each a little red tin box that had held dynamite caps and sent us on our way. I'm sure we looked like ragged little urchins.

We started school from this place that was nearly three miles from the Box Alder School. It was a long walk and night and morning we had to go through the cedar swamp. It grew dense and dark and tangled right up to the narrow road. The sun seemed never to reach through those thick dark green branches that drooped to the mossy ground. We were all afraid of what might lurk in there, bears, wolves, monsters –who knew what was waiting to pounce? My brothers were quite protective of me in many ways but in that swamp it was every man for himself and I struggled to keep up with them. Halfway through there was a large crooked tamarack tree and when I reached that, I knew I would soon be through. I wonder if Mom knew how terrified we were, as in her book she mentions walking through there at night. Now I think that someone must have teased us about imaginary dangers in this dense dark region and we built it up in our minds but we never forgot this.

We were poor and Mom had a hard time providing for us after our father died. We know that now, but suffered no feelings of deprivation at the time. We looked at the Eaton's catalogue and saw the wonders that it held, but we just knew that we could not have exotic things, such as the Eaton's Beauty doll dressed in silks and satins with hair in perfect ringlets. These things were foreign to us and anyhow I preferred the jackknives and BB guns that my brothers coveted.

My father died when I was past the age of four so I have just a few flashes of memory of him. I know he had dark hair and that he smiled at me. A child just takes many things for granted and I remember sitting on the bed with him, not knowing that he was very ill. He peeled a peach for us to share and this was probably not long before he died at our home.

Many years later when I was in Teachers' College we were watching a nature film from the National Film Board. On the screen came the image of a mother partridge and her big brood of little chicks. Suddenly I clearly remembered my father bringing a bunch of baby partridge home in his hat. It was such a vivid image and I could see his face as he bent over the tiny chicks. I wrote my mother to ask her if such a thing had happened. She replied that once Daddy was hunting and came across the remains of a mother partridge that a fox had killed. He gathered up the family and brought them home in his hat. They tried to raise them as domestic chicks but it was not long until they all died. So I had one more memory of my father to tuck away.

We lived at this place next door to Grandma and Uncle Tom until I was about seven when Mom sold the farm to J.A .Mathieu for his game preserve in 1942 and we moved to the farm that she bought from my grandfather George Strachan. This was where my mother had been born and was brought up.

My father had died in 1939 and Mom continued living on their farm until 1942. How she managed in those years I cannot imagine for there was no help from social programs available. Without doubt there would be support from her family. J.A. Mathieu bought the farm for his game preserve and moved the house for us, and Alan said that Lloyd Green from Box Alder was the driver of the big truck. The house was put up on skids and Alan remembered that a cow was tied on behind. I do know that we were all in the house as we moved. After the move we were not as isolated as we were closer to the school, church and neighbours and our world opened up considerably.

The house was not large or very well furnished by the standards of today but we were always comfortable. There were two small bedrooms and one big room at first. Our father had built a bay window with a seat and storage space under the seat. It was a cozy place to sit but probably not very practical. The chimney had a "cubby hole" with three drawers where socks and mittens and also books or a few toys could be stored. My father was quite artistic and also a good carpenter and had built a kitchen cupboard and desk that we always used. The house was built of cedar wood, with cedar siding, cedar shingles and insulated with cedar shavings. We did not live in a cedar swamp for nothing. My mother was fond of saying, "If this house ever caught fire it would go up like a paper box!" and was always particular about cleaning the stovepipes and keeping things away from the stoves. I do remember a chimney fire but no harm came of it.

Sometime after we moved, Uncle Bill Strachan removed the bay window and built a small kitchen with a sloping roof onto the house and brick siding was put on to make it warmer. There was a cook stove in the kitchen with a warming oven and a reservoir for heating water. Those old cook stoves were quite wonderful and our lives centered around it. We ate in the kitchen but if there was company we ate in the big room at the table that had leaves to extend it. This table was part of a set with the chairs and a buffet that held Mom's "good" dishes, the Aladdin lamp and many other things. Mom and Daddy had bought this set from Roy and Muriel Barker in 1934 when they sold out and moved to Geraldton.

Mom seemed to be able to do almost anything. She was a good cook and housekeeper, did all the barn chores, was wonderful with animals and took such good care of them. She harnessed and drove the horses, milked the cows, helped with haying, went for the cows, mended and patched, walked miles picking berries and fed a lot of hungry people. Of course we all learned to help and to do these things with her. From her I learned that there is a certain satisfaction to be had in hard work, that the sooner you get started at a task the sooner you are finished, and that any job that needs to be done, no matter how lowly, has its own dignity. Mom did not complain but just got on with the work. She was always able to see the funny side of things and she taught us to laugh even when things weren't going well. Heaven knows she had setbacks enough in her time, but she always remained a country woman at heart.

I recall the hog cholera when so many of the pigs died and the rest had to be destroyed. It was so awful to see the dead sows lying there with their babies all so sick. A huge pit was dug and the dead animals hauled away and dumped there. Lime was thrown over them and then a fire lit to burn the carcasses. What a loss that was to lose so many animals. The barn had to be cleaned and disinfected with Creocide and we all worked at that. Even Grandpa Strachan with his cane was out in the barn and I was complaining about the old broom I had to use. Grandpa said, "A new broom sweeps clean but an old broom knows the corners best." This is a good thing to remember, at least I have never forgotten it.

Mom liked to get the barn chores all done up at night before we saw to our own comfort. There were plenty of chores for all of us, especially in the winter. She would have started by the time we arrived from school about four-thirty. It was a tremendous amount of work as all the animals were tied in stalls. The hay had to be forked into mangers and some cattle or horses got oats or grain. The pigs were fed their chop and water, eggs were gathered and hens were fed. We milked the cows by lantern light in winter and the milk brought to the house to separate. The skim milk was given to calves or pigs or the barn cats.

The house chores were done also. We carried in wood and heater blocks and carried out ashes. We carried pails of water from the pump over the stile to fill the reservoir on the stove and carried the pails of drinking and cooking water. We emptied the slop pails and the chamber pails. Tubs of snow were carried in to fill the barrel behind the stove. These chores were done every day and many were done twice a day. I don't think that we complained too much as we knew that all our school friends were doing the same things. We took the chores for granted, as they were part of our everyday life.

There were tasks on Saturday added to our regular chores. The animals stalls were cleaned out and fresh new bedding put down. Gutters were well cleaned out and if possible the manure was loaded onto the stone boat and one of the horses hitched up to haul it away to be spread on the fields. In the house the ashes from the stoves were emptied, stoves were cleaned and all the nickel and porcelain parts polished. Saturday also was lamp and lantern day. They were filled with coal oil from the jug, the chimneys washed or wiped clean of all smoke or soot and the wicks trimmed. The Aladdin lamp required special care as it had a mantle and it gave a lovely bright light.

It was wonderful to get the chores done and the animals tended to. Then we could tend to ourselves and enjoy our evening knowing that our animals were warm and fed and dry. We knew them all by name. It was lovely to go into the barn for a final check with the lantern at night. The cows were lying down chewing their cuds, often with the cats sleeping on their backs. A horse would give a soft whinny of welcome. It was a pleasant existence for a child who had no worries or cares and we knew that we were helping our mother.

One of the best features of living on the farm was the big barn. Later I knew that there were many barns of the same type built about the same time. They were called, I think, Ontario barns. Grandpa's barn was built in 1918 and there are news items from the Fort Frances Times that tell of the "raising." Mom wrote much later that there was trouble with the barn almost from the start as the wrong kind of gravel was used in the cement and the foundation soon began to crumble. I considered it a magnificent structure and recall it with great fondness.

It was large and I believe it was about 60 feet high at the peak. There was the foundation with windows and doors on every side built into the cement. On the north was the gangway that enabled a team of horses to drive up into the lower part of the haymow. Under the top part of the gangway was a space where we would sometimes play. My mother said when she was young they had a swing under there until the sad day when a colt became entangled in the ropes and died.

There were nooks and crannies in the rocks that had been piled to build up the slope for the gangway. These little spaces were perfect for hiding things and leaving messages. I used to scribble songs and poetry and hide the volumes that I had penned. One day my brother Eric discovered my hiding place and became such an on the spot critic that I was very careful from then on where I left my writings.

There were hay mows on either side of the top part of the barn and on the east side the mow was built over the granary with its rows of bins. Some of these bins had chutes that would let the grain down to the stables. A fanning mill stood in the center of the granary with its many belts and sections to clean the grains. We used to turn the handles to see all the frames moving and shaking and to hear the rumble of it. There were perhaps eight bins in the granary and Marion and I once made a play house in the bin at the east end.

Slings had been used, but in my time the hayfork was used to unload the hay from the wagon. The big hayfork hung from the top centre of the roof and ran on tracks and would be pushed down into the hay as far as it could possibly go and then the ends of it could be fastened to hold its load. When the signal was given the person driving the team would start them out down the gangway. By the series of ropes the huge lift of hay would go up until it caught in the mechanism at the top of the barn, and then it would slide easily over to the mow. The cry "Trip 'er" would come and when the trip rope was pulled the bundle of hay was released. Four lifts emptied the wagon. I often drove the horses on the hay fork and after the last lift drove them safely over to one side until the wagon was backed down the gangway.

On either side of the barn, right at the very peak, were little windows that could be reached by ladders. The ladder on the west side was very long as it went right from the mow floor to the roof. The view from these tiny windows was lovely. My mother told of entering the barn one day and looking up to see my sister Marion who was perhaps five at the time at the very top, looking out the little west window. She did not call out for fear of startling her but just waited there until Marion climbed nonchalantly down again. The ladder on the east side was not as long as it was built over the granary, and at the top was a platform that had been built to enable men to work on the slings or hay fork.

I did not worry about the true purpose and it became a favourite spot, for there were quite roomy platform seats on each side and one could sit up there viewing the countryside. With visiting friends or cousins we could sit up there and talk without fear of being spied on by my brothers. My favourite activity was to take the book I was currently reading and a snack and sit in comfort and privacy, reading and munching on raw carrots or turnips. Many of my poems were penned from that vantage point as well. I was at times guilty of disregarding my mother's call to come and do some chore.

Two huge beams ran north and south to support the structure. Later I found a picture of lumber for this barn being sawed at Cornell's mill in LaVallee. The ladders were interesting as the rungs were not nailed but set into the long uprights. Is the term 'mortised'? Children braver than I could climb the ladders and step onto the beams and walk across. I could never do things like that, and I still get that same old sick feeling in the pit of my stomach thinking of it now. The workmanship of the barn was so beautiful, except for the cement foundation. At any time you could see evidences of the crumbling and I was once scolded for picking stones out of it.

While the upstairs with the granary, section for machine storage and the haymows was spacious and useful, the bottom part of the barn was the heart of it all. You could go downstairs from the mows by stair steps under the granary. At the top of this stairway was a nest where a cross hen sometimes sat brooding, and she would reach out to peck anyone that went by. Sometimes a batch of baby chicks would be hatched here. Down the stairs was the alleyway where the heads of all the horse and cow stalls were. The hay was thrown down the chute and the animals were fed from here. There was also a chute from the oat bin in the granary. Some animals were very good at opening chutes and gates and barn doors, so care had to be taken to be sure everything was secure. An animal can sicken itself by eating too much grain.

Each stall in the horse stable had a metal feeding bowl in the corner of the manger for oats. Some stalls were single and some were for double occupancy but all were very roomy and comfortable. The horse stable was on the east end and included a loose box where a horse could be put if it were sick or about to deliver a foal. Chief, a bright bay with black mane and tail, was our driver and had a stall to himself. It was near the oat chute and on occasion he was able to stretch his neck and head far enough to open the chute, thus letting out a large amount of grain that we had to try to salvage

The outside doors were in two parts, like Dutch doors and the bottom part could be shut to keep animals in or out. It was pleasant to let the sunshine stream in when the top part was open. Often cows would stand with heads hanging over the bottom door. The floors were of cement with gutters behind each row of cattle. The cow stable was in the center of the barn.

Each stall featured metal stanchions that were made, I think, by the Beatty Company. There was a Beatty barn book that we liked to look at with all the different furnishings that could be bought for barns such as ours. These stanchions held the cattle securely yet allowed them room to move their heads freely. There was room for eight cows to stand in four stalls. Daisy, the Ayrshire, Silver, a pure white cow, Button, a big red and white cow, Penny, daughter of Silver, little Jessie and others. I usually milked Silver, a good, even natured cow. It was rather nice to dig your head into the smooth warm flank of the cow, but the flick of a wet tail across your face was not so pleasant. Worse yet was the sudden forward kick that could knock you off your stool and spill the milk. The barn cats were quick to take advantage of this.

Off the stable was the separator room that was whitewashed and had to be scrubbed out regularly for use in the summer. The separator was sometimes in the barn in the summer, but in the winter it was a nuisance carrying pails of hot water to the barn to wash the parts. Usually we carried the milk to the house where the separator stood in the kitchen and the skim milk was carried back to the barn to be given out to cats, calves or pigs.

There were also pens for calves and some calves were tied. All these animals standing resulted in lots of gutters to clean out. I never minded the "barn smell." The west part where the young cattle ran loose was drafty and in the fall, Mom would collect cardboard boxes and tack strips over the cracks in the walls. She believed in making everything as comfortable as possible. There were doors and alleyways and passages to move easily from one part of the barn to another, closing each gate or door behind us.

There was what we called the root cellar on the north. I did not like this room. It was very dark and smelled musty and damp and was infested with cobwebs that caught in your hair. No doubt Grandpa had stored many crops of potatoes and turnips here for years which accounted for the bits of old sacks and twine on the floor and the damp earthy smell. Mom did store some of the produce on the shelves in here. A lantern was needed and even then the corners were always dark, and to a child like me, rather spooky. What a difference electricity would have made to that huge old barn.

    The barn played such an important part in all our lives. I played and worked there and when cousins came to visit we tried to sleep in the barn in the summer. We found that, although hay smells lovely, it is not really all that soft and that it picks and irritates your skin. Besides, mosquitoes quickly find their way to haylofts when bare flesh is available. Hay was great though, for jumping into from a beam or ladder. Tunnels could be made in hay and secret hiding places set up. Bins of oats were also made for jumping into and only later we found out how dangerous these activities could be.

    There were other big barns. The Cain farm had a similar barn, as did the farm of my great uncle in Box Alder. Many of these barns were built around Emo. Years later, when I would drive the back way I always looked for these barns. Some had begun to fall into disrepair and each strong wind or storm would do a little more damage to a once proud old structure. It was almost like watching someone die a long and agonizing death. I shed a few tears when one old barn, after a high wind, at last collapsed into a pile of rubble and twisted weathered boards.

    Sometimes in later years I would dream of the barn and I wondered why a place that had such pleasant memories for me could evoke such an unpleasant recurring dream. In my dream I am standing at the end of an alley way when the door bursts open and a stampede of sleek black cattle rush in. They have wide sweeping sets of horns and come at me with heads lowered and horns swinging. I have no way to escape and am paralyzed. When I wake I am terrified for a few minutes. Being a person who believes that dreams have meaning, I wonder what these wild black cattle signify.

I must confess that for some years our barn was far from my thoughts as I left home and pursued my adult life. The barn became more and more dilapidated and unsafe until at last Alan tore it down. It became just a pleasant childhood memory with the horses and cattle standing warm and fed and dry in their rows. When our brother Eric sent each of us an artist drawn picture of the old home place, Alan made frames for the pictures from the old barn boards. It seemed fitting somehow.

I have nearly thirty first cousins and am fortunate in knowing almost all of them very well. Sadly, some of my cousins, Lyle and Melvin Cain, Roxie Gingras and Gwen Cornell (Strachan family), George and Shirley Mudge (Adams) and David Anderson, have died. There is the wealth of second cousins and others that I just lump all together as cousins. Some of these we saw in school every day and others were regular visitors to our home. We all had cousins just our age and the older ones, such as Thelma, Lucille and Lyle Cain, I looked up to and admired very much. Melvin and Les were often with my brothers as were the Loney cousins from Emo, Dave and Larry, and Keith Strachan. Dave really enjoyed the farm life and would come in the summer and help with the haying and whatever else was going on. He has said later that those were among his happiest times and he was ready to pitch in no matter what the job.

We did not see cousins on the Anderson side of the family as often and I did not get to know the Mudge family, Shirley, George, Helen, Phyllis, Buzz and Virginia until they moved to Fort Frances from Mine Center and then we became good friends. Uncle Tom and Aunt Chappie Anderson had Bill and Iwins sons Dick and Don. I looked after these boys when they were children. Uncle Carl and Aunt Ruth's family, Elaine, David and Kathy, were also younger.

Ethel and Gwen Strachan came in the summer. Roxie was a year older and I have a memory of playing with her making mud pies while we still lived at the old place. We were making some lovely ones but were stopped by an adult when it was found we were using real eggs from the henhouse. Sharon was the baby in this family.

COUSINS-1938. L R: Keith Strachan, Ethel Strachan, Elizabeth Anderson, Roxie Strachan, Gwen Strachan, Eric Anderson

It seemed to be so very hot in those long ago summer days and we usually tried to sleep in the hayloft but we never made it through a whole night. We played endless games of Monopoly, played paper dolls and that card game "War" in the times we were not doing chores. At some time in the summer Marion and I were invited to stay with our cousins when they lived in Fort Frances. This was the height of sophisticated living for us and often included going to a movie matinee. These visits ended when Uncle Bill and family moved to Atikokan.

If it was not our cousins visiting, it was older relatives and often some of Mom's cousins, such as Hazel Wilson or Minnie Langtry would come for a meal or an afternoon. Mom's sister Grace Loney came fairly often with the children Bill and Judy for a day of sewing. Aunt Grace did not use the sewing machine and did all her mending by hand stitching. She saved sheets that needed to be mended or turned for Mom to sew on her treadle machine. Years later, my cousin Judy told me that her mother had one time run a sewing machine needle through her thumb and from that time on refused to use a sewing machine. On a Sunday in summer the Loney family would pick up our family and we would all go to the Point Park for a wonderful day of swimming and picnicking. How did we all squeeze into the family sedan?

FAMILY GATHERING at POINT PARK 1939. Back LR: Bill Strachan, Lawrence Loney, Grace Loney, Ivah Anderson holding Marion, Axel Anderson, Winnifred Strachan, George Strachan, Edna Cain, Albert Cain. Middle L R: Alan Anderson, Keith Strachan, Thelma Cain, Dave Loney, Lucille Cain, Lyle Cain. Front L R: Larry Loney, Eric Anderson, Leslie Cain, Roxie Strachan, (Elizabeth is behind Eric)

Hospitality was taken for granted and you shared what you had. If someone dropped in near mealtime, after a moment of "Oh dear, what will I feed them" Mom rose to the occasion and would tell us to set the table. There were travelers, such as cattle buyer Elmer McEachern, the Raleigh man, Edwin Persson, the Watkins man, Mr. Songhurst from Emo, (insurance), relatives and neighbours that ate at our table and seemed to relish the meal. My uncle Bill Strachan used to say, "No one can fry an egg like Ivah."

In those days, children were seen and not heard and we listened to our elders. When Pat Kerr, the Mothers' Allowance representative came, we were admonished to "not say one word." People receiving this were not to have too much or the allowance might be cut, and some thought that it was not right to even own a radio. That monthly allowance was $40.00.

Change came in the early 1950's. Both Eric and Alan left home to work in the west when the electric power was being installed in rural areas in Manitoba and Saskatchewan. Eric remained in Saskatchewan but Alan returned to the farm and took it over when he married. My mother went to work at Rainycrest. I began a modest teaching career and Marion went into nurse's training in Port Arthur General Hospital. We had lived on our farm only about ten years but looking back it seemed much longer and the memory of those years of growing up in Box Alder shines brightly.

In 1996 a cousin's reunion was held at this farm where Alan and Inez Anderson lived. Many changes had been made over the years and a new modern house replaced the small one built of cedar lumber and the big barn was no longer there, but when descendants of the original Strachan family gathered, all the cousins had memories to share of good times spent here in the past.

COUSIN REUNION-June 1996. Back L R: Sharon Braun, Gwen Cornell, Bernice Cain, Les Cain, Ethel Broski, Bill Loney, Dave Loney, Liz Donaldson. Front LR: Alan Anderson, Thelma Lindsell, Lucille Krishka, Marion Poutanen, Judy Klug, Keith Strachan

SATURDAY'S CHILD

I was born at the home of my parents on May 18, 1935. By all accounts it was a lovely day after a cool backward spring and, according to my mother's book, my father was getting ready to seed a little field to oats. My brothers had gone to Aunt Edna Cain's to help celebrate the birthday of cousin Lucille. Another cousin Keith Strachan was there as it was his birthday too.

My mother who was making bread and rhubarb pie had called a cousin Pearl Barker who often assisted the doctor at such times to come for the day, and Dr Young was called about ten AM. When he got there he made some reference to arriving on time as he did not when my brother Eric was born. I was born right at noon on Saturday, Pearl finished the pie and the bread and the men got the planting done. At that time a new mother was to stay in bed for ten days and Mom had another younger cousin Ilo Barker come to help. She said it was very hard lying in bed and would be so weak when finally allowed up.

I find biographies with accounts of others' childhood years intensely interesting. I have read autobiographies that told of the childhood years of titled people in England, that were so different as to be almost unimaginable to me, being raised as we were. They lived in nurseries on enormous old English estates, and like royalty were cared for by nannies and nurses and governesses. Some of them did play wonderfully inventive games, one family even having a nanny who taught the children shop-lifting. At four o'clock the children were made presentable and then taken at teatime to see their parents. After perhaps half an hour they were taken back to the nursery. It seemed the children spent very little time with their parents when they were very young. A description of one of those huge old homes said, "The nurseries were separate from the main part of the home, as they should be." Some of the children in these autobiographies seemed to be not very fond of their mothers. Perhaps that was from lack of mothering as we knew it.

My mother read to us. It would be evening when we all settled in for another installment of the current story. There were magazines with continued stories and we would wait eagerly until all our work was done and Mom had time to read to us. Stories read or told by her were distinctly dramatic or thrilling with pathos. She loved to laugh and instilled a sense of humour and of the ridiculous, as well as a sense of drama and love of literature into all of us. She often recited poems to us that she had memorized in school and she knew many. Mom also sang old songs that told a story such as, "Shadow of the Pines, which was so sad.

When young, every child may doubt that a parent could understand what is important and there were childish pursuits that did not include my mother or siblings. I much preferred activities that the boys pursued, like trapping and hunting and whittling things, or building huts in the woods. I considered it a privilege if they let me accompany them on their trap lines. Later Alan taught me how to use the little 22 calibre rifle. Every boy carried a jackknife, and jackknives, hatchets or hammers were preferred by me to dolls. A scar on my left forefinger, the result of whittling, is still visible. I liked boy's clothing. My ultimate aim was to be a Boy Scout because I liked the hats they wore and they carried jackknives and compasses and knew how to light fires by rubbing sticks together.

What kind of child was I? We all played and worked together but I did many things on my own. I was possessed of a very vivid imagination and even when quite young plotted scenes and activities where I played the leading role. Radio programs and reading influenced my activities. While riding with the Lone Ranger and Tonto in desperate pursuit of villains and rustlers, I carried on dramatic conversations with myself. (High voice), "But what have you done with Betty?" (Deep voice), "You'll never see Betty again." Imagine the joy when Betty was found and the thankfulness of her family after untying her bonds. "How can we thank you?" (Tearfully). "Don't thank me, thank my dog. He was the one that found where she was." As I say, my imagination was vivid and I had no trouble entertaining myself.

Does every child dream of flying? A little granddaughter told me of her attempts and brought back this memory. Superman was another hero to me, as "the mild-mannered Clark Kent" became Superman and just took off. When I was about seven I was sure that a cape was the only equipment necessary to be able to fly. I found a piece of material from the rag bag that would do and fastened it around my neck. It flowed behind me in a lovely way as I ran. Height seemed to be required so I struggled to get up on the fence post beside the stile. I poised myself ready for flight, jumped and crashed. How did Superman do it?

The nearby English Hay family with five boys received magazines and books from England, some titled "The Boys' Own Journal," and they would pass them on to our family. How I loved these books full of adventure stories that provided me with so much scope for my imagination. I would be going to the hen house to gather the eggs, and suddenly I was struggling through blizzards on the Alps with my sturdy staff searching for lost children, stumbling across some tiny hut, where miraculously the children were huddled. "We'll wait till this storm dies down and then the search parties will come for us," I would tell the clucking chickens. Again I was the hero, "If it hadn't been for you we would not have found these children." We were always able to find some "biscuits" to stave off hunger, though I was never sure just what these were like, surely not like my mother's hot fluffy creations.

Often I was a rancher protecting the herd from rustlers or saving an animal that had become entangled in barbed wire. This made getting the cows much more interesting. Someone would ask "Who were you talking to?' as I carried on my conversations with bad men or other ranchers or cowboys aloud. Oh, for a life on the open range! I sang cowboy songs to myself, "When it's Round-up Time in Texas" or "Bury Me Not on the Lone Prairie" being totally ignorant of Texas or prairies as they were far removed from Box Alder's bush land.

I wonder now that stories of this type were so often featured in the English children's books. There were people described as "Red Indians" and many a warpath I diverted by my skill and daring as I led the "Red Indians" on a wild chase on my spotted pony that was "fleet as the wind." Other times I lived in a wigwam and made pemmican or moccasins with the women. Mom's Pauline Johnson poetry books also fueled my imagination.

I began to write little scenarios, stories and poems. Writing material was not as easily come by in those days. A new scribbler and pencil or box of crayons were treasures. Mom saved every scrap of paper and ironed it to make us little booklets out of the brown wrapping paper used then, by sewing along the fold. My writing I kept hidden away in various places. Under the gangway of the big barn it had been built up with stones, and by removing one or two of these, a perfect hiding place was available. My brother Eric invariably found my "hidey-holes" and made great fun of my efforts. Once in anger I chased him up the ladder that led to the attic bedroom in the house. Every attempt to come down was stopped by me wielding a broom across his legs, until he screamed for mercy and for our mother to intervene.

Eric had quite an imagination himself. The last Christmas that we lived beyond the cedar swamp, I was given a doll. As it was wartime it was appropriate that this doll that I named Jimmy was a soldier dressed in a khaki uniform. Eric, influenced by the war news, decided this poor doll was a "Jap" or a Nazi and it was tortured, hung, buried, stabbed, tied up, imprisoned, drowned at sea or shot down in an airplane. Jimmy as an Allied soldier was decorated with medals and honoured as he mowed down the enemy. Not often was he on our side it seemed.

CHRISTMAS DAY AT GRANDMA ANDERSON'S-1941. L R: Ezra Craven, Elizabeth Anderson holding soldier doll, Tom Craven, Marion Anderson, Eric Anderson, Alan Anderson. Ezra and Tom Craven were living with my grandmother and Uncle Tom.

    I played and worked along with the family but my favourite times were solitary pursuits. Mom was very protective of us, yet allowed us amazing freedom and I roamed at will through fields, the bush and down to the LaVallee River. We would be gone for hours after being admonished to be "back by chore time." The big barn was a great place to play and it was always cool even on a hot summer day. It was easy to a burrow a little hiding place in the hay where I could stash my books and writing material. These, with a few snacks, were all that was needed for an afternoon of pure pleasure. If I heard

Mom call I was able to ignore her only so long, then would crawl out knowing that I was needed for some necessary chore.

We went to the river with siblings and neighbour children and there were many delights to take part in there. We all learned to swim in the LaVallee River and May 24 was the official first swimming day of the season. Usually it was a gentle stream with some surprising under currents at the little rapids at the sandbar below the bridge. We would start at the bridge and swim our way down to the sandbar. The water was quite swift there but not deep. Here we found good stones for skipping across the water, counting the skips. Deep down in the riverbed we could dig and find lovely, heavy blue clay. We carried gobs of this to the banks and used it to model things or to throw bits at each other. There were so many things to do at the river; gathering the wild flowers in the shade of the Box Elder maples, digging for clams and crawfish in the soft mud under the bridge, hiding in the overhang of the banks where the water had eaten the earth away, watching the birds and butterflies, swimming, wading and splashing in the amber coloured water. After an afternoon of such delights we trudged wearily home and were often surprised when Mom would insist we bathe. We also "swam" in sloughs and swampy places, any place that had a little water, wading through cattails and oozy black mud to get to the brown water in the center. Everyone avoided Mud Lake as we knew that the quick sand there would rapidly draw us under, never to be seen again.

As I grew older my favourite thing was going to the bush and lighting a fire to cook a little lunch. Mom gave me a potato to roast or a bit of meat to cook on a stick with bread. It was great fun gathering the best wood to make a little fire and I felt pleased with my world then. Victoria Day, May 24 was always a holiday and I invited friends from school to join me. One cousin, Ruth Barker really loved to come. Marion often came with me and she was such an agreeable companion that when I was feeling lazy I would say, "Let's pretend I have a broken leg." She worked hard at fetching wood and doing all the necessary camp chores while I lazed with my "broken leg" stretched out. I had favourite places in the bush and knew where the best berries or early flowers grew.

In the summer we played in the shade of the chokecherry bushes by the house. They were quite lovely in full bloom in the spring and the wild cherries were abundant later for jelly making. When they were ripe we would stuff our mouths full of the sour, almost bitter fruit and suck the pulp off. The pits we spat at each other and our mouths would be purple and puckered from the juice. We made dandelions chains and our fingers would become brown and sticky from the sap. On hot summer days we would carry pails of ice-cold water from the well to put in the big tin tub to warm in the sun. We could wash and bathe and play in it and Marion and I spent afternoons in the shade of the bushes keeping cool. Water was never wasted and later it would be splashed on the flower or vegetable garden.

About once a week we had to churn. The cream was kept in the little cellar that was under a trapdoor in the boy's bedroom. An area was dug out and there was even a natural stone step in one corner. Butter, milk, and cream and other food kept amazingly cold about three feet down in the earth. Cream has to be a certain temperature to be churned into butter and Mom seemed to know when it was ready. It was poured from the five gallon can into the crockery churn that was fitted with a wooden dasher. I often churned in the shade of the house with a cloth over my knees, against splashing, and with a book in one hand. If the book got too engrossing I would hear the command from the house, "Keep that dasher going" and churned with renewed vigor. Mom taught me how to work the butter with the wooden paddle, to remove all the buttermilk, then to wash and salt it, to press into molds.

Our animals were an important part my childhood and we knew them by name and by personality. Years later when I first heard the term "boss cow" used to describe female workers, I thought of Daisy our Ayrshire cow that was the undisputed leader of our herd. Many a brash young steer felt a jab with her horns when trying to drink before her at the trough. My mother said that Daisy with those horns could open any gate or door on the place. We had no fear of the cattle and went among them to pat or scratch them or pick off wood ticks. Cattle can be the most aggravating creatures if the notion strikes and the only time we ever heard my mother swear was during a particularly bad time of trying to chase them into a field. We all so shocked to hear a mild oath pass her lips, when time and again they turned tail and ran when approaching the gate.

Our work horses were dappled grey Percherons and Kate, daughter of Blanche, was the most respected of them. The term work horse might have been made for her, as my mother said she would pull her heart out no matter what she was doing. Duchess her daughter, also beautiful, could be flighty at times but she worked well with her mother in harness. All the farm work and transportation was done with horse power.

One time Duchess was injured in the bush and we could see the wound on her chest. The vet was called and Mom used all her skill in treating and caring for this and we would bathe it with disinfectant, but matter began to run down her chest and leg. One day Mom thought she could see something and finally a large piece of dried wood, four or five inches long, was pulled from the sore spot. Duchess healed up quickly after this.

Chief was a bright bay with black mane and tail and his main job was pulling the cutter in the winter or buggy in the summer. He did not have the kind nature of Kate or Duchess and would nip if he had the chance. He was rather lazy but could show spirit also. At twelve years of age I was considered old enough to take Chief with the buggy or winter vehicle, and drive to LaVallee to transact the family business. If I met a vehicle on the road I had to stop and hold Chief's head in case he decided to bolt. In LaVallee the cream was dropped off at the creamery and empty cans returned, mail for us and several neighbours was picked up at the post office, and groceries bought at Uncle Dave Strachan's store. At each stop Chief had to be carefully tied at the hitching posts. Once I had him shod at Ab Steele's blacksmith shop and that was interesting watching him pound the flat headed nails into Chief's hooves. Sometimes a visiting cousin rode with me and was impressed by my skill. Then I handled the horses with no fear but now I am nervous around the big animals.

When my mother was in Rainycrest and her mind was failing, I once asked her if she remembered the names of her children. "Of course," she said, "Kate, Duchess and Chief."

We also had pigs and chickens to tend and each species had their own characteristics and language and smell. Chickens tended to squawk and cackle and fly up into the air, acting as if they had never seen a human before when you first went into their building. Then they were fed and given water and the eggs gathered, Sometimes you had to reach under a hen on the nest hoping that she was not one that pecked. Some not only pecked viciously but also gave a little twist with her beak leaving a mark. The pigs loved to be scratched behind their ears, closing their eyes in bliss. A pig can look amazingly blissful and are very clean animals when given the chance with plenty of room and good bedding. There are few sights on the farm more charming than a batch of new born piglets suckling. Most days we made the rounds of the barnyard, checking on our animal friends.

We siblings all got along quite well but Eric and I had many a squabble, as we were close in age. Both strong-willed, we fought over who would push the old lawn mower first. For years I had a bump on my shin where he kicked me that time. He suffered a broken collarbone when he was giving me a ride on the crossbar of the bike. I can recall yet watching the silver spokes as we whizzed down the hill and thinking, "I wonder what would happen if I just stuck my toe in there." I did and the bike stopped abruptly. Eric flew over my head breaking his collar-bone on landing. I felt he was pampered unnecessarily during recuperation.

Alan once got a lovely green-handled jackknife for his birthday. He was so kind hearted and I wheedled it out of him to use for the afternoon and walked down the road swinging it on a string. The string broke, the knife flew, and though I searched frantically through the long grass in the ditch, I had to go home with the news that I had lost Alan's new knife. The thought of this still bothers me.

I know there were disappointments and disagreements and certainly we were poor, but I feel very blessed to have grown up secure in the love of my mother and my siblings, surrounded by aunts, uncles and cousins.

Not all childhoods are ideal and the accounts written by authors such as Frank McCourt in <u>Angela's Ashes</u> of their crushing poverty are heartrending to read. Charles Dickens wrote of the painful childhoods of fictional characters Oliver Twist and David Copperfield, but I was blissfully unaware of such hardships until later and no doubt thought every child was as fortunate as I.

The author Elizabeth Lawrence expresses this thought about childhood, and I sincerely hope that everyone has had a few such moments: "There is a garden in every childhood, an enchanted place where colours are brighter, the air softer and the morning more fragrant than ever again."

This seems true as I recall those long ago days with such pleasure. They seem to be strung together with a golden, hazy, dreamy quality. Did that happen to me or was it just some child that I watched from afar? I have often wondered if my children look on their youngest years with as much pleasure as I do mine.

School Days And Teachers

Working on the history book for the Centennial filled me with such feelings and "nostalgia for the irretrievable past." that sometimes I was in tears as I wrote. Our childhood worlds were so secure and we had no thoughts of the death, disaster and destruction that fill the TV screens each day now. Our world was comprised of the small community and we thought of little beyond its boundaries. Our father was dead and I missed him as much as I could miss the parent I had hardly known. We were concerned with doing our chores, taking care of our animals, entertaining cousins that visited and our life at the Box Alder School.

When we lived east of McFayden's corner through the cedar swamp the distance to the school was nearly three miles. It must have been hard for my mother to see her children start off on such a long walk especially on a bitterly cold morning. The cedar swamp always seemed sinister to us, but I feared it more in the summer months. I still harbour an irrational fear of bears.

I do not recall much of those early days but I do remember my first day at school, standing in the cloakroom with the "big girls" June Barker, Nellie Hyatt, and my cousin Lucille Cain, special because we shared the same birth date. I wore a dark blue dress made over from something Mom had cut up. She had embroidered little red and blue flowers in the lazy daisy stitch on the bodice and I had red ribbons tied at the ends of my brown braids. My brothers Eric and Alan were in grades three and five so I knew I had protectors. Mrs. Margaret Lichenstein was the teacher.

The school was the largest room that I had ever seen and, with the little platform where the teacher's desk stood, it was surely the most elegant. My desk was near the south windows where all the younger children sat. The walls were coloured some pastel shade and the floors were of hardwood. The blackboards that I loved writing on with the bits of chalk were on the west and north walls. A very small room in the northwest corner held the library books and science equipment and was the teacher's room as well. I loved that old, dusty schoolroom and thought our school very lovely. The school had one feature that some others lacked as it had a large bell that was rung by pulling a rope inside the school. The school bell could be heard for quite a distance.

The school was heated at first by a large heater that stood near the back of the room. Boots and mitts were placed near the heater to dry. At some point the school was raised, a basement put under it and a large wood-burning furnace installed. Then there was a big floor register near the front of the room and the heat spread around. The wood that was burned was elm and had a distinctive smell. A whiff of that kind of smoke now puts me right back into that classroom. Steps into the basement were from the back of the boys' cloakroom and had a slanted cover that we could slide down. There was an outside entrance with a similar cover. The wood was taken to the basement through here.

Chemical toilets were installed and a tiny cubicle was built in the corner of each cloakroom. The toilets were above large holding tanks that had certain chemicals put in. The basement was not a pleasant place as it smelled of these chemicals and of other things. I think it was about this time that a janitor was hired to carry the wood, stoke the furnace, tend to the toilets, clean and carry water. Up until this time the teacher and certain pupils carried out these duties. Bill Smith, an elderly Scottish gentleman, was the janitor I recall and I became very fond of him, as he was not as gruff as he first appeared, and I helped him with the dusting of the desks.

Madeline Hyatt, Jim McCoy and Garth Young were in the same class as I was. Madeline had a wealth of curly blonde hair. Garth later moved to LaVallee and we became friends again in high school. We were all good students but Jim and I had an unspoken gentle rivalry all through our Box Alder school days. When the Roy family moved into Box Alder Ronnie, the oldest boy, was in our class.

In the winter sometimes my brother Alan drove the horse and cutter as far as Uncle Charlie Strachan's where the horse would be stabled until after school. We would walk the rest of the way to school but, if we were cold Aunt Nettie would let us warm up in her big kitchen. She had a sharp tongue that we respected but she was kind to us. One time the Hay boys had caught a ride with us at the McFayden corner. Sometimes I stood on the runners to ride and this time I fell off and hit my head. I must have been dazed as I recall looking up and seeing all the faces peering at me. I thought I would bask in all this attention a while longer, so I closed my eyes and sort of pretended I was unconscious. This was quickly found out and I was bundled into the cutter by brotherly hands.

Often we caught a ride with the Bob McCoy family. Jim was in my grade, Edith was Alan's age and Jack was younger. We rode on the stone boat or the big sleigh all covered with straw and horse blankets. There seemed to be so much snow and it was so cold. Roads were not snow plowed in the winter in those days and walking was not easy after a big storm. Some children skied to school.

I learned to read from the blue primer called Mary, John and Peter. It was no time until I mastered, "I am John. I go to school. I am Mary I go to school. I am Peter. I do not go to school. I am too little." We were taught by the phonetic method that I think is a good way to teach children to read. There were little boxes of alphabet tickets and we were told to copy the words from the primer. I loved doing this and would spend any free time making words and sentences until the whole top of my desk was covered, but I was not quite as enthusiastic over the number tickets that were also part of the school day. Sometimes a rude boy would jiggle the desk and mess up my handwork or brush some of the letters onto the floor. In school we learned early to fight back and I found ways to retaliate, sometimes subtle and sometimes more heavy-handed. The word bully was not as common as it is today, but there were certain rough boys to avoid.

The school was small, ill equipped, unsanitary and poorly lighted but I liked it and that school was a very important influence on my life. It was the same school that my mother had attended. Many students there were second generation and many of us were related. It was nice to look across the room and catch the eye of a cousin. Some were cousins of cousins, some were second or third cousins—Strachan, Barker, Hughes, Cain, Anderson—we were all connected. The other families were the Greens, Grenniers, Browns, McCoys, Hays, Hnatiuks, Hyatts, Roys, the Fraser boys from Riding Mountain and the Tylers, children of the minister of the Gospel Lighthouse.

Sometimes if Mom found it difficult to scrape up enough lunch for us or was out of bread, she would call her sister Edna who would send extra with our Cain cousins for us. One unhappy day I had forgotten my lunch or it had gotten spoiled somehow. I was too shy to tell and cried at lunchtime until Irene Craven noticed my dilemma. Soon I had such stacks of sandwiches and cookies that it would have been impossible to eat a quarter of it.

The Cravens were a Children's Aid family. When they first came Irene stayed with Pearl McFayden and Ezra and Tom stayed with Grandma Anderson so they were like family to us. Ezra was in and out of our home often. Irene continued to live with the McFayden family until she married Don Redford. After Ezra was no longer under the care of the Children's Aid, he really had no home and stayed with our family when he needed a place. He was very fond of my mother and my brothers thought of him as a brother. Eleanor Watson who had health problems was another Aid child and so were Frank and Duane McLeod who were from Spohn Township. We came to know bits of their past lives and they all seemed to fit into our school years.

Some things stand out in my memory. Alan Hughes suffered from badly crossed eyes, a condition that nowadays would be corrected. Gentle and good-natured, he sat in school until he left school at fourteen. Nickie Hnatiuk, a slower learner also was sent to school. In those days there was no special help for children such as Nickie or Alan and it must have been frustrating for the teacher as well as for the child. We accepted such children as Eleanor Watson who had epileptic seizures, though the schools or the teachers in those days were not equipped to handle anything out of the ordinary. Everything stopped when Eleanor had a seizure and the teacher tended to her.

Another very pleasant memory was the day that my aunt Edna Cain picked all the cousins up at school, packed us in her car and took us to Fort Frances to see the movie "Lassie Come Home." That was certainly the first movie I had seen and I was very impressed with the luxury of the Royal Theatre. I had not often been to Fort Frances and that day held a great deal to absorb. The Internet gave the date of this movie as 1943 and I think it was about 1945 when we saw it. I find it odd that the main thing I recall of this momentous occasion was how wonderful the dark red velvet seats in the theatre were.

I quickly learned to read but as the reading material was limited I read the same things over and over. We were not supposed to read ahead in our readers but it was impossible to resist when there were such stories as "The Half-Chick" and "The White Rabbit" featuring Mrs. Jemima Puddle Duck. I look at that little book now with its 111 pages and wonder at how little it took to keep us satisfied, as this was the reader for the whole grade one year. Surely we must have had supplementary reading but I don't remember that. In grade two we had "A Garden of Stories," then followed "Golden Windows" and "Gateways to Bookland" in grades three and four. I was always looking forward to the next reader. The school library had sets of books such as Dickens, not well suited to the beginning reader but discovered and enjoyed later on.

On the bottom shelf of a bookcase there was a large dark green book that I would often choose to look at. In it were copies of old paintings that I would marvel and wonder at. They were of a classical theme, in black and white, with some figures sculpted of marble. One that especially fascinated me was entitled "The

"Burning of the Books" and in it there was a lovely woman in flowing robes. It may have been Diana at the Temple of Ephesus when all the literature that the priests deemed unfit was destroyed. I would like to see that old book again, but even then it was in disrepair. In another bookcase on the platform was a set of the "Books of Knowledge" and we were allowed to get these when our reading ability was sufficient. These held a wealth of information and I read on many subjects.

One time we played church and Sunday School with real fervour in the old woodshed preparing for the end of the world forecast by certain students. When the dreaded day and hour arrived and we were not "caught up in the clouds" we soon lapsed back into our old habits.

As we were going to school in wartime there was stress put on the war effort and we had Junior Red Cross meetings on Friday afternoons. These consisted of short programs by talented students and the latest news from the Red Cross Organization. Some children sang and some recited or gave readings. One vivid memory is of Phillip Fraser singing "The Spanish Cavalier" nearly every week. He had a good voice and loved this old song. We often sang patriotic songs such as "The Maple Leaf Forever", "Rule Britannia" and "Men of Harlech."

Then we would work on our projects. There were coping saws, hammers and little nails and glue and bits of wood, paint, raffia, yarn for spool knitting and other craft items. The idea was to make objects and then sell them to the community with proceeds going the Junior Red Cross. The day of sale was quite exciting with parents coming to view the work and to buy. The older boys made things like bookends and picture frames, Wayne Tyler once made a pair of bookends shaped like polar bears that I thought were really exquisite, but I knew that Mom could not afford them. We braided raffia to make hot pads, and sewed the strips from spool knitting into little mats. It was awful to see everything on the table sold except the thing that you had made. I wish I could recall more of these days but perhaps there is a reason that I don't remember. At any rate, we were all part of the war effort. When the war ended and word came to us at school, the school bell was rung loud and long. School may have been dismissed for the day and I recall Mom making a blueberry pie from her canned blueberries to celebrate.

Games were played with fierce intensity, especially after the Fraser boys came. Baseball was taken very seriously and the whole school had to play to make enough. One's athletic ability determined the order in which you were picked. I was neither first nor last and everyone was chosen from Edith McCoy, who was a natural, down to Alan Hughes who had eye problems. Our equipment was poor and bats were sometimes homemade but the game was the thing. In the winter we played Fox and Goose and threw snowballs when the weather was right. We chose sides and made snow forts where we took refuge from the barrage of snowballs. Some of the boys iced the snowballs into dangerous weapons.

We played Steal Sticks, Red Light, Green Light, Prisoner's Base, Kick the Can and Pump, Pump Pull away (at least that is what we called it), and I received my first kiss from a boy after being captured in one of these games. We played Anti-Anti-I-Over over the school. I can still feel the breathless suspense of not knowing which way the attackers were coming from. Often we all played these games but sometimes the boys followed their own pursuits, as did the girls.

Then we played Hopscotch and circle games. Hopscotch was fun but demanded great jumping power. I remember Maddy Hyatt and Shirley Tyler taking a run and then just flying to reach the seven and eight squares. We skipped rope and sang the rhymes as little girls have done for centuries. Circle games were played when the ball diamond was too wet. The girls and smaller children took part and sometimes the big boys would show some desultory interest. These games like skipping and its rhymes had been handed down through the generations. Farmer in the Dell was played by the whole school, as well as London Bridge is falling down and Drop the Handkerchief. I loved the one called "Fair Rosa" that seemed to be based on the story of Sleeping Beauty, as Fair Rosa slept one hundred years

There was another that I liked –"On the mountain stands a maiden, who she is I do not know. All she wants is gold and silver, All she wants is a fine young man." Then a young man would be called in by the girl in the centre with much giggling and blushing. I cannot remember how we acted this one out either. I believe some of these games were very old and alas, they have died out. I am glad that I played these games as a child, even if I cannot recall them in their entirety.

On bitter winter days we were allowed to stay in and read if we wished, or play paper or blackboard games such as Tic Tac Toe or Hang Man. Sometimes we played "Upset the Fruit Basket" or "Musical Chairs" while a student played the battered old piano. Such unsophisticated and old-fashioned activities provided us with entertainment and social interaction.

There were upsets and even fights when some of the boys would become riled up about some real or imagined slight cast on his honesty or strength. I hated the fights and could not understand why so many of the others would gather round to watch and cheer the fighters on. I always left and felt strangely sickened by the bloody noses or split lips that showed up in the classroom after. There were more fights after the Fraser boys arrived at our school. Years later Alan told me of the club called the White Hawk Band that some of the boys belonged to. They had a theme song and their only motivation was revenge against the enemy that varied from day to day.

We learned early to stick up for ourselves. Edith McCoy, who I think could trounce any boy in the school, often championed me so I felt quite confident. I often resorted to sheer language and would call others by some name or word that I knew they really had no knowledge of like scurrilous beast or contemptible idiot. Dickens was a great source of these phrases. All in all we got along very well and I look on my school days with great pleasure.

For some reason when I was in grade seven, the grade seven and eight pupils were sent to Devlin School. I am not sure why this was but perhaps Box Alder was overcrowded and Devlin lacking pupils, but by some agreement with the two school boards to Devlin

School we went. The seven of us were chauffeured by Elmer Berg in a panel station wagon. Elmer was always good natured and kind and laughed at our nonsense. He was especially affable some afternoons when he would pick us up a little late, red-faced and laughing. We never thought of telling our parents, although there were times when Elmer definitely should not have been driving at all, let alone driving a van full of school children.

Devlin School was very different as we went to the upper classroom of the big two-roomed cement block school. There we met many new friends and I have always been glad we had that experience. There were Greensides, McLean, Cooke, Caul, Kellar, Grennier (who had gone to Box Alder for while), Shine, Macedon, Teeple, and Venne families, plus Donnie Witherspoon, Alec Paterson, Earl Lalond, and Betty Hyatt who walked four miles and others. I have remained friends with many of these people to this day.

Miiss Fitzmaurice our first teacher was a tall elegant lady, not young but quite beautiful. However, she was not suited to teach a large classroom of rough and rowdy children and could keep no order at all. The schoolroom was chaos for a month when she left, as I believe she had severe health problems. We had supply teachers for a day or two at a time, even Mr. Parsons the minister. He liked to sing and taught us songs like "Do you ken John Peel with his coat so gay". That fall I fell ill with red measles and missed two weeks of school and some of the supply teachers.

About Christmas time Mrs. Mildred Mose came to our rescue and she is remembered with real fondness. She was red-headed, tough and strong and it was not long until the classroom was running smoothly and we were catching up on what we had missed. She kept excellent order, as she assured us early on that she had been helping her husband cut and haul pulp wood and her muscles were in good shape. We did not doubt her. Her three children Alton, Eddie and Ruth came with her and she played no favourites with her own children. Sometimes she would come out and play baseball with us and could she hit ! Everyone loved it. Mrs. Azaela Mac Quaker taught us after Mrs. Mose.

Then back to Box Alder we went to finish grade eight. The new teacher, Frank Markovich from Kirkland Lake, brought with him a different approach and attitude as he was the first male teacher in Box Alder for many years. I soaked up the history and geography and English grammar that he stressed and the poetry he quoted from the old poets. I have stayed in touch with him over the years.

GIRLS AT BOX ALDER SCHOOL-1949. Back Row 4 L R: Madeline Hyatt, Elizabeth Anderson, Ruth Barker. Row 3 L R: Alverne Green, Shirley Tyler, Marion Anderson. Row 2 L R: Annie Hnatuik, Arleen Cain, Greta Berg. Front Row 1 L R: Helen Hnatuik, Janice Barker, Helen Roy.

When I was in grade nine and talking to Grace McCoy one day at high school, we heard that a relative of ours had died in Box Alder. We could not think who it would be and when we got home found out it was little Leslie Hughes, son of Clarence and Rena. Marion was in school and told how the inspector Mr. Muir was there and Mr. Markovich stayed in at recess to talk to him. They had been working on building a skating rink and were using a large roller to flatten the surface. The smaller children were riding on the crossbar while the older ones pushed. Leslie aged seven slipped off and the roller went over him. It was such a tragic and terrible accident. Years later when Mr. Markovich talked to me of this incident the pain and sorrow were still very evident.

I remember little bits and pieces of those long ago school days—the smell of the wood smoke from the elm logs, cleaning the blackboard erasers, discovering Charles Dickens' writing, Philip Fraser telling me that pigs could see the wind and it is blue, syrup sandwiches, protecting my little sister and the indignation I felt when she was punished in her first days of Grade one, the sour, stale smell of our lunch pails, drinking from the communal cup at the well, Mr. Hickey and religious education, spelling bees and homemade valentines. the excitement when new families moved in, Eric getting the strap and the horror of that, Christmas concerts, throwing up on the story of "The Elves and the Shoemaker" in grade three, playing games like "hang man" at the board on stormy noon hours, having an appendectomy and missing the Christmas Concert the year I was in grade eight, warming Johnny Hnatiuk's frozen feet and finding the first violets in the school bush. This bush also grew jack-in-the-pulpits and lady slippers in its damp and mossy confines.

There were two major events in the school year, the Christmas concert and the school picnic that was held on the last day of school. The picnic was for everyone and featured races, ball ball-games, and a big community supper. The Ladies Aid had a booth and I remember having twenty five cents to spend. With that I was able to buy five different treats such as an ice cream cone, a bottle of pop, a chocolate bar, a package of Wrigley's gum and assorted penny candy.

Little old Box Alder School where I spent so many childhood years and happy days, days full of suspense and wonder, of laughter, of a few childish hurts, days of sharing and learning about human nature. It is easy to look back and almost glorify those days and think they were perfect. They weren't, of course, and there were hurts and misunderstandings, plus the bumps and bruises to the ego that go with growing up. I will never be sorry that I attended that old one room school and feel that the education I received there was quite adequate to enable me to build on to achieve whatever heights I have attained.

However, I left this school without a backward look when I finished grade eight went on to attend the Fort Frances High School. It continued to operate for another five or six years and the third generation of our family, Linda Anderson, attended the school. Things changed drastically and the whole municipality was on the way to becoming a township school area. Bud Cain tore the school down in about 1959 and by then I was married and raising a family. I did not think too much about it other than having a passing pang on knowing that both the church and school, icons of my childhood, were gone. The writing of the history book brought back many memories and an almost glorified remembering of my days of growing up in Box Alder and of that particular part of my life.

Teachers at Box Alder School

I asked an older cousin who her teachers were at Box Alder School, but she could not seem to recall that, which rather surprised me, as I supposed most people remembered that. My mother often spoke of her teachers and was especially fond of Miss McRae who was a niece of John McRae that wrote "In Flanders Fields" and of Miss Jessie Young, whose sister Letty drowned at Big Fork in the Rainy River. She spoke also of Belva Tanner and Muriel Sanderson.

Alan's first teacher at the Box Alder School was Hildegarde Halliwell and I knew that she had red hair and that she smoked. This was notable to me at that time as I thought only men smoked.

My first teacher was Margaret Lichenstein. At the time she taught in Box Alder the family lived in Devlin and her children attended school there. I think that she walked the three miles to our school but she may have had some arrangement for rides. She taught at Box Alder for a number of years and was my teacher from grades one to four. She could become very angry at the shenanigans of the boys. The school was quite large at this time with the coming of the Grenniers and the Fraser boys. Strapping was allowed in those years, but whether or not it was a deterrent is another story.

Mrs. Lichenstein had beautiful handwriting and was very artistic and tried to teach us some of the rudiments of drawing. We each were given an art book with soft drawing paper. The pages were perforated at the edge for removal but usually all the pages remained in the book. Each Friday afternoon we were given an art lesson and sketched in pencil or coloured chalk and or crayons. The older children were allowed to use paints that came in green tin boxes, from I think the Reeves Company. Colours were mixed with water in the back of the lid. The school day in those times was very structured.

Mrs. Lichenstein was notable in my mind, as she liked my brother Eric. Eric was high strung and lively and could be somewhat of a trial but Mrs. Lichenstein seemed to enjoy his high spirits. They shared the same birth date of March 5 so that was another bond. One morning after we had moved to Grandpa's farm Eric was riding me to school on the crossbar of his bicycle. I remember that the spokes of the front wheel looked solid silver as we whizzed down the hill. What would happen if I just stuck the tip of my toe into that shiny wheel? I did and Eric went headlong over me as the bike stopped abruptly. My mind is a blank after that.

That is truthfully all I remember but in some of Mom's writing she says that Uncle Charlie Strachan found us and took us to Emo to Dr. Young's office and phoned her from there. Eric had a broken collarbone and was taken care of accordingly. It bothers me that I can recall none of the details after sticking my toe in the spokes. How could I not remember a trip to Emo in Uncle Charlie's truck and Eric's arm being put in a sling, to say nothing of the stern, terse professionalism of Dr. Young and the gravity of the situation? What I do recall was that Eric was somewhat pampered by Mrs. Lichenstein. It was near Easter and she came to see Eric with a gift. She had blown out the contents of an egg and carefully poured melted chocolate in so that he had a solid chocolate egg. We all coveted that egg. Years later when I visited Mrs. Lichenstein in Rainycrest she asked about Eric.

I have the written report of my year in Grade one. Mrs. Lichenstein wrote that I had made good progress and that I tried to be neat and exact but "Elizabeth's only fault is her desire to talk. I am thankful for her wonderful sense of humour but she will have to control it in class." I also recall a report where the progress of all three of us, Alan, Eric and I, was written on one small sheet of paper.

Mrs. Iona LeBlanc was the next teacher at Box Alder. She was married to Clement LeBlanc and they had two small sons Jackie and Bobbie, not of school age. Mrs. LeBlanc and the two little boys boarded with Mrs. Hay through the week and then Mr. LeBlanc came for them on Friday to take them home to Dearlock. It was likely in the years that she was there that the Fraser family moved to Box Alder and the four boys started school there. There were nearly forty students and it cannot have been easy, as at that time grades nine and ten were also taught in some rural schools. Mrs. LeBlanc had a temper and one day she used the strap on Eric with some severity. He took it without flinching and then bolted for home. Mrs. LeBlanc did the best she could but it was hard controlling a large unruly group.

The next teacher was another middle-aged woman named Mrs. Barbara Wiggins. She had two children who both came to school with her. Again I believe that all three stayed with Mrs. Hay. The children Marilyn and Bruce were both in the higher grades. I was in Grade six that year.

Mrs. Wiggins was a lovely looking, well-dressed woman with soft white curls and pink cheeks. She must have been beautiful as a young woman when she was, as she liked to tell us "Barbara Schweitzer." However, this gentle looking person also had a temper. I did not seem to mind Mrs. Wiggins and at her worst I would concentrate on counting the ruffles on her lovely blouses or gazing at her jewellery.

I recall good things about all my teachers. We did learn and I could always escape into a book if necessary. We just accepted them as our teachers, even if they were cross at times, and thought that is what teachers were like. For some reason in grade seven we were sent off to Devlin School with the grade eight pupils. When we returned after a year and a half in grade eight, Mr. Markovich was the teacher. He was young and had such a different attitude that it was a new experience for us and prepared us for the male teachers we would have in High School. He gave an air of suspense and interest even to subjects such as history and geography.

I consider that I was very fortunate to attend that little one room school and to have the teachers that I did. They all added something to my life's experience and how to deal with people. My years at Box Alder School prepared me well for my high school years

Christmas

When you reach a certain age it is impossible to get through the Christmas season without letting your mind go back to the "ghosts of Christmases past." The Christmas of today is so far removed from those of the long ago days.

I have only one memory of Christmas at our first home through the cedar swamp. There is a picture of my siblings and me with the Craven boys, Tom and Ezra who were living with my grandmother. Eric has said that one year we came down and stayed at Grandpa and Grandma Strachan's for Christmas but I have no clear memory of that.

In 1942 we moved to Grandpa Strachan's farm and then memories of Christmas are clearer. Mom would begin her preparations and send the Christmas order to Eaton's catalogue service. Money was scarce but she tried to see that we got one small toy or book and then some needed clothing. The day that parcel came in the mail or to the station was very exciting as we could only dream about what was in there.

Mom made wonderful fudge of brown sugar and chocolate that she tried to hide until the big day. We became experts at finding it and having tastes until there would be hardly any left and Mom would talk about the lack of sugar and work involved. Remember, this was wartime and sugar was rationed. We also made a fruitcake and I think we all helped with the cutting up and dredging of the dried fruit with flour. The cake was always dark and there were three layers of graduating size cooked in pans lined with brown paper. The woodstove oven was hard to control to maintain the low heat needed and sometimes a portion of the cake would be scorched just a bit. These bits were trimmed off and the cake wrapped in cloths and put away to ripen for several weeks. A few days before Christmas we decorated the cake. Mom had a lovely cake plate on a pedestal and this held our cake. Each layer was iced and the layers put together. The first layer of icing had to set then the second layer was applied, as smoothly as possible. The decorations were put on and we outlined each layer with those little silver candy balls–dragees. The finished product was quite beautiful and rather like a wedding cake. It stood on the buffet to be admired until Christmas Day.

Christmas seemed to be proceeded by an air of mystery and excitement and we would be wild with glorious anticipation as each step was taken. It is impossible to describe the feeling of intense excitement that built as the day approached. Sometimes I think it would be nice to feel even one little twinge of what we felt then but now I see it through the grandchildren. One small granddaughter expressed it by saying, "Dad, my heart is glowing."

At school we practiced for the concert that we knew would astound our parents with the perfection of our performances and after the concert there were only very few days until THE DAY. We put up the Christmas tree of spruce or balsam only a few days before the 25th. It was erected as far from the heater as possible because of the danger of fire. Mom told us that in her day there would be real candles put on the tree. All the candles were lit and the children called to see it and then the candles extinguished as quickly as possible.

We put up streamers that crisscrossed the room and were caught up in the middle with one of those tissue paper creations that opened out. Ours was in the shape of a bell and was carefully saved each year. We did not have many decorations and most of them were homemade. The one that I remember most was a bird of lovely coloured glass with a tail of some shiny fibers. There are reproductions of this type of ornament now. With these decorations and a few boughs decking the windows the house looked and smelled very "Christmassy."

We always hung up our stockings on the long mouthpiece of the old wall telephone and there would be a "Jap orange" in the toe of my ribbed cotton stocking along with some candy, nuts in the shell and a small toy or box of crayons. The stockings seemed to have lovely, interesting lumpy shapes.

On Christmas morning we could open our stockings but then the chores had to be done. It seemed always to be very cold. The wood box had to be full and the water pail and reservoir filled ready for the days cooking. We zipped through the chores as quickly as possible and then we had our breakfast. After the dishes were washed and the house tidy it would be near 10:00 a.m. and then and only then were we allowed to open our presents. We always were allowed to open one gift on Christmas Eve and it would be so hard to choose. Mom saved all the paper and would smooth it out to iron later. We did not have scotch tape that ruins the paper now.

We children somehow would manage to get a present for our mother, one year it was a rose bowl that cost forty cents. There were no fancy or expensive gifts. We would get new mittens or a scarf that Mom had knit. Often there would be a book or a colouring book and crayons. The boys would get jackknives or woolen socks. Eric always preferred a hard present to a "soft" one that he knew held socks or mitts or a sweater. Aunt Edna was always so kind and often gave Marion and me pajamas or blouses that she had sewn. What Aunt Edna was really famous for in our eyes was her wonderful homemade candy. We loved opening her box of the most exquisite treats, lovely white divinity fudge, chocolate fudge and maple cream candy and her own marshmallows rolled in toasted coconut, pink and green mint fondant patties. The memory of those wonderful boxes of candy is still with us.

Muriel Barker, my mother's friend from Geraldton, also sent a box of books, magazines, clothing and treats like Velveeta cheese. A box of canned goods and treats came from the Loney Cloverleaf Grocery in Emo. Mom's cousin Ivah Ford, for whom Mom was named, often sent a box. These were toys that she had played with as a child, beautiful dolls with china porcelain heads and jointed bodies made of kid skin and exquisitely made doll clothes. One year she sent a fur muff that I thought was the last word in elegance but my brothers kept threatening to shoot it. When she sent clothing for Marion and me it was usually too small as she did not realize how sturdy Ivah's girls were. The only thing that has survived is a doll dresser that Emily now has.

Chickens were roasting in the oven and vegetables ready to cook as we prepared for company. Sometimes Uncle Bill and Aunt Orph and our cousins came and we had such good times. There was not room at the table for everyone as Grandpa and Grandma and others were there, so Mom would fix the cedar chest as a table for the little girls and we sat around this on cushions as we visited. The meal would be very large and Uncle Bill always praised Mom's cooking which made me feel very proud of her. There would be pie or suet pudding and sometimes homemade ice cream to eat with the dark fruitcake. It was a wonderful family time. When the company went home in the late afternoon there were chores to do again before we had a late supper in the lamplight. The phrase "tired but happy" could have been penned for us.

Sometimes we went to Uncle Bill's or Aunt Edna's for Christmas dinner and that was exciting. I remember walking to the corner as the roads were not snowplowed at that time and Uncle Bill picked us up. When we went to Aunt Edna's we would go in the cutter around the road by Barker's. If the snow were not too deep we could go through the bush with the big sleigh and that was much shorter and very pleasant. The magic of those days is with me yet and I feel very fortunate to have such positive memories.

At Christmas in 1945 Grandpa and Grandma Strachan came and stayed several days. With them came Cousin Rachel Barker from Geraldton. She was about eighteen, very pretty and vivacious, and we all thought she was wonderful. When I look back now I wonder where we all slept as our house was not large but everyone was accommodated and it was a memorable holiday.

In 1946 near Christmas my grandfather was very sick in Emo. Mom had gone to be with them all and I wakened to the sound of Mom fixing the fires when she came home very early in the morning of December 22. Grandpa had died in the night and I wanted so badly to comfort Mom but did not know how. From the wisdom of my young years I said, "He's gone but not forgotten." It was bitterly cold and we had not kept the fires up and all the houseplants were frozen. Grandpa was buried on December 24 in the Box Alder Cemetery. Mom made Christmas for us just the same.

Those days were so different from now. We had so little outside influence, rarely went anywhere and the few square miles of Box Alder encompassed our whole world. No wonder we so intensely awaited Christmas with its mystery and suspense. Santa Claus did not really enter into it very much. We had a Santa at the concert but he had the same voice or wore the same boots as one of our neighbour so he did not seem very real to me. Our mother was the source of all the good things that Christmas brought to us.

The Two Churches In Box Alder

I was born and brought up in Box Alder and I lived there only 18 years but they were my youngest and most formative years, so the memory of them has never left me. In the early 1950's I began a modest teaching career, marriage followed and I lived in Burriss for nearly 50 years and grew to love that community. I still thought of Box Alder as home and my husband used to find it annoying when I spoke of going "home" when I went to visit there. I meant no disrespect but have never been entirely able to shake that earth from my roots, nor do I want to.

What an insulated and sheltered little community we were. Many of the families, descendants of the early pioneers, were related. Most people had radios but with no daily papers or television, no easy access to the news media and limited means of travel, everyone just went about the business of making a living from the farm and being involved in local affairs.

We were very isolated living beyond the cedar swamp until after my father died. We first three began school from there with a walk of nearly three miles and of course that broadened our lives a certain amount, but I was not aware of church affairs until we made the move to my grandfather's farm in 1942. Here we were so much closer to the centre of Box Alder, the school and the church.

The church was built about 1906 by Hastie Jack from the Emo area on land donated by that prominent citizen C.W. Hughes. Nearly all the early settlers in Box Alder were of the staunch Methodist faith and the church was named Grace Methodist Church. It was quite a large building, covered outside with squares of pressed tin, and pressed tin of a different design covered the walls inside. This type of tin has become quite popular when salvaged from old buildings. My son Jerry and daughter-in-law Nancy bought an older house and have carefully preserved the ceilings that were made of this type of patterned squares.

Inside was a high platform or stage reached by three or four steps on either side. A wood stove provided heat and stovepipes meandered through the room. The pews were solid and plain, painted brown and had been made by some local carpenter. On the platform were the pulpit, chair, the old style pump organ and a few other bits of furniture. A communion table stood in front of the pulpit. Dusty, dark green curtains could be pulled to close off sections for Sunday School. It was a large plain building inside and out, as the early churchgoers did not believe in ornamentation. Behind the church was the horse barn. In the early days all the churchgoers arrived by horse drawn vehicles and the horses were stabled. There was also a decrepit outhouse that was used only in the direst of emergencies.

The attendance in those early days was large, as these settlers took their religion seriously. The church would be filled with Strachans, Hughes, Barkers, Hatherlys, Ings, Greens, Scobies, McFaydens, Fergusons, Watsons, Rosses and Shutes. My mother often spoke of these people and I liked to imagine what it would be like to see the church full on Sundays. They would be dressed in their Sunday clothes, the ladies in their long dark dresses, all wearing hats; while the gentlemen of course removed theirs. No man would appear in church without a suit. The little girls would wear their best starched white "pinnies" over their dresses, and long, black stockings with their high, black laced up boots. The boys would struggle against the restraint of suit coats and ties.

Church was a serious part of life to be endured at least twice on Sundays. At home they engaged only in quiet conversation and suitable reading of the Bible or Sunday School papers. No unnecessary work was to be done and the women worked extra hard on Saturday baking, cooking, cleaning and getting clothing ready so they too could have a "day of rest." My mother often spoke of these early days. Later I knew the stories and that Aunt Edna Strachan's was the first wedding that took place in the church. Surely they decorated for that. My step-grandmother Charlotte and great grandmother Janet Strachan who died the same day were buried from that church on the same day and a long funeral cortege of horses pulling buggies and wagons, all draped with black crape, wended its way to the Box Alder Cemetery. There was the funeral of young Earl Strachan who died when a wagon loaded with grain went over him, crushing him. My grandfather sternly told a brazen young man who lit up a cigarette at the Christmas concert that was always held there that he was not to desecrate the House of God. In modern words "Butt out."

The Methodist religion had such marvelous old hymns to be sung with enthusiasm and vigor. My mother taught us many of these and she never forgot those beloved old songs even when there was very little else she remembered.

It would be in the early 1940's when I first remember much about church. By then it was the Grace United Church with union of the Methodist, Presbyterian and Congregationalists having taken place in 1925. The Devlin Church had been of Presbyterian faith and the Church at LaVallee was also Methodist. The care of these three churches along with the Presbyterian Church in Emo was made into a four-point charge. The first minister Mr. Hockin lived in the manse at Emo.

After church union things stayed much the same and an old book of minutes of the Box Alder Social Club showed the names of all the Barkers, as the club put on suppers, concerts and teas to raise money to support the church. This changed about 1930 and the names of the Barkers no longer appeared on the roll.

It is very likely that there had been rumblings of discontent and that some people missed the older evangelical style found in the Methodists. About this time the Pentecostal movement had its beginnings in the area and the first Pentecostal camp meeting was held in Emo in 1932. Certain members of the Box Alder congregation had felt the call of this movement and the "Gospel Lighthouse" was built in the early 1930's about one half mile from the United Church on land donated by Alfred and Mary Barker. Now Box Alder had two churches and the membership of the new church included all the Barker families, some of the Hyatt families, the Green family, later Mrs. Fraser and others. Yearly camp meetings began to be held in Box Alder on the bank of the LaVallee River and were attended by many in the community.

To me it has always seemed odd that a force that should unify people should cause so much distrust and division. Religion seems to be at the root of so many of the world's problems. Even back in those days there were hard feelings and as someone said it was better not to mention religion in Box Alder. The fact that many of the people in Box Alder were related made it a little harder. Years later I knew that religion divided families as well as the community.

Some of this feeling of course trickled down to the children and we were always a little conscious of what was called "the split' as we discussed these things at school. Those children seemed to have such excitement in their church. The camp meetings were well planned affairs with huge tents set up to feed the people and to hold the meetings. The public was invited to some of the general meetings and they were so emotional and stirring. The singing of those Pentecostal hymns was carried out with such fervour with their irresistible rhythms. The ministers and speakers pleaded with the unsaved to come forward. The emotional impact of this was noticeable even to a child.

I was about nine when we attended one of these meetings and I was so susceptible and caught up by the emotion and sheer drama that I rose, ready to come forward and be saved. My mother grabbed my coat tails and plumped me down again. After, she tried to explain why it was not appropriate for me (or anyone) to do something swayed only by emotion. It was not an easily forgotten scene. My grandfather was with us, walking with a cane by then. The speaker took his arm and said, "Are you saved, Brother?" My grandfather said quietly, "I accepted the Lord as my saviour when I was seventeen." The man shouted, "Hallejulah, Brother!"

Special meetings were held where baptisms took place in the LaVallee River. These, our school friends told us were total immersion, much superior to the sprinkling of the United Church, as all sins were then washed away. They told us other things too about the mystical speaking in tongues and told of one of the school children that had done this, although he looked no different to us. We were sometimes labelled as sinners. What could we say? We had nothing to come back with as thrilling as this. My brother Eric, rarely at a loss for a comeback, would sum it all up by quoting biblically, "Judge not and be not judged." I do not think the adults of either church knew how seriously the children took religion.

One time some of the children came with the sobering and frightening news that the world was going to end at a certain date and time. I did not tell my mother of my concern. Some scoffed but soon all of us were going to "church" in the school woodshed at recesses, singing hymns, learning Bible verses and doing our best to be ready when we met our Maker. The suspense was almost unbearable as the day grew near and at last came like any other. We watched the clock and, as the prophesied time came and went, we sneaked glances at the ones who had been most sure that doom was upon us. The world did not end. Soon we back at our old pursuits of skipping and baseball. A lesson had been learned.

So we went to our church and heard of some of the events in the other church and basically got along well. I recall just a little of the York family but have clear memories of the Tyler family. There were four children, Wayne, Mervin, Margaret and Shirley. They fitted into our school as they were all well liked, and all athletic and lively. Wayne became a minister in later life.

The people who attended our church were neighbours and attendance varied of course. The church would be filled at

Christmas and Easter or special occasions. Then we would see Clarence and Rena Hughes with their family. Clarence was Mom's cousin and was a short stocky man who worked very hard at the same steady pace.

Transportation was a problem as not all the families had cars. Clarence had a very old Model T type that Eric always thought would never make it up the hill when they came to visit us. Evelyn Brown with her family also would come at special times There were others like the Cadds and the Redfords who came from different communities for a time. The McCoy children often came. There was a group, however; the regulars during the 1930's and 1940's and these are the ones I remember the best.

First in my mind was my mother, granddaughter of George Strachan Sr. one of the founders of Grace Methodist, who recalled their stern and strict background. She remembered that her father had taken "the pledge" and was very much against the consumption of alcohol. This concept stayed with Mom and she tried her best to protect us from the evils of alcohol and tobacco. One must admit that the misuse of alcohol has caused untold misery through the years. My mother was very proud of her heritage and was one of mainstays of the church for many years. We did not often miss church and Sunday School.

I can see her in my mind's eye wearing her black winter coat with the big fur collar. No wonder I recall that coat as she wore it for eleven years. At that time all ladies wore hats and gloves. Women did not wear pants or slacks except for barn chores, and the men always wore suits and ties. I can only wonder what these old disciples of the church would think of the modern and casual garb at church now.

We walked to church summer and winter unless in bad weather someone offered us a ride. Once after Eric had acquired an old Buick, Mom decided to take his car. I was amazed as I had no idea she could drive. Then she told us tales of driving the Model T's and a 490 Chev truck belonging to her father and of having an arm broken by the crank recoiling.

At church we sat together and knew that we were not to wriggle or squirm or look around and above all not to laugh. It was then that I found out how very funny things could seem in church and how hard it was to suppress a laugh when a door would slam or cousin Melvin Cain would pretend to trip or an older cousin would wink or make faces and try to make me laugh.

The first minister I remember was Mr. Harry Kay. One Sunday his wife and baby came with him and Mrs. Kay set the baby in a little chair in the aisle. The baby dropped a toy fairly close to me and Mrs. Kay motioned for me to pick it up. I was only eight years old and was so sure that we were not to move that I stolidly sat there and would not help out. Mr. Bray was the next minister and then Mr. Parsons who died tragically.

The ladies of the churches took turns in giving the minister his noon meal as he started quite early in the morning at the first of his three charges and then went on to Emo. This was often a source of worry to Mom and I am sure to the others. Mom would decide whether to make scalloped or mashed potatoes to go with the cold beef or roast chicken. She often served tomato aspic and beet pickles and her famous lemon snow dessert. We children liked this Sunday because of the meal and then we were able to ride to church with the minister.

My grandfather and grandmother attended church. Grandmother Strachan named Winnifred, was Grandpa's third wife and the only grandmother we knew. Grandpa had had two or three strokes and walked with a cane and with some effort. He was a truly good man trying to live by the old standards set down by his father and all those sturdy Methodists from his past. He had lovely snow-white hair and bright blue eyes, the Strachan trademark. My mother had both. Grandpa had had a sad life but we were unaware of such things then. Grandpa was highly respected in the community and later when I would tell people that I was George Strachan's granddaughter that seemed to be a mark in my favour. Years later Rosella Galbraith said that her uncle had worked for him and that George Strachan was the only man who paid him more than they had bargained for before the job.

Winnifred made a deep impression on me. She played the organ at church and would seem majestic as she took her place at the front. She was a tall woman with an innate dignity that nothing could fluster. She wore gloves and a hat and linen suits or dark patterned dresses, always looking cool and elegant and completely ladylike. Indeed, she was of that generation that produced "ladies." One time my mother had made me a new little coat that pleased me. After church I stood out on the step telling people as they came out, "This is my new coat. My mother made it from an old one." I remember no one's reaction except my grandmother's. She whisked me aside and told me sternly, "A lady never discusses her clothing, Elizabeth."

The church was full for Grandpa's funeral on the day before Christmas 1946 and Grandmother died six months later.

There were the four Cain families, Harry and Tillie, Aunt Edna and Uncle Albert, Earl and Vera and Clifford and Lorraine. They all had families and lived in close proximity. Going there was exciting as some of the children were our cousins, some were second cousins and some were cousins of our cousins, not related to us but all like one big family. They all came to church, at least the women and children did and the men came occasionally. The Cains had a car before others in the community and would all pile in or perhaps make two trips to get everyone to church. They worked with communal property like the car.

The Cain men were all tall, lean, quiet and fast moving. The men worked in bush camps in the winter and Harry, the oldest, was a boss whose boundless energy and drive earned him the nickname "Hurri-cane." Tillie was a sweet and gentle lady. Albert married our Aunt Edna and we were often in their home. Albert was quiet but liked to tease us just a bit at times. Edna was hard working, and always kind and generous to our family.

Tillie and Edna were stalwarts in the church until their families moved. By the late 1940's Vera and Lorraine and their families were the ones that attended. Vera was Mom's first cousin. After my grandmother left Vera played the organ, walking in her sedate fashion to the front of the church. In later years Earl came to church with her and the children Raymond and Arleen.

Lorraine and Clifford had a family of four, Joan, Kenneth, Ronald and Lyn. Clifford did not go to the camps as he ran the farms and did the barn chores in the winter. He was always quiet but seemed amused by our chatter when I would visit my friend Joan. Joan played the organ for Sunday School and sometimes for church.

Bud Cain, Harry's son, married Oda Klassen, a gentle and loving person after the war. They had a large family and had sorrow in their lives as they lost a baby and later two young, teenaged sons. They were in church no matter what and kept that church going ethic.

The English Hay family had five sons, Jim, Gilbert. Ken, Gordon and Paul. Mom and Mrs. Hay were close friends, although they never called each other by first names. Mrs. Hay was a nurse and people in the community were well aware of her skill and kindness. I had reason to bless her years later when I had a very ill small son. Her skillful hands and confident manner made things look not quite so bleak. Mrs. Hay had beautiful deep brown eyes and she just exuded compassion, love and concern as well as good humour.

Mr. Hay was so scholarly and well versed and well educated and he never seemed like the typical farmer type, but rather like an absentminded professor. He had a quiet, dry sense of humour and he and Mrs. Hay would laugh and joke with Mom when they were together. His views on religion did not seem to quite fit and Mom had one cryptic entry in her diary from this time, "Disagreed with Mr. Hay." I would think that this was about religion.

Bill Smith, janitor at the school was another regular. He was a Scottish veteran but of what war I do not know. He lived in a small house that was actually in Lash Township and walked everywhere. It was known that Bill "drank" but that seemed to be taken into account and he took part in all social activities in Box Alder. Bill loved to sing and he had a good Scottish tenor voice. He was none too clean and I recall the black that was engrained around his fingernails and in the creases of his neck. Bathing facilities were often limited in those days. Children notice such things but are not unduly bothered by them. I liked Bill and we became quite good friends, dirty fingernails and all. I cherish a little note and a picture that I have of him and recall the Scottish songs that he loved to sing.

Uncle Charlie and Aunt Nettie Strachan were churchgoers. Uncle Charlie had a short temper and, believe me, as children we were on our best behaviour around them. Their family attended church also until they moved away. Earl had been killed in a tragic accident close to their home. Harvey, Milton and Meryle were there sometimes with families but it is Dean and Mary that I remember best.

Dean took over the Strachan farm and the big brick house that was and still is beautiful, now owned by other people. Dean farmed and Mary kept an immaculate house with their two children, Billie and Connie. Dean and Mary were always kind to us as young teenagers and we were very fond of them. It seemed that they never went anywhere without a group of young people in the back of their truck.

Christmas was an exciting time because the concert was held in the church. The church was larger than the school and had the bonus of having portable wings that were put in place and made it much easier for entrances and exits. I imagine that these were made when the Box Alder Community Club, as did all the communities, put on plays on a regular basis. I thought that having the wings added an air of professionalism to our programs. When the church was packed on concert night and the air smelled of balsam fir and the gas lanterns hissed away as they spread their glow, it was a truly exciting event in a child's life.

The church was used by the Ladies' Aid for their fund raising events. This group of ladies worked tirelessly to raise money, to pay their share of the minister's salary, keep the church in good repair and help pay for maintenance for the church manse that was in Emo. Their major fundraisers were the tea and bake sale and the annual fowl supper. Both these events were held in the church. Before the church was renovated I think that a wood-burning cook stove was brought in to cook the vegetables. The chickens were roasted at home and each lady would bring three or four of these, plus pies, pickles, vegetables to be cooked, coleslaw, dishes and cutlery.

It was a major operation and the whole community helped out. Men were delegated to set up tables on sawhorses, and do any of the heavier work. Men with cars also picked up donations of food, as many people at that time had no vehicles. The young teenage girls acted as waitresses. Even those who were not regular church-goers donated pies or a roast chicken. When the Catholic Roy family moved in in the late 1940's the ladies did not ask for donations, but were very pleased when two lovely chocolate pies were delivered

This little group of women, faithful to their cause, worked so hard and took their responsibility seriously. In 1948 their receipts for the year totalled $429.73. The fowl super brought in $124.70 and the bazaar in April $66.70. These women were the social leaders of Box Alder as they provided concerts, ice cream socials, sold treats at the school picnics, bought candy for the children at the Christmas concert, remembered the sick, the births and the bereaved with flowers or fruit. Their work was organized through the United Church.

In 1950 the church celebrated the 25th year of church union. The church was renovated and re-dedicated at a special service. The high ceilings were lowered and a small room was made at the back by dividing the large one. The high platform was reduced to a much lower one and the interior painted. Most of the work was done by volunteer labour. One of the major changes was the installation of electric lights and power. This made a vast difference and things went along very well for a few years. However, big changes were just ahead in the rural churches.

This was still a four point charge (Emo, Devlin, LaVallee and Box Alder) which was quite a heavy one for a minister. Congregations began to decline as communities changed with the coming of electrical power and increased modes of transportation. People went further afield for entertainment or work.

In Box Alder membership dwindled. Mom came home from church one day to report that only she, Mrs. Hay and Vera Cain were there. The minister went through the whole service as if every pew were filled. Soon after this the Hay family moved away. My mother, due to changes in our family, took up employment in Fort Frances. The older Cain families moved away. Others followed and as it was the same in the other communities, the Box Alder church closed and then the LaVallee church. The churches in Devlin and Emo became the focal points of the former 4-point charge and remain so to this day.

By then I was away from this community also and took little note of what was happening in Box Alder. The small fenced in area where the church stood kitty-corner from the school is still there. As far as I know it has never been able to be cleared from the United Church ownership to belong to Brian McCoy as the rest of that section does. The school and church, both icons of my youth were torn down in the late 1950's. I still feel a pang of nostalgia when I drive past that corner.

The Gospel Lighthouse? This little church built by volunteer labour is still in operation with Delbert Barker as the minister. This building has a distinctive architectural style that it has retained after being rebuilt in the 1960's. The sign, in Gothic style lettering, always interested me as it was said that my father had painted the original sign for the church. The little church looks very nice nestled near the banks of the LaVallee River. It is good to think that there is still one church with roots of those pioneers of the old Methodist faith in Box Alder.

High School Years

Was I ready to take the big step from our one room rural school to the world of higher education in Fort Frances? Even the thought of Fort Frances was intimidating as I had been there very few times. I had little idea what was in store and yet when I came home after my first day of high school I told my mother," I think I'm going to like it."

Both my brothers had made attempts at high school. Alan walked 3 miles across country to take some grade nine courses at LaVallee School. Later he boarded with Mom's cousin Hazel Wilson in Fort Frances and took an after school job delivering groceries at the Food Basket, a grocery store run by "Tud" Truax. One day I came home from school to find my Aunt Edna there, and I remember the shock when she told me that something had happened to Alan and Mom had gone to Fort Frances. An older man from Emo was driving with his windshield almost completely covered by frost and he struck Alan's bicycle and ran partly over Alan's chest. The man was charged and by all accounts felt really terrible about the accident. I think Mom said that he paid Alan's hospital bills.

Alan was taken to the hospital and was quite badly hurt and said he remembers the doctor saying, "I think he's gone." When he came home he looked so pale and sick. I think his high school ended with that experience and he started to work at different jobs and the farm when he recovered.

Eric did not have to board in Fort Frances as the year he started, John Hyatt had been hired to transport students starting from Aylsworth and all along the way to Fort Frances. This vehicle was simply a large wooden box set on the back of a one ton truck. There were wooden benches around the sides and in the winter a small wood stove provided heat. There were few rules and regulations in those days and the farm students had the opportunity to attend high school and yet stay at home. There are stories about this school bus that may still abound, but the ultimate was the day it tipped over, woodstove and all. No one was hurt, no one seemed overly upset and this bus continued to run for about two years.

Eric was not a model student and did not really take to high school except for the friends he met for a smoke or for skipping school. A good friend was Roy Dick who often came home with Eric for the weekend. He liked the things that the boys did, like hunting and farming and seemed to fit into our family quite well. Mom and Mrs. Dick exchanged ration coupons, butter for sugar. On Monday the boys would set out for school but would sometimes return, saying that they had missed the bus. The large tree near the corner conveniently hid them until the bus passed and then they would have one more day roaming the woods or doing chores. Eric did not finish grade nine and then he was away to the work world also. Many years later he got his high school diploma as an adult in Saskatchewan,

In 1948 the route was taken over by Clarence Wright, Fort Frances Bus Lines and the driver was Art Wood. I began high school in September 1949. My friend Joan Cain, a year ahead of me, was able to tell me a little bit about behaviour and clothing required. I bought my saddle shoes for $3.95 and white bobby socks with the tops that turned down, from the Eaton's catalogue with my baby sitting money. Sweater sets with a short sleeved pullover and a cardigan of the same colour were the fashion at that time. I did not have one of these sets, but Aunt Edna made me several cotton blouses. Mom thought I needed at least one good black skirt to supplement my meager wardrobe so that too was ordered from Eaton's. Slacks were not allowed to be worn in school.

I was taller than the average girl and certainly chunkier than the average, so getting clothing to fit was always a problem. The length was rarely right for me and everything had to be let out or let down. The new black skirt was no exception and Mom let out the hem as far as it would go, faced it with strips of an old black slip and hemmed it neatly. The day before school began I was given the job of pressing the hem.

We were still using flat irons that were heated on the woodstove. I was carefully pressing the hem with a damp cloth and I got dreaming, no doubt about the day at hand, when the odour of scorched wool alerted me. I lifted the iron and could see the whole shape of the iron burned right into my new skirt. Horror filled me, as this was the only really good piece of clothing I had. I called Mom and stood there holding the iron. Mom had a number of mild expletives and on this occasion she gazed speechless at the skirt and finally said," Well, Lumping Lupiter!"

Although later we laughed and laughed at her strange expression, at that time it was terribly serious. I was in tears and had decided that my schooling days were over forever. My mother, always resourceful, set briskly to work picking out the scorched edges. (Those old irons were smaller than modern irons.) She cut up some garment of hers that matched the material and carefully sewed in a patch. When finished and due to the position of the burn at the hem it was barely noticeable. She was excellent at this kind of thing.

So I started high school in a patched skirt and a dark green cardigan sweater with my saddle shoes and short socks. Everything was so new to me and I did not know one other person in my Nine A class. The boys and girls entered by separate doors and lockers were on different floors. I shared an assigned locker with Marion Angus from Burriss. You chose either the commercial or general course determining whether you became a teacher or nurse or a secretary. The classes were 35 minutes long and there were some double classes for Home-Ec or Shop. We were given one hour at lunch and I think there were nine classes a day. The changing of classes and having so many teachers was very confusing and exciting and I learned to follow the crowd. Sometimes yet I have a disturbing dream of trying to find my way to classes and being hopelessly lost among the crowds of students and having many obstacles in my way.

One thing did change. Up until then I was called by my full name Elizabeth but in high school most fellow students promptly began to call me "Liz." Most people who have known me longest still call me Elizabeth. I never cared to be called "Lizzie", although Uncle Tom and Mr. Grennier the mailman always did.

It is unnecessary to say how different times were over 60 years ago. If I earned a little money looking after children or at other jobs I usually spent it on clothing. Slacks were not allowed and stockings were not fashionable, so we often froze our knees. In the coldest weather I would wear slacks to walk to the corner and then leave them and my overshoes in the anteroom of the church before I got on the bus. Anything to be in style! I set my hair in pin curls as 99% of the other girls did then.

At that time there was a certain stigma attached to being a farm or country student. The bus students could not take part in sports or activities after school, as there always the bus to catch. I made friends with the other students from the bus and there were others that I knew like Grace McCoy or Valerie Langtry who were related to me. There was an "in group", as there always is, that was above us in popularity if not in intellect. If there were snubs we discussed them later with stinging retorts that we might have made.

The fall that I started high school a bad fire destroyed the east wing of the school and caused much smoke and water damage. After a few days, arrangements were made for classes to be held in various other places. I was among those that went to schoolrooms at St. Mary's School. The bus still picked us up at the high school and the bus students had to rush across town to catch this bus at 4:00 P:M, as we all seemed terrified of missing our ride home. There was a large auditorium/gymnasium and cafeteria, as well as new classrooms when construction was done.

I was a fair student in most subjects but math remained a bugbear all through school. We had such a variety of teachers. Miss

Simmie, a small older woman taught art and geography and for the first time I heard terms like the Canadian Shield and The Group of Seven. We began instruction in that foreign language French from Mr. LeBlanc who taught us rollicking folk songs. Mrs. Alma Henry, a severe grey-haired lady, presented history and also led the school orchestra. Mrs. Henry had been at the school for many years and seemed rather stern and ageless but we learned history! Mr. Fleurie, a younger teacher, also taught history and in Grade 11 taught the Ancient History that I really enjoyed. We studied Deeds of Gods and Heroes in grade nine. Mr. Hamm taught the science and chemistry classes very well and had a good dry sense of humour. These subjects were all new and foreign to me, as we had not deviated very much from the little grey course of study used in all the public schools in Ontario.

Leroy Newman was the principal. Miss Yakimischak taught Home Economics and Miss Jackson was the teacher for Physical Training or PT as it was called. Young and energetic, she flipped around in little, short full skirts with her whistle around her neck. There may be readers that will recall those blue cotton gym suits that we were required to wear. There were other teachers such as Mr. Houghton, Mr Ross and Mr. Book that I did not have for classes. Mr. Steele was a wonderful English teacher and one of my favourites.

We did not take part in high school social events. I had come to know the Devlin students well when I attended school there and often stayed overnight with friends Iris Mclean, Betty Hyatt or Lois Cooke to attend a dance or event in the Devlin Hall. It was not the modern building that is so well used today but it was large and had a good dance floor. When built it was a two storey structure with a large upper room that you entered by an outside staircase. I remember going to a dance there held by the Junior Farmer's and the floor was actually swaying. It was later condemned and all functions were held downstairs. The music was often supplied by Smith's popular three piece orchestra who played wonderful old time and popular tunes and square dances.

Grade Eleven and Twelve were the best years as I had made friends and felt more confident. Helen Mudge, my cousin from Mine

Centre, had entered high school by then and she was placed in my homeroom class. I have such memories of fun and laughter and incredible mix-ups in Home Ec and science classes. We would laugh until our sides ached and try to stifle the giggles. We joined the choir as the practices were at noon and if there was an event to attend I stayed with Helen or Aunt Chappie. There were not many boys so Mr. Krawetz, after listening to my voice, often had me sing bass. Helen and I found this hilariously funny. One time we sang at the Music Festival and the required song was," Music, when soft voices die." It was a difficult piece and when we finished the adjudicator was not kind. Poor Mr. Krawetz was crushed and had tears in his eyes and we all felt sorry for him. I think our best song was, "Smoke gets in your eyes."

In the last year of high school our family lives changed and one could say our home was broken up. Alan had married and took over the farm. Mom, Marion and I went to live for the winter in the big Roy house down the road that was vacant. It had never been properly finished and was very cold. In March Mom applied for and got a job as second cook at Rainycrest Home for the Aged. Mom asked Mrs. Hay if I could stay there to finish Grade Twelve and she made other arrangements for Marion. I was very fond of Mrs. Hay and even though she had other boarders, she promptly agreed. I helped her as much as possible with the work and really enjoyed the atmosphere there.

I was glad to leave high school behind me and my mother was there to see me graduate. She had never had this opportunity. When we played Scrabble she would often win by a good margin and then she would say, "Not bad for person who never went to high school."

There are things that stand out in my memory of high school, going to Ray Holmes Confectionery and having a lemon coke for 5¢ at noon hour, or with three friends ordering one of their delectable sundaes with a spoon for each of us. We never had lunch downtown but always brought it from home. Occasionally I bought lunch from the cafeteria that opened after the fire and I had my first taste of chili there. I remember when a fellow student was killed in an accident and the shock that ran through the whole school. I never attended a foot ball or hockey game as "bus kids" did not do these things. It is rather strange to meet some of those lovely young girls or handsome boys now and to see what time has done to all of us and to realize that many are no longer with us.

I recall with shame skipping school and I do not advise that for anyone. Sometimes with friends we would walk across the river to look around Woolworth's big store and to buy cigarettes. I had started smoking, as nearly everyone smoked in those days and we were allowed to smoke on the bus. I write this now just for information and not because I am happy about it.

I attended the Graduation Dance at the end of June with Bob Fisher, a friend who was also going on to Summer School and this was officially the end of my high school days. We wore long white gowns and carried bouquets to graduation and wore corsages to the dance following. In a way it was more like the Prom that is held in high schools now.

At that time there was a shortage of teachers and a program was in place where, by attending two summer school sessions and teaching for two years, we were eligible to attend Teacher's College in North Bay. With a group of friends, Jean and Alec Ogden, Garth young, Jean Whiddon, Bob Fisher and others, I took this way of entering the teaching profession and went to Port Arthur in July, 1953 to the six week summer course. I would be teaching at Burriss School in September.

My high school years were good years, but I was very glad when they were over. I do not recall them with the same fondness or acute nostalgia as the time I spent at the Box Alder Public School, but my high school years were good years and a necessary part of growing up and preparing for the next step.

My First Teaching Job

From the time I was twelve years old a teacher was what I wanted to be. I knew that Normal School, as it was called at that time, at North Bay was a requirement and wondered if I would ever be able to attend.

During my last year at High School in 1953 I learned of the program to recruit new teachers and decided to enroll. This involved two summer sessions while teaching and then attending Teachers' College. Norman Muir, the school inspector at that time, was involved and set up times that we could observe teachers in their classrooms. I spent a day in the classroom of Audrey Livingston at Sixth Street School and was very impressed with her handling of the Kindergarten class.

I had applied to several schools and when Angus Hyatt, chairman of the Burriss Consolidated School Board, came to interview me I accepted his offer of a salary of $2000 a year. When I met with the school board to discuss salaries, Mrs. Hyre the principal was present also. When my salary came up Jack Booth, the Chairman, said that since I was just a young girl starting out they were offering me $1800 instead of the $2000 that was advertised. Either amount seemed monumental to me and up until then I don't think that I ever had even $100 in my possession so I was ready to accept. I caught Mrs. Hyre's eye and saw the sight shake of her head and said in my most businesslike manner that I would expect the $2000 that was advertised.

Just after July 1st of that year, a number of fellow students and I boarded the train for Port Arthur (no highway yet) for six weeks of intensive training at the old Lakehead Technical School building. Jean and Alec Ogden, Jean Whiddon, Bob Fisher, Garth Young, Glen Ewald, were among the group that I remember most. It was the first time I had been away from home and friendly faces were important.

When September came school did not start at the usual time due to a polio outbreak, as it was deemed unwise to have large groups of children assembled. It was mid September when I, after six weeks of training, faced my first class of 28 pupils. This was the grade one and two children, Dave Ogden had the middle room with grades three, four and five, while Mrs. Helen Hyre, the principal, taught grades seven and eight. She helped me over many a rough spot.

I began to jot down first impressions and observations and many of my pupil's original words in old work books, with pencil or using one of those early ballpoint pens where the ink soaked through the page, often in a near illegible hand. In 1957 I decided to decipher and preserve what I called my "gems" in a better fashion and that book lay among my papers for over 50 years until I recorded and saved them on computer. At first I thought it would be good to divide my recollections into categories but then decided to copy just some of what I had written. This is a very condensed version. I did not use last names but if any of those students should be reading this they will know who they are.

Even after so many years I can close my eyes and see that old classroom and those rows of children that I remember so well. No other group has stayed in my memory as clearly as those children that I had the privilege of teaching in those two years.

*S*EPTEMBER, 1953:

September is nearly over and I have been teaching twelve days. Although I am dreadfully inexperienced I have developed some sort of routine and learned to deal with certain situations in an adequate way. It is certainly interesting and we were all impressed when one day I momentarily lost my temper.

On the first day of school Bobbie confessed with tears spilling from his eyes, "Teacher, I can't read and I can't write." I nearly wept with him while reassuring him, for I felt insecure also.

Dianne told me she had saved eleven cents to buy me a concert present. Anita told me, "I like school and you and everything." Some are so independent like the one that insisted on sharpening her pencil "her own self" and others are just the opposite and have to have their oranges peeled and zippers zipped. Clare likes oranges and doesn't often have one. She will see a grade one child struggling to peel an orange and offer to do it. Then she will say. "Now you have to give me half, I peeled it for you." Usually a bargain is struck without my intervention.

I have done my first register and it balanced. I have also received my very first pay check from Mr Maxwell and I intend to spend every cent of this one.

*O*CTOBER:

Mr. Hickey was here today for religious instruction and the children were restless. He asked a question obviously wanting angels as the answer. I tried not to grin when 'fairies' was the closest he got.

When I told the children to put on their coats and go for recess Leslie said, "The cow got my coat off the clothesline." Being a rural person I understood this kind of thing.

The children were very skeptical about the bulbs that we planted so I hope they will grow. Just in case they don't bloom Bobbie brought me more flowers.

Barry has new shoes and exhibits them so proudly and even said a few words out loud. He has only whispered so far.

Larry approached me timidly and said, "Please teacher, I'm hot." I was concerned and felt his forehead as Larry had just had his tonsils out, but he said, "Please teacher, I just got my winter underwear on." It was a warm day.

Judy said they never drank milk. I asked if they had cows and she replied cheerfully. "Nope, just two bulls."

Bobbie always wants to sing "Too Old to Cut the Mustard|" in music period and likes to sing it for us.

*N*OVEMBER:

A new month and "the day is cold and dark and dreary." It is such a dismal day. The Halloween party went well and the children had a joyous time but my legs ached that night.

Cleanliness was the topic and we were discussing the virtues of a clean neck. After the lesson Roger said," Jackie has a dirty neck." Clare indignantly said, "He does not!" standing up for her cousin.

Such a day! Katherine dropped Aurilla's hat down into the toilet, the old fashioned chemical type. Rilla said, with arms akimbo said, "She just dropped it right in!" We had Kathy fish it out with a long furnace poker.(Now I am not sure why) Then Donna vomited all over. What a mess, over her sweater, desk, dress and floor. After I got her cleaned up as well as I could she said quite cheerfully, "I sure feel better now." I can't say that I did.

Edgar rushed up at lunch to tell me that Larry had 18 sandwiches in his lunch! They do keep close tabs on what others have in lunch pails and sometimes trades are made. They also are very interested in what I bring for lunch and often check it out. They eat most of their lunch at recess and one of them asked if I only ate at lunch because it wasn't worth while getting mine out at recess.

Near the end of the month a new girl came into grade one. I heard her being questioned by another pupil as to what her mother's name was. Then she said, "Is your mother good?" The new girl replied, "Well, she's my mother, ain't she?" Good answer and I did not correct her grammar.

The Christmas spirit just exudes from me at the first snow. The children gambol and cavort like puppies. Roger asked if we could sing about Redolph the Rude nosed Reindeer.

December

December 4th and only eleven pupils are here so far this snowy day. The children think it is quite a joke and snicker when they catch each other's eye.

Sidney asked just before recess if he could leave the room. I asked him if he could wait and he said he could. A second later he said, "Please, I can't wait," and it was obvious he couldn't, so off he went.

They preface everything with "Please" or "Please Teacher" and I don't know how that came about, perhaps passed down from generation to generation.

Mr. Hickey asked what Christmas was. Christine said, "A great time." Bobby replied that we get toys and there were similar answers. I think the poor man wanted answers along a more spiritual line but he phrases his questions rather poorly at times.

December 17: The odor of tangerine oranges fills the air. I love it. Edgar said proudly, "We've got our Christmas oranges, do you?" I always think of a tangerine in the toe of a Christmas stocking. We are up to our ears in concert today. This is our first big practice downstairs on the stage and I hope we all know our parts.

One of the children has reported at home that I ordered haircuts and shampoos for everybody for the concert! After our dance practice Leslie said, "Whew, that wears a guy right out." He brought an old suit coat for the play and told me that his mother said that "it was not to be threw around."

January 1954

A clean New Year to fill with triumphs and mistakes. The kids are the same except for a few missing teeth and scrapes and bruises. Joyce opened her mouth wide for me to see "that black filling down there."

Anita said so proudly, "My aunt set my place at the table this year." It takes so little for a child to feel important and I wondered if her aunt knew how happy this small action made Anita.

One day we were talking about beards and Larry told me that his dad had a beard but he shaved when he went to town and that he even did it for the concert this year.

On January 7th When I was giving out new workbooks Gary remarked, "We are sure going to have a tough time getting through these books."

Some girls were noting their progress on the spelling chart. Christine pointed out. "Only one wrong for me. That means that every day I'm getting a little more gooder." Sometimes a grammar lesson does not really seem to apply and would spoil the effect of such a revelation.

Evelyn was not in school and Leslie told me that she had put her tongue on the meter box. (Does every child do this? I remembered putting my tongue on the well pump on a bitter morning.) I asked if she were badly hurt but Leslie said, "Oh no, it only took the tip of her tongue off."

Yesterday Bobbie had a heart spell. Poor little boy to have such trouble. His mother had told me that he was a 'blue baby' and she wrote me such a lovely note.

Karin asked to go for a drink but since it was ten minutes until recess and as such things lead to a chain reaction, I refused her request. Irene came to me shortly after to tell me that Karin said that she hadn't had a drink all today or yesterday. I still refused.

Roger came in just splitting with laughter (he is such a jolly little boy) to tell me, "Alan just went outside singing ki-yi yippee-ippee-ay and he hasn't got a coat on."

Subject was germs and Dianne said, "I had the measles and the chicken pops." Gary not to be outdone said, "I had mumps, pneumonia and the whooping cough—I think."

I had to miss a day of school and Donna told me that "she sure missed me yesterday".

FEBRUARY

Their conversations which I love to listen to cover so many topics. Some of the little girls were talking about having boyfriends and one of them said, "Shame on you—a little kid like you having a boyfriend." Another reported that Clare had gone "clean crazy" over one of the grade five boys.

Gary is, oh so serious most of the time and is obviously a deep thinker. This morning he said to me confidentially, "Elephants have big ears, don't they? I think they're about as big as a cabbage leaf."

The Valentine's Day party was long anticipated and went very well.

MARCH

Mr. Muir, the public school inspector was here yesterday March 4th. The children were angels and the pupils that he talked to displayed their knowledge creditably. I was so proud of them and they were all so good and when I praised them afterwards they were very proud of themselves.

In our morning discussion Shela told me, "Last night Christine and I went to bed at 10 after. " When I asked 10 after what, she replied, " Well, I don't know," giving the impression that I was an utter idiot for even asking.

Larry said in a surprised tone, "I can see with one eye." He also asked me if the world would quit. He must have been talking to Gary.

Today a little girl told me she was not in school yesterday because her mother only had enough bread and butter for the older sister. I remembered when my mother would have to call my aunt to send some extra lunch for us when times were so hard.

In health class we were discussing the topic of danger. Roger confided. "My grandfather got his foot cut off with the axe and it bled." They are so serious when they tell these things and are not above trying to outdo each other with similar stories.

I love the notes that I get and I keep some of them. Today I had two: "I kept Evelyn out of school as she had laryngitis and Leslie had a pretty bad cold," and this one, "Donald has been rather sick and is still not feeling good. But he is that crazy to get to school that I am letting him go. Would you see, dear, that he don't stay out too long as his ears bothers him and you will see that he is somewhat hard of hearing." One girl after an absence told me that her mother was too weak to write her note.

April

I just fell part way down the stairs carrying the screen for the film projector. Dave, the middle room teacher, rushed out shouting, "The screen—did you hurt the screen?" The school had a Bell & Howell film projector and screen and we were able to order educational films from the National Film Board. No one had television yet and the films were greatly enjoyed on a Friday afternoon and I recall watching the wedding of Princess Elizabeth and Prince Philip.

Aurilla has an interesting way of talking. She does not say 'underline' but 'lineunder.' She will say things like 'pop coaket' for coat pocket,' and 'postfence' for 'fencepost.' She tells me that someone has a 'richwatch' and spoke of someone who fell 'fat on his flace." It is quite charming and I am sure she will outgrow this way of talking as her articulation is very good.

It is damp rainy day and the children smell like small wet dogs – not at all unpleasant.

Gary has drawn a prehistoric monster with fins all down the back and when I admired it and asked what it was called he said it was a "dinocerous." (There was not nearly as much known about dinosaurs at that time and the topic did not come up often. Thank goodness, as I knew very little about them.)

April 26: Today I have four beginners. At that time children of the correct age were allowed to come to school after Easter for a sort of readiness preparation for Grade one in September. Little Tommie was sick and unable to come. Jimmie refused to move into the seat allotted to him but preferred to sit with his brother. Larry was so embarrassed and told me, "Please Teacher, Mommy said Jimmie was supposed to do what you told him." I assured Larry that soon Jimmie would want to be in his own desk and he did. When Jimmie did a bit of work I gave him, Larry reported proudly, "Jimmie's working now, Teacher." It is heart warming to see how protective these older children are of their younger siblings. Elizabeth is the first of her family to attend school so has no protector but she is lively and not as shy as some. David has to be escorted to the 'baf room' by his older brother Gary. It has certainly livened up my classroom having four newcomers and my regular students are feeling quite superior to these unschooled beginners.

To paraphrase an old quotation-Those whom the gods would destroy, they first make new school teachers.

May

May 4: Today I have only 13 pupils so I am not too busy. The weather is extremely unseasonable and unreasonable. It began snowing Friday night and by the time the dance in the hall was over it was very bad. It snowed all day Saturday, Sunday and

Monday and now on Tuesday there is still snow in the air. We have about 15 inches of snow and roads are nearly impassable. The snow plow has been dismantled so we'll be here until it melts. Cars and trucks have been stuck several times on the hill. Milton Smith with his school bus was stuck on the highway. It has been drifting of course and the drifts in front of the doors are sometimes quite a surprise. One of the worst things to see are the pretty little songbirds lying dead on top of the snow. Hay is scarce and the cattle will suffer for this more than we will. Maybe someday I will tell my grandchildren about the spring of 1954.

May 5: Larry is such an amiable little fellow with a wide grin. Roger doesn't always take his work as seriously as he might but when he grins at me I find it impossible not to smile back. And can he draw! His pictures are treasures. The Taylor children have such beautiful posture.

Burriss School-1954. L R: Eddie Taylor, Liz Anderson, Bobbie Taylor

Elizabeth is unsure of herself and I make sure to praise her every effort. She is very affectionate and likes to be near to me. More and more I feel such a kinship with these little people and every one of them has endearing qualities. Jimmy now comes up in class without being persuaded. Dennis is a wonderful boy and he is quiet but only because he has important things on his mind. He reads every chance he has and that is so good to see in a child. A person who reads is rarely bored or lonely.

One child told me this, "When I get going good I can't stop and when I don't get going good I can stop." That is quite a discovery to make early in life.

Karin said, "Anita doesn't believe that every kind of pie tastes the same but I do."

Edgar took a ballpoint pen apart and blissfully rubbed the ink into his hands until they were a deep, deep blue and I caught him at it. It does not come off easily.

When the children draw pictures they like to put signs on them and they have often asked how to spell DANGER or BUMP. The latest one is SCHOOL-DRIVE SLOWLY. They are drawing pictures today depicting rain and as it is raining they have plenty of scope. I love rain at this time of year but rainy day recesses are chaos. They never tell you about these kind of things when you enter the teaching profession.

Our topic today was 'When I grow up". There was excited talk of cowboys, nurses, ballplayers, doctors and fishermen. Larry said thoughtfully, "When I grow up I'm going to be a father."

On the last day of May Roger told me that he had found 'a little blue egg about so round', and that he made a nest and took it into the house and was going to hatch an egg.

*J*UNE

This morning Roger brought me a tiny broken robin's egg.

There is much talk about the school picnic and the races and ballgames that will be held. This and the Christmas Concert are two very big events in the lives of these children as everyone in the family attends both events.

This ended my first year of teaching. During the year I had boarded with Melta Farmer and could not have had a better place. Other teachers had stayed with her and when I approached her she said that I could come on the condition that I did my own cooking. Melta was somewhat of a free spirit. She was in her fifties and had never married and was quite a remarkable and capable lady. She drove one of the school buses and often chauffeured people around the area and did not want to be tied down making meals at specific times.

Melta was very well known and as the school year progressed the two of us were often invited for supper at various homes in the community. I got to know many of my pupils' parents this way. Some of the homes we visited were Mrs. Marion Smith who read teacups and told fortunes, Jean Booth, Manson and Wendy West, Frank and Teenie Kennett, Vivian and Milton Smith, Dorothy and Charlie Taylor, Fred and Reta Topham, Derward and Helma Angus, Dick and Kate Norris, Morrison and Bessie Birrell, Donna and Reg Morrish, Dave and Janet Clark, Violet and Len Angus, Elsie and Alec Clark, Mrs. Mattoon, Bob and Marion Greenner. These visits were so enjoyable. Jean Booth told me that when she heard that such a young girl was hired as teacher she was not pleased but she said, "I take that back now and you are a good teacher." I thanked her for being so forthright and we were friends for many years.

I returned to Port Arthur for my second year of summer school and then came back to live with Melta and teach at the Burriss School again. We shared a love of picking berries and before I left in June, Melta had suggested that I buy some sugar and that she would pick strawberries and make jam for me in the summer. When I returned there was a nice little row of strawberry jam in my cupboard. Dave Ogden had moved to another school and Peggy Jo Norris who I knew from high school took over the middle room.

SUMMER SCHOOL-1955. Liz Anderson and Jean (Ogden) Corrigan

Liz Anderson holding a lamb at Norris Farm 1954

September

It was nice to come back and be greeted so warmly and the children of course were full of news. Larry told me that they had had a pig last year. When I asked if they were going to get another he said, "No, Dad was going to get one but he had a flat tire."

Aurilla told me that Robert her older brother had caught a rabbit in his trap and it looked just like her cat. Aurilla also asked, "What are them things that have a point on them and they are kind of like a rat or mouse?" She meant a mole.

Bobbie coloured a pig red and black all over and when one of the girls said it didn't look very nice, he replied that it had just rolled in the mud. They always have an explanation, perfectly plausible, for what they draw.

One day at indoor recess I asked a noisy child, "Can you talk in a normal tone of voice?" Sidney interpreted for me, "Teacher says to stop yelling."

December.

For the Christmas concert my class performed a simple version of Jack and the Beanstock. They liked the lines in it, "Here came the giant, Clump, Clump." Mrs. Hyre was a wonderful pianist and very talented at putting on these concerts One of the classes danced in a lively fashion to 'Christmas in Killarney' that year. Every child, dressed in his/her best, had a part whether large or small and the parents were not disappointed.

I remembered this concert for another reason. My brother Eric, always lively and exuberant, had just arrived home for Christmas and came to the concert. He bounded across the floor to give me a big hug and whirl me around. This was upsetting to my image as a staid, dignified and serious teacher. The children could not wait to ask if that was my boyfriend. They are quite conscious of boyfriends.

January 1955

Aurilla asked, "Was that dress you had on at the concert taffeta?" When I said it was she said proudly, "Well, so was mine."

Bobbie tells me that he is going to Winnipeg tonight for his operation. He is so brave.

It must be awful to be a little girl and have all your garters come undone at once. I have fastened two sets this morning. (One of best invention in children's clothing was tights. Before this, girls wore long brown cotton stockings that stayed up by fastening garters to a garter belt. In winter long underwear was often worn under the stockings, resulting in a rather lumpy look. Children's clothing has changed and improved greatly since those days)

I spent considerable time helping the girls with various aspects of their dress and I did not mind this at all, but on one day that must have been particularly busy I wrote:

If I ever have a daughter I will not permit her to have: Clip-on braces-garters-barrettes-overshoes that tie-corkscrew curls-dresses that tie in the back-garlic-shoelaces-buckles-safety pins instead of buttons-onion sandwiches at school. (though I love them myself.) Thereby I will save some poor teacher a lot of time and frustration.

I was skating today. The children were thrilled and some were amazed. Karin remarked. "I thought it would look funny to see you and Miss Norris skating but it don't."

Beverly calls marshmallows "mushmarillas."

Health Inspection: Teachers and students of earlier generations will remember this ritual. Hands were laid out on the desk to be checked, front and back, for cleanliness and fingernails checked. The child was to tell if he had brushed his teeth and was to display a clean handkerchief. Other children were monitors and results were entered on the health chart. Ideas of cleanliness varied and, heaven help you if the monitor had a grudge against you, for your name would have a bad mark beside it. Paper tissues were not widely used at that time and sometimes a grubby handkerchief was furtively passed from one child to another. It was rather a brutal system when you think of it and since the children drank from a common cup at the water cooler one wonders at the effectiveness of it as far as transmission of germs was concerned.

One morning Larry came to me weeping bitterly his hands spread out, "Teacher, they're not dirty." It was such a touchy situation and I conferred with the monitor and others were called to give opinions, in a judge and jury type of thing to take the pressure off the monitor and me.

Children have such a wonderful imagination and sense of anticipation. Beverly said, '"I asked Grandpa if he was going to the skating party and he said "Yes" but I didn't tell Momma and Grandpa will say, "Who's ready?" and Momma will say, "Where are we going?" and Grandpa will say, "To the skating party," and I won't be ready and he will have to wait on me and Momma will be surprised!"

I like the quiet times when they all pretend to sleep and some even snore softly.

*F*EBRUARY

Last year Dave Ogden had taken an interest in sports and the boys' hockey team and was helped by Rollie Hyre. Green and white sweaters were acquired somehow and the boys did very well when they played against other schools such as Devlin, LaVallee and Big Fork. One time for some reason I had to accompany the team to Big Fork with Rollie, in the capacity of teacher representation, certainly not as coach, as I knew next to nothing about hockey rules. It was just another experience and Earl Allen was teaching at Big Fork at that time. We met years later and talked about those "good old days."

Borrowing an expression of Anne Shirley's I wrote that I had a "Jonah day" when everything went wrong and I lost my temper and got cross with the children. I hate that and I cannot remember what caused the flare-up, only that I lost my temper and was ashamed of it. They are a very forgiving little bunch though.

The Valentine's Day party has arrived and some of that fudge looks good. February is half over and right now I feel half dead.

I am reading one of Dale Carnegie's books and find he quotes one of my favourites, Salutation of the Dawn –"Each day well lived makes every yesterday a dream of happiness and each tomorrow a vision of hope."

A little girl in a foster home situation was with us for a short time. Poor child, she became sick and then homesick and sobbed her heart out to me in my little storeroom. "I've been a bad girl before but I'm going to be good now." My heart ached for her and why she thought she had been bad.

Irene told me that her Grandma is sick and has to eat through a needle. Barry confided that Len and Cliff have new skates and won't be grousing all the time now. Sometimes I wonder if the parents have any idea the things the children tell me.

Aurilla asked if there were two kinds of boats, the kind you ride in and when you 'boat' for a party.

MARCH 21

Spring at last if only by the calendar. Gary and David are sporting new jeans and denim shirts and are trying not to appear conscious of them but nothing looks quite as new as new jeans. The kids all look so clean and scrubbed on Mondays mornings with clean clothes, shampooed hair and "shining morning faces."

A child asked me worriedly if he would have to go to high school if he didn't want to. I always pray my answers are adequate.

APRIL

Donna came to me, shy and blushing, "Teacher who put that red tape on your shoe? April Fool!"

Four beginners arrived today, Helen, Eddie, Orval and Kenny. They all have an older sibling in class. When they drew a picture of something they liked to eat Orval drew ice cream, Helen bananas, Eddie carrots and Kenny drew plain old potatoes. I'm with Kenny.

At some point in this year the house of Alex Maxwell, the secretary/treasurer of the school board burned to the ground destroying some of the school records. He was an elderly Scottish man living, I thought, up to the Scottish reputation of being saving. He would come on the very last day of the month at four o'clock with our cheques, peering at the cheque then at the recipient just to be sure. Then I was offered a grubby wintergreen candy dug from a pocket full of unknown items and offered on the flat of his hand. He would wait and I dared not refuse it. If the last day of the month was Saturday or Sunday the cheques were not given out until Monday. Sometimes we would like to have the money to go to Fort Frances after school on a Friday. I remember Dave Ogden and I going to his home after school and while he obviously did not want to, he would get out the books needed and slowly and laboriously write the cheques. I felt almost guilty accepting it and not quite sure I had earned it yet. We were not offered candy on these occasions.

After the fire and loss of records, the board persuaded Gale Donaldson to take over the job of getting things back in order and then we were able to get our cheques on the last Friday of the month with no problem.

*M*AY:

We had our first polio shots today. Only one child cried and one got sick. It was a cold dreary day.

I had two little frogs living in a fish bowl. I slipped a tadpole in there and soon after Bobbie reported, "There is already a tadpole borned in the fish bowl."

I am sitting gazing benevolently out over my class, as they all work busily at printing. They do work hard and they do want to please and they are wonderful children.

May 18: The children have discovered that today is my birthday and this was the day that Kenny got a little ring of Elizabeth's stuck on his finger. His finger was so badly swollen by the time he showed it to me that it looked like a little purple sausage. Peggy and I tried the usual things to no avail and I said, "I will have to cut it off." Elizabeth burst into wild tears and said, "Don't cut Kenny's finger off. Mama will be mad." I soothed Elizabeth, Peggy found a small file in her car and Kenny stood stoically while we filed the ring, not the finger, off, while Elizabeth sobbing, stood closely by.

Tommie asked. 'How old are you anyhow?" I asked them what they thought and Gary looked seriously at me and replied, "About a hundred, I guess."

June 29:

Well, it is over and I will go to Teachers' College in September. How many slivers have I dug from flinching hands? How many small injuries have I treated? How many shoelaces have I tied? How many answers to serious questions have I fumbled for? How many arguments have I settled? Will I ever get the stains from the hectograph off my hands? How many garters and buttons have I fastened? And how many times have I dashed to the privacy of my little storeroom to laugh and laugh and laugh?

Some of the questions the children asked me: What colour are a pig's eyes? What is another name for a dinosaur? Does the world stop? Did God bring me? Is that girl a fish? (mermaid) How many lights does an airplane have on both sides? Is there teats on a mother lion? Can ladies draw better than gentlemen? Can you really see the sky moving? Do clouds come down? Can a buffalo run faster than us? Could an eagle pick us up? Do you know what butter is called in India? (This was obviously asked to test my intelligence and I did know, having read Little Black Sambo.) Where did Eskimos come from? Do Eskimos have bathrooms? If an Eskimo gets a nosebleed what does he use for toilet paper? Why do they call them Northern Lights? Do alligators have big ears? Can a crab eat a turtle? What does a rabbit say? Does calves come out of cow's stomachs or does men bring them in the night? Who made the first hen? After explaining how the little chick broke out of the shell when he got too big–If we got too big would we break out of our shells? How come I feel sick but I'm not? Will orange peelings make you deaf? When we grow up will our mothers be our grandmothers? Can you cook soft-shelled crabs and eat them? Is a boy's nose the same as a girl's? Is Mississippi a man or a woman?

I have learned so much from these children that I think no other pupils could mean as much to me. I have made mistakes that I will not make again. Any mistakes I make now will be fresh new ones.

During this summer I worked at the Northwest Bay Trading Post operaled by Lyla Armstrong. Working at a tourist camp was another great experience, entailing hard work and long hours. There was no indoor plumbing or electric lights, although there was a gas generator that was turned off at night. Doreen Armstrong was the other cabin girl, Helma Angus was the cook and Derward Angus was the guide. Marvin Laycox tended to carrying wood, water and garbage and many other duties. It was a very good summer with one weekend off and I returned there the following summer after attending Teachers' College.

Nostalgia

"Nostalgia is the file that removes the rough edges from the good old days."
D. Larson

- Christmas Concert Time
- The Kitchen Stove
- As Time goes By
- Corsets
- The Shadow of a Doubt (fiction)
- Warmth

Christmas Concert Time

The Christmas concert of the early rural schools has stayed in the minds of the vast majority of those who experienced one. It was a tradition begun many years ago that each teacher would present to the parents of her pupils and the general public the best concert possible. Often a teacher's reputation was judged by the concert that she/he could produce

A few years ago I attended a school Christmas program. The children were excited and performed their parts well, as their parents looked proudly on. There were plays, songs and acrostics just as usual. Microphones, speakers and special lighting were used in the acts, some of which took their theme from television shows. In the manger scene lighting was used to full advantage. with the final scene bathed in a soft blue light, while a choir sang softly to the accompaniment of taped music. It was very effectively produced.

It was easy to drift back in memory to a cold clear night standing under a brilliant star-lit sky listening for the sound of sleigh bells. The horses' hooves crunched in the snow and they snorted out great gusts of steam as they drew to a halt. We clambered into the back of our neighbour's hay-covered sleigh and were glad to pull the heavy blankets over us in the wintry night. When we reached our destination the horses were stabled with others and we entered the church. The feeling of suspense was almost unbearable. This was the night for which we had practiced many days. It was the biggest night of the year with drama, music, dance, culture and spirituality, along with the anticipation of a treat all rolled into one exciting package.

Many of the early rural schoolhouses were small, so the concert was often held in a church or hall. No matter where it was held, the building would be lit by gas lanterns with their gentle hiss or some of the parents' best lamps placed strategically and safely. The air smelled of the evergreen tree, decorated with homemade paper chains and lanterns, strings of popcorns and garlands of tinsel kept from year to year. No candles adorned the tree, as that was too dangerous. Sometimes the smell of smoke from the wood stove that warmed the interior was stronger than usual. The odour of barn and horses was often quite noticeable, but no one minded that for, after all, we were rural folk.

The Christmas concert was a community affair. If need be the fathers erected a small stage or made any props necessary. They were also in charge of bringing the lanterns and lamps and sometimes of keeping the fire in the big heater stove at the right temperature. The mothers were on hand to help make or sew costumes, help with the teaching and singing of the songs and hymns and coaching the children in their parts. They also prepared the lunch in the days when it was served after the program. Often the chairman of the school board was the master of ceremonies and he had to be prepared to entertain the crowd while the next item in the program was being readied. Sometimes he would get carried away in appreciation of his own humour and the children would stand waiting as he told yet another joke.

The teacher had the enormous responsibility of preparing a program that lasted up to two hours, seeing that no child was left out. The community expected a full range of entertainment with solos, duets, plays, skits, dance routines, carols, acrostics, drills, monologues, recitations and the climax of the show, the manger scene. Her raw material was chosen from perhaps twenty children with varying talent, ranging in age from five or six up to pupils in their teens. Every child had a part, whether it was a simple verse or being a sheep in the manger scene. The older children often had to act in several plays, perform in the drills, and sing to round out the program.

A mother who could play the piano or pump style organ provided the music. Many practices were held until near the time of the concert, when the mother was asked to come to a rehearsal and then the singers had to adjust their pitch and style to the music. Sometimes a student or two would act up or show off to the acute disapproval of the others and the teacher. Occasionally a wind-up gramophone was used for certain numbers and this gave an air of professionalism to the evening.

The philosophy of the day seemed to be that a teacher who was able to put on a well-organized program with pupils well disciplined was a good teacher. Parents in rural areas reasoned that if the program was good that the children were receiving training in memory work, reading, language and literature. Besides this the children learned to speak in public, sing in choirs and perform in rhythm bands, to march in drills, act in plays and just generally benefit from the organization, more than making up for any lessons that the children might have missed during the weeks of practice.

The rural Christmas concert lasted virtually unchanged in form for well over half a century. There are people who will claim there can never again be anything so wonderful and exciting as "concert night." It stands clearly in my mind and I can recall some of the acts that were presented in my time. One I especially remember was "The Alice Blue Gown" drill performed by the older girls. The costumes for this were quite elaborate and were made of crepe paper sewn by the mothers. They wore long dresses, little frilled hats and carried parasols. The girls sang the popular song,

"In my sweet little Alice Blue gown,
When I first wandered down into town,
I was both proud and shy as I felt every eye,
And in every shop window I'd primp passing by—"

It was quite beautiful to watch as the girls performed their drill, sang again and finished with a graceful curtsy. The costumes that could be made from crepe paper were beautiful and were saved from year to year.

I also remember the "Parade of the Wooden Soldiers" drill with the little soldiers walking with a stiff-legged gait. The drills were formal exercises performed to music and the marchers made different patterns in the stage often following lines and markers. They marched, they wheeled, they turned, they crisscrossed passing each other, all to whatever music was available. One of the most intricate drills was the Star Drill, but there were many others in the books that gave suggestions and directions for concerts.

The programs definitely had a religious flavour and featured the old familiar Christmas hymns and recitations about the birth of Christ, and without doubt the crown of the evening was the nativity scene. The 'shepherds' in long robes and towels tied on their heads carried their crooks and followed the star that led them to Bethlehem. Small children played the parts of sheep and cattle. The choir of angels sang "While shepherds watched their flocks by night and "It came upon a midnight clear." The wise men in crowns and robes carried their precious gifts. Mary and Joseph were in the stable with the babe in a manger. The choir sang "Away in a Manger," and "Silent night" and "O, Come all ye Faithful." The angels were often arrayed in loose gowns made of cheesecloth. Ours had little loops where we could place our thumbs to pull the cloth up into wings and we wore little crowns made of tinsel. It was a beautiful scene and viewed by the audience with total appreciation. We knew our parents were proud of us.

In early days a hearty lunch was served with tea being made in boilers on the stove and served in big pots and sandwiches and cakes were passed. Santa Claus presented each child with a small gift and a bag of candy to end the evening. No wonder it was called the biggest day of the year.

It may not have been the most brilliant display of talent. Often the speakers could not be heard over the noise of crying babies or people coughing. The children would forget their lines and little girls would stand twisting their skirts in an agony of shyness. People were crowded into a small room that could be icy cold or boiling hot. The commotion of students moving was almost constant, but everyone loved the concert.

The true spiritual meaning of Christmas seemed to be shown when the children sincerely acted out the nativity scene. The parents were pleased with seeing their children on the stage. The teacher was happy that the concert had been a success. Everyone learned to cooperate, to improvise, to make do and to share. There was really no other form of entertainment that could match it at that time.

Christmas programs still exist in most schools today but with large classes and nine or ten classes to perform, they of necessity have a different form. The fact that there is so much more to entertain people now makes a great difference. It is still pleasant to attend a program and see that the children have caught some of the old excitement.

The drama, the excitement, and the joy of those old concerts will not be forgotten or surpassed by those who recall them. Cameras did not play much part in rural occasions in those day and I do not recall ever seeing a photograph of one of our concerts but people of a certain age will be able to see a scene or two in their memory. The feeling of nostalgia for those days comes to the surface at concert time, as we remember the biggest night of the year.

The Kitchen Stove

The old wood cook stove was really the heart of the home as so many activities took place in the farm kitchen. This appliance was a most necessary fact of life, as the ashes were first stirred into life in the morning and banked the last thing at night. The stove was large and stood off the floor on curved iron legs, had a black cast iron top with four or six burners, a reservoir to heat water and a warming oven above the burners, as well as the baking oven. There were dampers, drafts and little doors that one had to learn to operate and it was fastened to the system of stovepipes that ran through the house. Some stoves were ornate with much shiny nickel to polish and porcelain behind the burners and on the front of the oven door. Sometimes the porcelain was light blue or green instead of white. These stoves bore trademark names such as McLary, Renfrew, Findlay or Home Comfort.

There were big cast iron griddles made that fit right over the two front burners and many pancakes could be cooked at once. A lid could be removed and a cast iron pot or kettle put right over the open flame to hurry things up. Most teakettles had a well blackened bottom. A kettle could be boiling furiously on a front burner and another simmering gently on a back burner. We learned early to keep something on the back burner.

The stove was so versatile. Food that was cooked could be kept warm in the warming oven until ready for the table. The oven door could stand ajar to put the bread to rise when the house was chilly. Sometimes a pail of some mash for an animal or water warming for the chickens would stand on the back of the stove. Water for the week's washing was carried and heated in the boiler and the irons were heated on the stove and wiped on a cloth to remove any soot before doing the ironing. The stove was one of the most essential of all household equipment.

In winter a clothesline was often strung in the kitchen and baby's diapers or wet socks and mitts dangled over the stove to dry for morning, while wet boots dried out under the stove. The dog slept behind the stove on an old coat and sometimes the cat curled up in the wood box that stood beside the stove. Sometimes a weak lamb or calf was brought in to be babied and baby chicks often spent their first day or two near the warmth of the stove. In the winter the snow barrel stood near the stove providing nice, soft water from the melted snow. Stoves were useful as garbage disposals and garbage did not build up to any extent, as so much of it was just popped into the kitchen range.

Coming home from an evening out it was pleasant to sit around the stove and warm up with the oven open. Toast made over the open fire was a wonderful snack at these times. Some may remember bathing around the old stove in the kitchen. A sheet or two could be draped over some chairs for privacy. Towels were warmed by hanging them over the open oven door. Some hot water from the kettle on the stove or the reservoir was added to warm up the water for the next bather.

Skill was needed to operate these stoves and certain things had to be done to keep the stove in prime condition as so much depended on it for heat and cooking. On winter nights the fire was "banked" so embers were there to stir up and kindle the fire in the morning. The ashes had to be emptied from their special drawer and a little chamber near the bottom of the stove was opened to scrape out the soot. The reservoir on the side held quite a few gallons of water and another chore was carrying the water to keep it filled. To the children it may have seemed as if the wood box was always empty, as the stove could consume wood at an alarming rate on baking or canning days.

On Saturday the stovetop was cleaned and rubbed with stove blacking and polished with crumpled up brown paper or newspaper. The porcelain parts were wiped off and the nickel polished with Bon Ami. With its coat clean and shiny it was ready for another week's service. Several times a year the stovepipes had to be taken down and outside to clear them of soot. Stovepipe cleaning days are not among my favourite memories of the "good old days."

Stoves could be temperamental and were fussy about what kind of wood they liked to burn. They did not like damp, soggy poplar or wood that was too green. This would cause the stove to sulk and smoulder and not give out the heat needed to bake the bread. Mother would send out for some dry wood to see "if we couldn't get some heat out of this stove." The stove also preferred certain kinds of weather and a wind from the wrong direction would have Mother adjusting the dampers and drafts while brushing smoke from her eyes. On a clear bright day with some dry tamarack or birch wood the stove could be depended on to cooperate to heat the oven for a good baking day or ironing day.

Those old stoves were such a source of warmth and comfort and had much more personality than the white sterile appliances we use now. Replicas of these beautiful old kitchens stoves are still being made and used by people with a yen for the past. However, they are generally used now as a backup source of heat or cooking and are not the centre of the home's comfort and food supply as in days gone by.

As Time Goes By

Time is such an unfathomable concept. I heard a man, a scientist and an expert no doubt, on the radio say that there is no such thing as time –it just is—and we just float along apparently without any respect paid to time. There is no such concept as time- it just is? I do know that there is no way that we can harness or stop time even for one little second. I probably did not understand what he saying but I have pondered this, and wondered if is this is so. why are we so caught up and obsessed with time? Lost time, extra time, fast time, the right time, the wrong time, next time, quality time, bad timing, time will tell, time after time, another time, the list is endless. According to the expert no such concepts exist but to me the importance of marking time is illustrated, when every four years we have a whole extra day, February 29, to use or squander as we wish. I do not possess a scientific mind.

I love the words of that old hymn, "Time like a never-ending stream bears all its sons away," as it evokes a lovely image in my mind. I am very conscious of time passing, and as I age it seems to fly faster and faster. When I was a child the summers seemed endless with the long hot days stretching ahead of us. At a time of anticipation such as Christmas the days crawled by with maddening slowness. Now, the heightened commercialism seems to make the seasons all blur together. Thanksgiving is over, and without a pause Christmas is thrust upon us with Easter waiting to pounce.

Now I tend to think more about the past, and the people who filled my younger days are often in my thoughts. I will dream of a relative or person long since dead and then thoughts of that person will stay with me for days, as I relive times spent with them. When we have much more behind us than ahead of us, we might seem to dwell on those old familiar times.

I wonder if we ever really see the past clearly and objectively. It is easy to glorify the past, as my Uncle Tom did in his later years. Things stayed the same as they were in perhaps the happiest time of his life, that of life on the farm in Box Alder. No one had ever died and I'm sure his mind was full of conversations with Pa and Ma and his brothers and sisters. He could easily visit "Long Bill" or Harold Green. The past was his to do with as he wanted. What a wonderful way to be unless someone rudely jerks you back to reality, such as the time I told him that Axel, my father, had died some sixty years ago. His eyes filled with tears as he said, "I wish someone had told me."

You can do what you want with the past because no two people remember a person or event in exactly the same way. There are as many versions of a story as there are people to tell them. Some will omit certain things, others will add and embellish as they recount their memory of an event. The past can be elusive, and try as you will, you can not quite remember as much as you would like. As younger people we probably all remember a senior family member or "old timer" telling stories of long ago and often telling the same story over and over. All of a sudden, it seems, you realize that you are telling and retelling bits from your past history and that you may have already told the listener about the terrible snowstorm 60 years ago. This is another illustration of how things come full circle.

Sometimes you might think, "Do I really remember that or did someone tell me?" My two brothers could never really agree on who owned the Mickey Mouse balloon that landed on the big thistle and burst. Good things can be told in great detail, just as less perfect memories can be pushed to the back of the mind or repressed entirely. It has been said that anything that ever happened to you is stored in your mind and can be brought back to you by a scent, a bit of music, a word or sight. Nearly everyone has had flashes of this type of evoked memory.

I have thought of how much the early part of my life was like that of my mother. We were both bereft of a parent, although I know that I did not miss my father as much as Mom suffered from the loss of her mother. She grieved for her mother all her life and maybe that is why she was such a strong maternal influence on all of us. I have talked to others who lost their mother at a very young age and they too have spoken of the terrible sense of loss they always felt. One is never ready to lose one's mother.

When Mom's mind was failing she often thought I was her sister or her mother. Time had slipped a cog somewhere for her. "Are you my mother?" she would ask, peering into my face. They say that you are not to let a person like this be deceived but rather to drag them back to reality. I have heard Mom do this herself. When a lady in Rainycrest roamed the halls looking for her deceased husband Mike, Mom would say firmly, "Your husband is dead, Mary. Go back to your room." I would gasp at the cruelty of it, but Mom declared that the nurses told them to do this.

So when my mother would grasp my hand and ask imploringly "Are you my mother?" I sometimes did not have the heart to say, "No, your mother died years ago." I would smile and nod and ask what we should do today and did she want to go to have tea. Sometimes she would ask where I had tied the horses, and instead of always saying that I drove the car, I would say that they were tied out front with a little hay for them.

The rural way of life changed fairly slowly in the first years of the century. Time was divided into work time and relaxation time. There was plenty of work as we had no electricity and used coal oil lamps, and burned wood in our stoves. We carried water and melted snow for washing and household use. We helped with the farm work and the care of cattle and horses. We loved our animals and knew their personalities and also knew every nook and cranny of the big barn that Grandpa had built where the livestock was stabled.

I walked the same dusty road to attend the same one room school that my mother had attended and went to the same church. I grew up with stories of former neighbours that Mom had known until I felt I knew Mrs. Ferguson and Mrs. Sexsmith. My mother was a child during the horror of World War One and she often spoke of neighbour boys that never came back. I was a child in the days of World War Two and I remember the young men of our community, Donnie McFayden, Jack Judson and Jim McMahon that did not return.

We travelled to LaVallee to get the mail and to shop for groceries at the same store and I was as awed by Uncle Dave Strachan as my mother had been. We also travelled in the same mode, that of horse and buggy in the summer and by cutter in the winter.

We ate simple food with no items such as fill the menus of today's families. Cinnamon and sage were the only seasonings used to any extent. Much of our clothing and bedding was homemade or bought from the Eaton's catalogue, and was warm and comfortable if not stylish. Hand-me-downs were received gratefully. We learned to "use up, make over and make do."

Entertainment and relaxation activities were home made. We did have a radio but it did not always work. There were wonderful radio programs and we sat in the circle of light of the oil lamp to listen to "Ma Perkins," Lux Radio Theatre", Fibber McGee and Molly, "The Lone Ranger "or "Jack Benny." We played games, read, talked, sang and looked forward to the weekly newspaper and farm magazines. The Christmas concert and school picnic in June were major events in our lives. It was a simpler time then and we were rather insulated from world events. We were shielded and sheltered from any adult topic with the explanation that we would understand when we were older. Alas, there are adult things for which I still strive to find answers.

I roamed the same fields and bush that my mother had in her childhood. Mom and her sister Grace had many special places in the bush and I knew them all. We all knew where the "plank" was, though it had rotted away years ago. One time my cousin Ethel and I saw bear tracks in the soft mud at the plank. We rushed home as terrified as if we had seen the bear itself. They scoffed at us at home until Uncle Bill walked back with us and was surprised to see that a bear had been there. I have always been afraid of bears and for many years checked under my bed each night.

We picked berries and knew where the best saskatoons grew and climbed through brush piles to where the raspberries grew in abundance. Our bush had only a very small bit of muskeg and we knew where to cross the swampy part to check for blueberries. The bush was so lovely and I spent time there whenever I could. We would listen for our cowbell and then strike out to bring them home for milking. I knew that my mother had done this many times also.

Life was pleasant in most ways and our lives were very sheltered and far removed from any violence or war or crime. Looking back the edges of our life were soft and blurred and we hardly knew these things existed. We seemed caught up in a timeless dream. Yes, in many ways my life was like that of my mother's a generation before me. My sense of time was perhaps much the same as my mother's had been when she was a child.

The changes that took place in the 1960's were inevitable I suppose. Technology was advancing rapidly and soon we had radios that did not need batteries. We heard of the television that would make us a global community rather than just our own tight little communities. We heard of the computer so large that at first it filled a room, never dreaming that some day we would sit facing our own personal devices. Now it is impossible to escape events, some good and some so terrible, as to be unimaginable to one brought up in that other time. Do we become somewhat hardened or callous for our own protection? Children can be affected by knowing too much too soon, and having knowledge but not understanding.

Now time's "ever-rolling stream" has borne all these older things away, and though we may gasp at the newest advancement, we still wonder "what next?" I am thankful, though, that I do have memories of that other time. I do not live in the past as my Uncle Tom did, but it is a nice place to go back and visit.

Corsets

*M*ost people are familiar with those old movie scenes of beautiful young women hanging on to the bedpost and "sucking in" while someone pulls her corset strings in tighter. Scarlett O'Hara boasted a seventeen-inch waist but was unable to eat her barbecue supper due to the constriction of her stomach. The barbecue sounded so delicious I wondered how she could resist.

These corsets or waist cinchers that made the waist smaller while causing the hips and upper body to flare out attractively were very different from the undergarments in the pages of Eaton's catalogue. I was told by my elegant grandmother. "A lady never discusses her clothing, Elizabeth." I instinctively knew that underclothing especially was never to be mentioned but I found these pages to hold a fascination, as did the men's underwear pages.

The corsets, often manufactured by the Dominion Corset Company, encased the female body from the breasts to the tops of the thighs and fit securely over the buttocks. Straps went over the shoulder and four garters were sewed to the bottom edges to fasten to your stockings. The deluxe models had an inner belt and six garters. Pantyhose were far in the future, hence the garters. The material was of strong, finely and firmly woven cotton. Sometimes an embossed design of satin thread was a feature. They were of the colour described as nude, a pinkish orange hue, or white.

Some elastic inserts allowed for a little ease or stretch. Sewn strongly into the material at strategic points were the stays or bones of perhaps 8 to 10 inches long. In the early days corset stays were made of whalebone but in the time I recall they were made of thinly coiled strips of flexible metal. They fitted over the hips and waist and up the sides of the bust. As the name stays implies, they were meant to control any bulge or ridges of flesh or fat.

There were also sections of lacing in the sides that allowed for some deviation of body weight. You could lace quite tightly to fit into last years' dress or loosen up the lacing to allow for more comfort while working. If you rested in the afternoon you could loosen your corsets. Many ladies had two sets, a "good" one for social events, and the older looser set for everyday.

I remember these garments, as my mother wore corsets and so did most of the women at that time. You could tell the women that wore these garments as they had such firm, smooth, controlled body shapes with never a ridge or bulge showing. Most women that wore these garments had to sit up very erectly, as the strength of the material and the stays did not allow for a relaxed looking posture.

A silky undershirt made the garment a little more comfortable. The woman then stepped into the corset and pulled the straps over the shoulders. The bottom part opened in two parts and this was arranged around the body and then fastened in the front with strong hooks and eyes fasteners. The hooks extended up over the bust section and when the corset was all hooked and laced up, the other clothing ,slip, underpants, stockings, dress and apron, was added.

Instead of purchasing such a personal garment from the Eaton catalogue there were women called corset ladies that made their living measuring and fitting women for their garments. One such company was the Spencer. Spencers were the Cadillac of these corsets. Some advertised their garments as giving a feeling of security in an uncertain world. Perhaps if your body was encased rigidly, laced and hooked in, you may have felt ready to face almost anything.

There were drawbacks of course. Sometimes a stay would work through the material. I recall spots on Mom's body where a stay had rubbed and actually pierced the skin, resulting in a "corset sore." Then a patch was sewn over the offending stay and the spot on the body had to be padded until it healed. Mom always had tender skin and suffered from various rashes and skin eruptions. She applied large amounts of powder or cornstarch before she put on her "garment" and I sometimes rubbed the starch over her back to help protect the skin there. Sometimes a bit of flesh was pinched in and not noticed at once. This could be agonizing as the day progressed and it was impossible to release the sore spot without undressing. Another hazard was being at a social occasion and having a garter stick into the back of your leg when you sat down. You would try discreetly to squirm into a more comfortable position but eventually would have to find a private spot to refasten the garter. Mom would tell us of these hazards often in a joking way and act it out to make us laugh.

In summer these garments were insufferably hot and of course became saturated with sweat. On the hottest of summer days the corset was not worn and what a relief it must have been, although I know that Mom preferred to wear the thing if possible. Mom sometimes hung her garment over the clothesline to air it out between washings.

The memory most associated with corsets is of Mom getting ready for bed. I lay in the bed after the lamp was blown out where sometimes she, my sister and I all slept, hearing the unhooking of the garment and the audible sigh of relief and pleasure as flesh that had been constricted all day was released to the air. Then the scratching and rubbing of tender spots took place with little sighs and moans of sheer satisfaction and relief. This was a nightly ritual. One time I was visiting my aunt and as my uncle was away, I slept with her. I took it as a matter of course, as I heard the unhooking and the same satisfied sighs and the scratching with which I was so familiar. The relief must have been immense. I have always associated corsets with the pleasure felt by these ladies when they took them off.

Why did they wear these torturous garments? For many years women had worn some type of restrictive undergarments. They had been brought up in a corseted era and likely a rite of passage for a young girl was getting your first corset. They say that women's clothing was designed by men and that men set the fashions that sometimes seem torturous now. Think of the famous hourglass figure, the bustle, the small waists achieved by lacing. They all seemed to involve a cruel, unnatural sort of reconstruction of the body to achieve the desired fashionable contours. The forties and early fifties were the tail end of this fashion and so women were still wearing corsets that were uncomfortable and restrictive. With the advent of pantyhose, undergarments changed immensely. It seems that some form of corseting will always survive, even worn outside the clothing, such as the bustier that Madonna displayed.

Women's clothing has seen many extremes of fashions and sometimes certain things are revived. I somehow doubt that these older restrictive types of undergarment will return.

The Shadow Of A Doubt
(Fiction Based On Truth)

*I*t had been a lovely Halloween party but now we were hurrying home facing the gusty wind, knowing it would be dark early. In our dinner pails were the remains of the feast, a half-eaten apple, kernels of popcorn and the delightfully sticky and chewy candy kisses saved for later. Some of us had black, store-bought dinner pails but blue Bee Hive Corn Syrup or red Domestic Shortening pails were more popular. Bobbie Watson had no pail at all but carried his sandwiches in a small crumpled grocery store bag that he folded carefully after each lunchtime and shoved in his pocket.

Bobbie's mother Lily had married our bachelor neighbour Caspar Yenkowitz. Caspar at that time in the 1940's was known as a DP, although we were not really sure what that meant. We knew he had come from Poland and that made him different from our other neighbours that we knew so well, as he spoke with an accent. Caspar was a lean, dark complexioned, intense and hardworking man determined to get ahead and he began to accumulate cattle and horses and build up his farm. As did many of the men he worked in the bush camps of Northwestern Ontario in the winter. Most men left their wives and children to take care of the barn chores while they earned some money to keep the family and farm going. Those winters were cold and lengthy with deep snow making life harder for the animals as well as for their caregivers.

Caspar at first was alone but then he married Mrs. Lily Watson, and there were jokes in the neighbourhood that now Caspar had someone to do his chores in the winter months. There were many comments such as, "Oh, she'll earn her keep all right." Some said other things that I did not understand. No one knew where Lily had come from or where she and Caspar had met but suddenly Caspar had a wife and a stepson Bobbie.

The presence of a new pupil at our school was always of intense interest and Bobbie was no exception. He was not like some new boys who tried to impress or show off with amazing feats of strength or daring. He never once tried to jump off the woodshed roof or climb to the top of the trees. Bobbie never pulled the girls' pigtails or tried to trip a fellow student in the aisle but he soon earned our respect. He was never bullied as some new children are. There was something about Bobbie Watson that was just different from the usual rough and tumble farm boys, and sometimes when he looked at you with his black eyes you wondered just what he was seeing. You knew instinctively that Bobbie was not afraid of anything.

When I think of Lily and Bobbie Watson I see only black and white images in my mind. They both had heavy black hair of the kind that shows no highlights or gleams. Bobbie's hair stood up in little peaks around his ears and on top of his head. They both had white skin and their faces showed no tinge of colour in their thin cheeks. Their hands and fingers were long and thin and white. Their eyes were huge and dark, deep set and sad looking under the arch of black eyebrows. The clothing that they wore was always of material that was dark in tone. It seems to me now that even if their photographs were taken in colour their images would emerge in black and white.

Bobbie carried bits of paper in his pocket and spent any spare time drawing strange figures with his short thick pencil. There were creatures that had scales and forked tongues and long claws that seemed to writhe and twist on his paper and he would laugh at our expressions of wonder. He drew queer angular people with pointed faces and the exaggerated features of beings that belonged to another world. His trees reached out with limbs like arms that might clutch at you if you passed too closely. These sketches did not fit our wholesome "John, Mary and Peter" type of art. The pictures that we drew had sturdy square red houses set in the middle of the page with trees shaped like lollipops on either side and a sun with bright rays in one corner.

Bobbie's art had a fascination for some of us. Where had he seen such creatures? What else was stored in that black head? I realize now that he had talent far beyond his years, as the mythical creatures that he drew came alive as you looked at them. The teacher after a few efforts to make him stop let him alone, for he did all his work neatly and efficiently before he reached for his scraps of paper.

He and his mother Lily both worked very hard on Caspar's farm and the winter must have been especially difficult for this frail looking woman and her young son. Cattle needed to be fed and watered regularly. Caspar had taken the horses with him to the bush camp so Lily did not have their care, but the winter chores took up much of the day. The neighbour women were kind and did what they could to welcome her into their ladies' groups and afternoon gatherings. When my mother and her friends talked of her they always seemed to end their conversations by sighing and saying, "Poor Lily."

In those long ago days we sat and read by the light of coal oil lamps beside our wood burning heaters. It was sometime a struggle just to keep warm enough as the wood stoves consumed their fuel so quickly. Lily and Bobbie persevered through one long winter and of course Caspar was home in the summer working long days to get his hay crops gathered so his growing herd of cattle could be fed in the winter.

Only once were we in the house when Bobby and Lily lived there. It seemed so clean and bare and plain. The dark chairs were lined squarely against the wall and there were few softening touches such as curtains or pictures. There were no books or magazines, games or puzzles such as graced our home with casual clutter.

On the table sat a red geranium covered with bright blooms. Lily caught my eye as I looked at it, and when I smiled shyly at her she responded with a warm answering smile. I was glad she had the flower to look at.

Bobbie liked to come to our home. He came to listen to the radio programs on our little battery radio and especially liked the scary, heart stopping ones like the "Green Hornet" and "Inner Sanctum" that started with the eerie, long drawn out sound of a creaking door. Our favourite was "The Shadow." I can hear it yet, "Who knows what evil lurks in the hearts of men? The Shadow knows." Then would issue forth a maniacal laugh that sent shivers down your spine.

Remember, we had only the voices from the radio and the rest was up to our imaginations. Bobbie did not sit in the circle of light from the coal oil lamp but preferred to sit back in the shadows. He did not talk or smile but listened intently. Once a week when "The Shadow" was on Bobbie would appear at the door to slip into his favourite corner and then would walk home again, not seeming to mind the dark. My imagination had filled the dark with creatures that lurked ready to pounce on anyone that ventured out, but after listening to "The Shadow" and after seeing Bobbie's drawings, nothing could have induced me to leave the house alone in the dark.

On this wild wet Halloween afternoon so many years ago we rushed home. The wailing winds tossed the barren branches of the trees and threw sudden gusts of rain and sleet into our faces. We hurried through our chores eager to reach the warmth and safety of our house, with the smell of the pot of soup that my mother had simmering on the back of the wood stove. The rap came at the door. It was Friday night and time for Bobbie's favourite radio show. I cannot remember the plot of any of those programs or why they seemed so frightening but I do remember that on that Friday night they seemed more spooky and chilling than ever. Bobbie listened with quiet satisfaction then rose to go, declining my mother's offer of soup.

My brother in a rare gesture of kindness said, "I'll walk out to the road with you, Bobbie." Bobbie pulled his thin dark jacket closer around him and answered, "No, I'll cut across the field."

My brother and I looked at each other. Across the field on such a night? We watched as the dark swallowed him up. He would have to go by the swamp where heaven alone knew what terrifying creatures, perhaps like the ones that he drew, might be waiting to snatch him up and drag him down into the depth of the ooze and slime. The thought of these creatures, evil, sinister denizens of the swamp, made us talk in hushed voices of his bravery. Didn't he care? Wasn't he afraid?

Bobbie was not in school on Monday morning –not then or the next day. We never saw him again

Adults did not talk as openly in front of their children as they do now, when they discuss things that I still consider not really meant for children's ears. Near the end of the week one of our classmates came with the news. Caspar had been getting things ready to go to camp again. He had gotten a good price for the load of young cattle and hogs that he had shipped to market. When doing some repairs to the roof of the barn he slipped and fell, injuring himself and breaking a leg badly.

Back at home with his leg in a cast and crutches Caspar lay helpless and in pain in bed. No one knew the whole story, but they say that Lily moved his crutches out of reach, took the wallet from his pants pocket and coolly removed the wad of money and left by some previously planned method. The neighbourhood buzzed with the story of Lily's betrayal, although there were still a few women who wistfully said, "Poor Lily."

There was no mention of Bobbie. My brother and I hoped that Bobbie had survived the walk home across the field that Halloween night and got to leave with his mother.

Warmth

*M*y mother was a woman who believed in warmth and comfort and she took loving care of her children and our animals. In the fall our little house was banked with straw or hay and then often snow was heaped over that. Cardboard was tacked over drafty places. She would pack old rags around the front door that was never used and did not fit very well. Mom knew that the winters were long and cold and prepared for it as best she could. Our house was small, built entirely of cedar lumber and not insulated as houses are now. She would often say, "If this house ever catches fire it will go up like a paper box." That was not a very reassuring remark, but I do not recall ever being unduly alarmed.

I am sure that the winters were more severe in those days of the 1930's and '40's. The bedrooms were icy cold and the frost an inch thick on the windows and we dressed by the warmth of the heater. On the cold bitter mornings our clothing would be thrown over chairs to warm by the wood heater. Our boot tops were turned down to the warmth of the heater and extra socks were warmed as well. We often wore leather moccasins with heavy socks and these would be lined up ready to put on.

Mom believed in a good warm breakfast. We had porridge or warmed over potatoes with a fried egg on the side, and toast made over the open flame of the cook stove. Cocoa or good, hot strong tea finished the meal. An aunt once said that 'Ivah spoiled her children' and maybe she did, but we thrived on the loving care. Fortified by a wonderfully hearty hot breakfast we would don our warmed outer-wear ready for the walk to school.

Clothing then was so thick and heavy to provide the needed warmth. Girls and boys alike wore fleece-lined underwear of a creamy white colour with blue streaks of colour through it. It would be changed once a week and would become quite stretched and baggy. We girls had to carefully fold it around the ankles to be able to pull up the long brown cotton knit stockings. Even so, your legs had a definite lumpy wrinkled look. Bloomers of navy blue or brilliant pink also featured strongly, worn with undershirts, garter belts, the cotton stockings and cotton slips. Over these came our sturdy cotton or woolen dresses or blouses and skirts.

I much preferred the "breeks" made of Melton cloth worn by my brothers. Coats, jackets and snow pants were all made of this heavy woolen material that the snow would stick to and gather in clots in warmer weather. Breeks flared out like jodhpurs at the thigh then were laced up the side below the knee where they ended. Long heavy socks pulled right up over the lacing. Not many girls wore these but I would have loved to wear them. Scarves, mittens and hats were usually hand knitted but the boys sometimes had helmet type leather hats that fastened with a buckle and strap under the chin. Coats were often made over from some discarded adult garment. There were not many fashion statements made in those days.

Sometimes we would take a spoon and carefully scrape away a peephole in the thick frost that covered every window. The bedrooms were so cold that if your hair was damp from a bath at night it could freeze, as the tip of your head was all that showed. Mom loved flannelette sheets but we often had ones made of used flour sacks. Five sacks made a sheet, four were opened out and sewed together, then one was split in half and sewn across the end. One time Uncle Dave from the LaVallee store gave Mom a pair of flannelette sheets and she was so happy with them. Our comforters were made from old coats or the best parts of old blankets cut into squares and sewn together. Some type of backing was put on over the batting and then the quilt was tied together with bright yarn and knotted. Several of these would be needed on a bed. On extra cold nights a heavy coat or two would be thrown over the bed.

The water pail would freeze at nights and house plants had to be kept close to the warmth of the stove but sometimes they were touched by frost. When Mom set bread at night, as was often done in those days, it would be wrapped in a clean old quilt or blanket and then set on the open oven door. Sometimes the home canning jars in the back cupboard would freeze and break, but these things were taken as a matter of course, as everyone had the same problems.

If my mother spoiled her children it might also be said that she spoiled the animals. Mom also believed in making the animals as comfortable as possible. In the fall she would start patching holes and cracks in the barn and outbuildings. A plaster could be made with cow manure but I am not sure if other ingredients were added or not. Like the house, buildings would be banked with straw or snow. She looked with delight on a cardboard box and saved all she could. Cut into strips and tacked over cracks, they provided some insulation from the bitter winds. I remember coming home from school and finding her working cheerfully away at this task. When I look back and think how hard Mom worked I feel ashamed at my life of ease.

Chores had to be done no matter how cold or stormy. Often on a cold winter's morning there would be a pail or two sitting on the stove. Mom would be warming water and mash for the chickens or making something for a calf or the pigs. The chickens were at one time in a separate building and if you went in on a bitter cold morning the hens would be moving so sluggishly, sometimes with the tips of their combs drooping with the touch of frost. Their eyes were dull and lifeless, their feathers ruffled and puffed out. They did not fly up squawking and fluttering nervously as they did in warmer weather. You knocked the ice from their water pan and poured in the warmed water and gave them the mash and scraps and potato peels. They would be heartened for a little while and perhaps reward us with an egg or two. We would sometimes find a frozen egg. Mom always seemed to be going to the barn or other buildings with a pail in each hand.

It seemed to be so cold and the snow was piled in huge drifts around the barn. After a storm and a bad blow all the paths would be filled in and it would be hard to get down the drifts to where it was sheltered around the barn. It was especially hard if you were carrying two pails. Little steps could be cut down the snow bank.

The animals were stabled in the barn and would be turned out to find their way to the water trough. The pump in the well-house was primed with a pail of warm water from the house. The child whose turn it was to pump would try to get a head start filling the ice encrusted trough before the cattle got there. They would come in a long line and the older cows, the matriarchs would drink first, dipping their muzzles in then flinging their heads back from the first touch of the ice-cold water. They drank and drank while we pumped and pumped. The younger cattle drank next. If they tried to get in with the cows they would be chased aside by a cow that knew they had no business there yet. It seemed as if those cows would drink forever but you kept pumping away. There was a trick to it. At the end you did not want to have too much water left in the trough to freeze, for if there was a lot left you had to dip it out. When the ice built up too much leaving little room for the water, the trough had to be chopped out.

One cold morning I was pumping and became almost mesmerized by the glistening green painted metal mechanism of the pump. I thought "I wonder what would happen if I just put the tip of my tongue on one of those raised letters?" I soon found out and left a bit of my skin stuck there as I pulled free. I never did it again.

When the cattle were finished drinking the horses came plunging through the snow to drink. They did not seem to drink as much as the cows. If the day was not too cold the cattle were left out to lounge around the south side of the barn where some hay would be thrown out from the loft window for them. Otherwise, they and the horses were put back into the cleaned barn, bedded down, to be warm and comfortable.

South east Corner of the Barn with Young Cattle.

We would trudge back to the house to see to our own comforts. There was a certain satisfaction to knowing that both we and the animals were warm and dry and comfortable. If there was a storm brewing Mom marshaled us all to extra activity when we got home from school, get the barn chores done up a little early, make sure the wood-box was heaped and some piled at the door, fill all the water pails and the reservoir and empty the slop pails. There was a certain sense of urgency in the air and inside there could well be a stew simmering and loaves of fresh bread turned out on the table.

Even today if a storm seems imminent I feel a little of that urgency and apprehension and want to check to see if everyone got safely home. I want to make vegetable soup and have hot bread or biscuits, as they are comfort foods for me. I realize that this goes right back to those childhood days that always seem to stay with me.

Family & All That Kind Of Thing

"Call it a clan, call it a network, call it a tribe, call it a family. Whatever you call it, whoever you are, you need one." Jane Howard

- Branches on the Family Tree
- Family Matters (Our Life In Burriss)
- Hockey
- Chickens, Geese, Turkeys, Quail
- Raising Cattle
- Fire At Donaldson's
- The Old White Chev

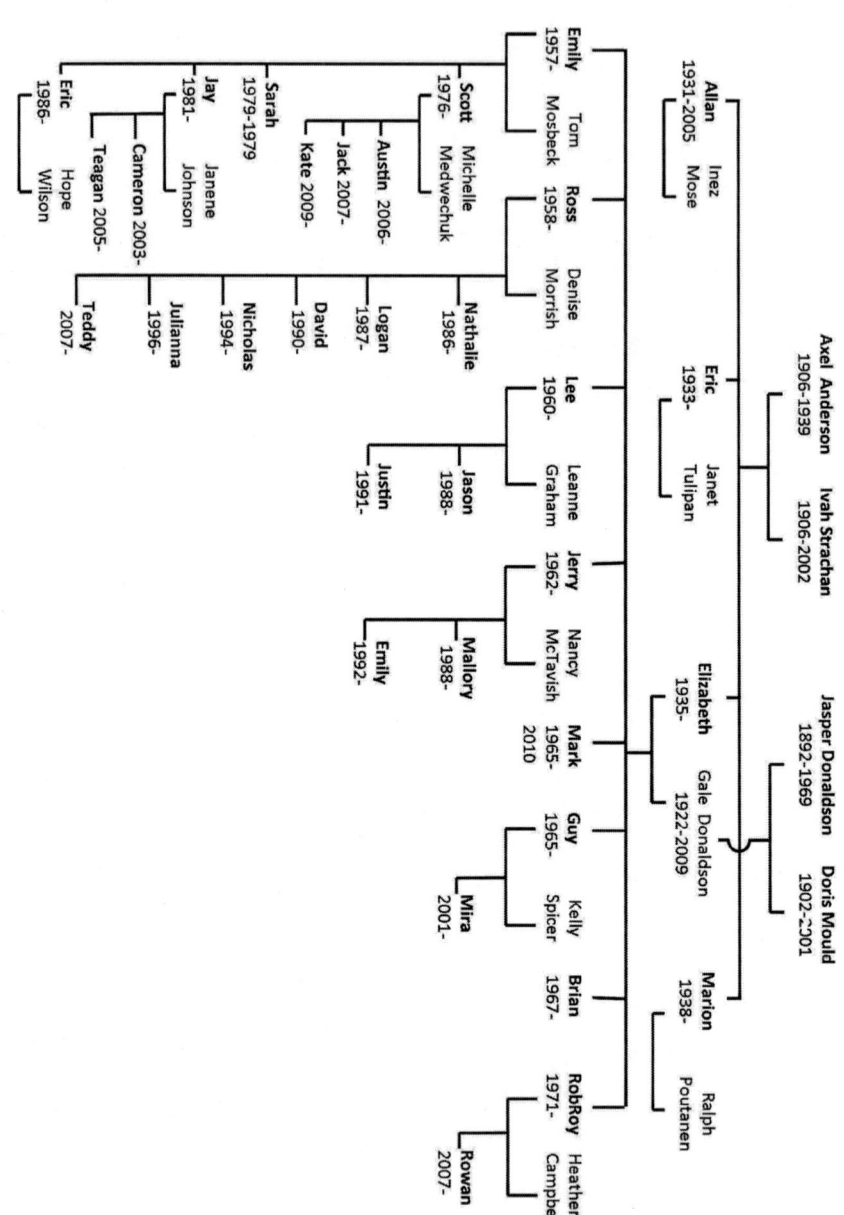

Family Tree Page

Branches On The Family Tree— Donaldson-Mould Branches

Both Gale and I were interested in genealogy and we discovered a great deal about our ancestors. It is hard to explain just why it is so exciting and satisfying, but in the past years many people have been hit by this same desire. The Internet has become a valuable tool, and by this source and old records we found more than we ever thought possible. The problem is that the more you find the more you want to know. I am not the only one that wishes that more attention had been paid when the older people were talking or that more questions had been asked.

The first Donaldson family came to Burriss in 1898 from Ohio. Through a special arrangement with the Canadian government and immigration agent R.A. Burriss, only settlers from the United States were allowed into Burriss Township when it was first opened for settlement. In 1898 Jared and Belle Donaldson with family William, Guy, Jasper and Emily and extended family arrived from Ohio and homesteaded on the property that is still in Donaldson hands today.

Gale's mother, Doris May Mould, was born in Nelson, England and her family emigrated to Saskatchewan in 1907. Gale was born in Nokomis, Saskatchewan where his parents had met when Jasper went west to work in the grain harvests. They came back to Burriss when Gale was three. Our son Lee once quipped that when Jasper married Doris we first got the "mold" on our family tree. Grandma was amused!

Gale's brother Lyle, who was an excellent carpenter, died of leukemia in 1958 at the age of thirty three. Gale had two younger sisters, Crete who married Lawrence McLeod and Sheila who married Glenn Manty from South Gillies. Crete and Lawrence had two daughters, Maureen (Lorne Ricard) and Dianne (Don Debenedet). Sheila and Glenn had two sons and one daughter. Donnie married Shelly Brandrick and Kenny married Cindy Hodge. Heather is married to Joe Miller. These nieces and nephews are all married with children.

DONALDSON FAMILY. L R: Sheila Manty, Olive Nicholas (visiting cousin), Doris Donaldson, Gale Donaldson, Crete McLeod.

Anderson-Strachan Branches

My maternal grandparents were among the early wave of settlers that arrived in the Municipality of LaVallee to homestead in

Box Alder in the mid 1890's. Both the Strachan and Barker families were large and probably the thought of free land for the young people was hard to resist. George Strachan Jr. married Elizabeth Barker in 1898 and after having five children Elizabeth died in 1907. Ivah, the youngest child born in 1906, was my mother. Her siblings were Ethel, Edna, William and Grace.

My paternal grandparents were both born in Sweden. Abel Anderson and Anna Olson immigrated to the United States and came to the Minnesota and Wisconsin areas as so many Swedish people did, met and were married in 1903. Abel had one son Carl from a previous marriage. My father was born in Lac du Flambeau, Wisconsin in 1906. Katie and Thomas were born in Wisconsin and Helen and Emma were born in Fort Frances after they came to Ontario. The Anderson family moved to Box Alder where my father met my mother and they were married in 1929.

My father Axel Emil Anderson had a very unfortunate accident when he was 12 years old. His brother Tom Anderson told of this accident, "Axel and another boy had been making some skis and were steaming them in a large barrel at the Border Mill. Somehow he slipped into the barrel and his legs were badly scalded. He ran home with the hot water burning in his wool socks. Later when the doctor had come and gone, a mistake was made in the kind of linseed oil used to wrap his legs and when the bandages were taken off much of the tissue came with them." The family never forgot the terrible suffering of the young boy and the memory seemed to shadow them all their lives. When he recovered enough his siblings pulled him to school on a sleigh in the winter and a little wagon in the summer. Axel completed high school with honours.

This accident affected him for the rest of his life and I believe from the things that my mother told me that the injury never completely healed. She said that he had virtually no flesh on the back of one leg. He did have years when he recovered enough to play some sports, to work and also to marry and have a family. Years later when he went to work in the bush camps he was given the job of camp clerk, as he could not stand to work out in the snow and cold.

The Depression was a very different time with no social assistance and it seemed you just scraped to get by and trusted to luck. People in those times did not depend on doctors as we do now. Coming home from camp in the winter of 1938, Axel's leg was very bad, and he had to have rolls of bandages made from old sheets to cover the open wounds. He went back to camp, saying he would see a doctor in the spring. He did see Dr. Young in Emo who said he was sure it was cancer and that amputation was the only course. This was done in Duluth in April 1938 and when Mom wrote of this time later, she said that he did quite well after the amputation with crutches and was fitted for an artificial leg. I remember both the crutches and the artificial leg.

While the amputation probably took away some of the pain it did not solve the problem, for the cancer had progressed into the groin and then further into his body. He died October 19, 1939, aged thirty three. It is difficult to read the account that my mother wrote of those last months. Thinking of that accident when he was just a young boy, and the crude treatment he had for those severe burns, and his later suffering is not easy. From anything I have ever heard, my father Axel lived and died with courage and his last thoughts were for my mother and his family. He had had the foresight to take out a small life insurance policy. I have a few memories of him, just flashes really, but I cherish them as part of my parent's history.

My mother Ivah's early life was not quite as smooth as that of some others, as her mother died leaving five young children. Her father later married twice more, trying to provide a stable home for the family, so there were stepmothers. I know that my mother understood their point of view better when she was older and regretted some of her actions. I did not know Charlotte but I remember Winnifred as our grandmother.

When Charlotte died, both sisters Edna and Grace were teaching school. Mom never got to go to high school as they had and she became the house keeper, with according to her, varying degrees of success. The two older girls and her brother Bill came home on weekends to help with the house and farm work but the responsibility was great for a young girl. Her father thought that she should have something also and when she was 16 she attended a term at Success Business College in Winnipeg, being able to stay with some relatives. She did well, excelling in writing and spelling, and graduated in 1923, receiving an enormous certificate (15 by 23 inches) that is among relics of the past.

She and Axel were married in 1929, a marriage that lasted ten years and produced five children, one deceased as an infant. Left with four young children at the end of a historic depression, she faced life head on, bought her old family homestead and farmed for over ten years. An old diary written in terse phrases tells of the years 1945-1950 and there was so much we would not understand until we were adults. The next phase of her life was beginning a 20 year career as cook at Rainycrest. Years later she made a rather triumphal entry into the new Rainycrest for what she called "Rainycrest the second time around."

I have written of my parent's short stay in Prairie River and of the birth and death of their first child William Allen. Alan Norman was their next son and he was born at Cuthbertson's Nursing Home in Devlin April 21, 1931. He worked for a while for Manitoba Power after schooling but took over the family farm when he married Inez Mose from Emo. Alan and Inez had five children Linda, Daniel, Douglas, Kevin and Kathy. Alan loved the farm but like many farmers he found that other employment was necessary to provide a living and he worked at the paper mill in Fort Frances for many years until his retirement. while Inez drove a school bus.

Always having a talent for wood working, Alan took up carving and that grew into a hobby and passion that surpassed even his own imagination. The carvings of his ducks and other water birds are familiar to many, and when he began entering them in craft shows all over the country he won many prize ribbons that he liked to display in his work shop.

Many of us are proud owners of some of his carved handiwork and he gave each of his many nephews and nieces a carved duck. Alan had some health issues but we were all shocked when he died very suddenly in December 2005. The family farm was sold and Inez lives in Fort Frances.

Eric Strachan Anderson was born March 5, 1933 and my mother often said that Eric was different from her other children, as he rarely cried when he was a baby. Grand mother Anderson predicted that he would not live long but he is still with us. Both Eric and Alan loved hunting and fishing as young men, and as well took over much of the farm work as soon as they were able and did the work of men. When the electrical power was being installed in rural areas in the west they both worked at that, Alan in Manitoba and Eric in Saskatchewan.

Eric grew to love Saskatchewan and stayed with Saskatchewan Power Corporation, later being a district manager. He married Tanyss and they had three children, Nathan, Guy and Joan. They divorced and he and his second wife Janet Tulipan, a teacher, now reside in North Battleford.

Eric also enjoyed working with wood and made cedar chests, stools and many other things, but after his retirement his talents showed up in other ways. He always had a flair for the dramatic and became involved in Saskatchewan Little Theater. He acted in many plays and won Best Actor awards for some of his portrayals. In October 2001 Guy and Kelly with baby Mira drove me to Moosimin, Saskatchewan for the Saskatchewan Drama Festival. This one was special as Eric was acting in a play that he had written. A number of plays, six I think, were presented and judged and it was wonderful to see my brother win awards for acting and for writing the best play. He said that he usually played the parts of grumpy old men and didn't even have to act, but that is only partially true.

Eric is the sibling closest to me in age. I was born May 18, 1935, attended Box Alder and Fort Frances High schools and later North Bay Teachers College. I married Gale Donaldson and we raised eight children on the family farm in Burriss.

All of our family was born in the Depression with Marion Helen arriving September 15, 1938. This was the fall when fires were raging everywhere due to the dry conditions and Marion was about three weeks old when the Dance Fire took the lives of seventeen people.

Marion was just over a year old when our father Axel died. After high school Marion began nurses' training at Port Arthur General

Hospital and graduated in 1959. She married Ralph Poutanen and they have three children Paul, Allen and Neil and have seven grandchildren. Ralph was involved in mining activities and was Mining Recorder for Thunder Bay District when he retired. They reside in Thunder Bay.

After retirement, Marion was very involved with the production of a history of Port Arthur General School of Nursing. With two colleagues she did much of the research and writing of the book entitled *A Time and a Place* that was published in 2000. Marion, though retired from nursing, keeps very involved with community and also helps many people that come to Thunder Bay for medical treatment. Marion is the traveller of the family and she and Ralph have visited many provinces, states and countries from Cuba to South Africa. I always experience a great feeling of relief when they arrive safely home again

People that were born in Depression time often seem to remember these times with a sort of nostalgic pride, as we have all heard the stories of hardships told by our ancestors. As children we felt no sense of hardship or deprivation. Our family is no exception and we love to talk about those days with others with similar experiences.

ANDERSON FAMILY-August 1999. L R: Eric Anderson, Marion Poutanen, Elizabeth Donaldson, Alan Anderson.

After Gale and I married many branches were added to the family tree. Our children all attended Burriss, Cornerbrook and Fort Frances High Schools and some took further education. I have stated that it was not my intention to tell my children's stories but will give a brief summary of them.

Donaldson Children page

Emily married Tom Mosbeck from Emo who is associated with one of the district's earliest businesses, Tompkins Hardware. They have three sons and five grandchildren. Scott married Michelle Medwechuk and their children are Austin, Jack and Kate. Jay married Janene Johnson. Their children are Cameron and Teagan. Eric married Hope Wilson in 2011. All the families live in Emo, with Scott and Eric being employed in the family business. Jay is an entrepreneur, working as a pilot, a versatile carpenter and has other interests as well.

GREAT GRANDCHILDREN. Back L R: Austin Mosbeck, Cameron Mosbeck. Front L R: Jack Mosbeck, Kate Mosbeck, Teagan Mosbeck

Ross has worked as a building contractor among other things and is a carpenter by trade. He married Denise Morrish and they live in Burriss. Their children are Nathalie (Matt Calder), Logan, David, Nicholas, Julianna and Teddy. Ross is employed at Tompkins Hardware and Denise as an educational assistant. At present Ross is Reeve of the Township of LaVallee. They have miniature horses on their farm.

Lee married Leanne Graham and they now own the original Donaldson homestead in Burriss. They have two sons Jason and Justin, both at university. Lee works at the Beer Store and Leanne at the Fort Frances Times. They do some gardening and farming with their Belgian horses and we all enjoy the sleigh and wagon rides there.

Jerry has worked at several occupations and is employed now at Tompkins Hardware. He is married to Nancy McTavish who works at the Hammond Greenhouse. Their two daughters Mallory (Bob Flegel) and Emily are both in University.

Mark attended but did not finish university in Ottawa. He worked at various jobs and with his brother Ross in construction. He died suddenly at age forty four in 2010.

Guy and Mark were twins. Guy married Kelly Spicer from Thunder Bay and in the past they operated Robins Donuts and Curves in Fort Frances. They have one daughter Mira and live on an island on Rainy Lake. Guy is employed at Revco Carpeting at present. In August 2011 right on her tenth birthday Mira was diagnosed with Type One diabetes. With the excellent care from the Thunder Bay Diabetic Clinic, support and guidance of parents Kelly and Guy, Mira accepted that challenge with maturity, poise and intelligence. She is involved in learning about the nature and treatment of the condition while keeping up with music and her school work.

Brian trained for occupations in the medical field in Winnipeg and then Vancouver. He now works as a biomedical technologist with Gambro Inc. and lives in Thunder Bay. He travels to hospitals all over Canada working with dialysis machines, installing and maintaining them.

Rob Roy attended Lakehead University in the educational field. He married Heather Campbell and they are both employed with the Rainy River District School Board. They have one son Rowan and live on Reef Point Road on Rainy Lake.

I am happy that most of the children have stayed in the Rainy River District and that the families and grandchildren are close by. It is good to have some of them residing in Burriss where they all grew up and where we all like to return at times.

Family Matters—Our Life In Burriss

Writing about my family, the thing that matters most to me, may be the hardest thing to do as it seems difficult to compress so many memories into a few pages. I find I cannot write in chronological order but just as memories occur. It is not my intention to tell my children's stories here as I will leave that up to them. Their memories of childhood will differ from mine and that is as it should be, as no two people remember things exactly the same. Perhaps now as adults/parents they will understand the past a little better.

While at Teachers' College I was offered a position with the Atikokan School Board on the recommendation of a friend Ken Hay. The salary quoted was an astounding $3900 and after some deliberation, I accepted this. During the summer, Gale and I decided to get married In December 1956. He was offered a job in Atikokan with Newman's Ford but decided against that and we went ahead with plans for a quiet wedding.

Atikokan was booming with the mining activity at Steep Rock Iron Mines and things were very different in school from my little class in Burriss. Classrooms were bulging and I taught one of the two Grade One classes in Rawn Road School. Both classes had about 42 students and they had not had the benefit of Kindergarten. I had some specialized problems such a girl that would not speak and a boy who could be violent. He also did not speak and at times had to be isolated from the rest of the class but the students as a whole were excellent. The principal was Frances Rawn who had taught at Box Alder school as a young teacher. The Inspector visited the school twice. His name was Mr. Partridge or Mr Parrot and since I could not seem to remember which I tried not to call him by name.

I enjoyed my year in Atikokan and was able to stay with relatives. I made new friends and never regretted my decision to go there even if it meant separation from Gale for a time.

Our marriage may not have got off to the best start as it is not good for newlyweds to be separated, but we were. Gale and I were married in a quiet ceremony on December 22, 1956 and I returned to Atikokan in early January. At that time you could only get there by train service, so when it was convenient we travelled back and forth on the night train until the end of the school year. Then, though it is not good for newlyweds to live with a set of parents, we lived at first with Gale's parents in the big cement block house in Burriss. They were extremely kind but I wanted my own household. It is not good for newlyweds to have no definite plans for the future but we did not. Besides this, we were expecting a child who arrived on October 7, 1957. Both Gale and I had come from what I considered the perfect family of two boys and two girls. We exceeded that modest ambition by having seven sons, and as Gale liked to say, "Every one of them has a sister."

It was not long until I realized that Gale would have been perfectly content to go on living in his parental home, and that is no surprise because that is the way he was brought up. In his early home there had been thirteen in all, elderly grandparents, uncles, parents and siblings, cousins and even a neighbor who "came in out the rain and stayed for twenty years." A man's point of view for such a household is probably quite different than a woman's and I did not think it fair to his mother. Besides this the big cement block house was infested with mice, the foundation was crumbling and it was not possible for anyone to spend another winter there.

Liz and Gale Donaldson in Kitchen of Old House 1957.

After the death of Gale's brother Lyle, Gale's parents purchased a trailer home in 1958 to set up on the property and that winter Gale and I rented a trailer and lived in Emo with baby Emily and Ross who was born December 19, 1958. In May we moved back to Burriss to live in the big house that was perfect for a family, fine for summer but beyond repair. By then we had plans for building a new dwelling.

Things never go quite as planned and it was a very cold fall to build but we moved into the basement of what would be our house on December 22, 1959. It was quite roomy, cozy and comfortable but we never thought that we would live there for seven years. Gale at that time was employed with the Stratmat Mining Company in

Emo and I turned down a teaching job offer or two as I was enjoying being a fulltime mother.

Except for two small oaks there were few trees in the Donaldson yard and at the end of May, Gale and I dug up and planted 74 small spruce trees in the west of the yard and they all thrived to make a lovely windbreak. Lee was born that year on November 13, 1960, right on his grandfather Jasper's birthday and Jerry arrived December 29, 1962. Each child was welcomed by his siblings to the point that Lee put a chew of gum in baby Jerry's mouth. This was the family of four that I had often thought of as the perfect family.

Life was simpler then. We had no indoor plumbing and TV was not widely available. We seemed unaware of the big changes that were coming in the 1960's, being quite content with our country life and raising the family. It was so interesting watching the personalities of the children develop and we were often amazed at the strength of mind of such little people. Gale's parents were living in the trailer and were on hand when help was needed. Although my mother was employed as cook at Rainycrest she often helped out, and many times over the years I said a fervent prayer of thanks for grandparents. There were aunts, uncles and cousins which added to the enjoyment, as I remembered this kind of childhood. It has been said that cousins often are the best friends most people have as children. I knew that, and that no one understands your family as your cousins do.

In mid December 1965 I was leaving the doctor's office after a prenatal visit when Dr Johnson said "Hey, come back here," ushered me into the X-ray room and soon gave me the stunning news that I was going to have twins. I went to the waiting room to see that Gale had not returned for me yet, but I did see Vernon Armstrong, a close friend of ours. Blurting out the news that I was going to have twins, Vernon replied, "My God Liz, how is Gale,?" in what I thought was a typical male response.

The babies were due on December 31 but arrived a week early on Christmas Eve, beautiful and healthy, and we named them Mark and Guy. I had felt very well before they were born and continued to feel well after which was fortunate. I had told someone that after the third child it was easier and, though I might not be believed, it was true for me that being experienced, I was able to handle two babies quite confidently.

DONALDSON TWINS-1966. L R: Guy Donaldson, Mark Donaldson.

There was no kindergarten for the four oldest children but Emily and Ross were in school by then, and when they were home Emily was proving herself to be a very capable and helpful child. They played endless games in which she was usually the leader. Like all children they played school and "house." It was amazing and amusing to hear my words and even my voice inflections (not always flattering) come from their play. They also played Sunday School, as Mr. Hickey was part of the school curriculum. Usually the boys acknowledged Emily as teacher or leader but occasionally Ross would not conform, and one day he was especially obstreperous. I listened to see how soon I would have to step in but then heard Emily say in exasperation, "Well, all right. Let's see what the Scriptures say!" and things settled down quickly.

As we were still living in the basement, the arrival of two babies made us even more aware that we needed more room. This was really driven home in the first week in March 1966 when the worst snow storm in many years snowed us in for five days. In our cement block basement with blocks painted white inside and all the windows snowed completely over, the comparison to an igloo was inevitable.

Entrance to Basement Home. Children Sitting on Top of Snow-covered Oil Barrel.

Work was begun on the upper part house of the house in the spring and we were ready to move in just before Christmas. As the boys were still sleeping in downstairs bedrooms, I worried the first night that I would not hear them if they called out for me. I need not have been concerned as they were hit by a contagious stomach flu and I was up and down those stairs all night. There were many episodes like this, living in such close proximity no one escaped being infected. The whooping cough siege was the worst. They had had shots and contracted a less virulent form of that childhood disease, but it was long lasting.

I never knew what real worry was until the children were sick or hurt and always imagined the worst, and though there were some very bad times things turned out fine. There were cuts, bumps, bruises, doctor's appointments, stitches, burns, nosebleeds, allergy shots, black eyes, sprains, frost bite, broken teeth and all this kind of thing but there was never a broken bone, although as Ross said later "Some of us tried pretty hard."

After the twins were born we were a bit of a novelty for a while. Many family and friends stopped by to view the new babies, often comparing them for size and looks, but I recall one lady who stood and looked at them for quite a while and said not one word. My friend Yvonne Hyatt was there one day as I spooned Pablum into one open mouth, then the other." Now you know how a mother bird feels," she said. Her son Tony was born not long before the twins, and neighbours Tom and Shirley Morrish had a daughter Kathy about that same time. The heavy snowfall that year caused problems for all of us.

The four older children were an amazing help and the experience of having two babies was interesting and enjoyable. They slept one at each end of a large crib and it was no time until they were moving toward each other. I would come to find them close or see one lying across the legs of the other. Unlike some twins they did not have their own language later but did communicate closely. I thought of them as a "force" as they seemed to know what the other had in mind and it was often done without words. When they were about four they had wrestling matches which seemed to involve no rancor, but I had to intervene. Perhaps it was about this time that I found myself saying things to them and the other children the things that mothers have passed down through the ages: "if you're going to fight go outside," "if you break your leg don't come crying to me", "because I said so, that's why," or "finish your supper or no dessert." Gale had his own unique phrases such as, "First one to sleep gets a peppermint," and he was a master at reverse psychology.

Two more sons were born, Brian on September 25, 1967 and Rob Roy on June 18, 1971. I was ill after Rob Roy was born and had to return to the hospital. Emily was nearly 14 and she took over the care of the new baby and helped the grandmothers look after the rest of the family. Times were changing and Rob Roy was our "new age" baby as he the only one of the children that used disposable diapers and plastic bottles. Later Rob Roy was the first one to have a computer, when on the suggestion of principal Jerry O'Leary we purchased a little Commodore VIC 20 for him.

In spite of the newer technology Gale and I always read to the children. We had plenty of children's story books and also a big brown book of stories for children. Now it seems odd but there were no coloured pictures in that book, just the old fairy tales and the Rudyard Kipling stories and others but the children were quite content to just listen. Grandma Anderson liked to give books and we had many of the Thornton Burgess Bedtime Stories that are still somewhere in the family. Like other small children they liked to hear the same story over and over, and you dared not miss a word or you were reminded of the omission.

Eight children were born to us in fourteen years but there were other large families, Hyatt, Meyers, Morrish and Galusha, in the area at that time. You do not often see families of that size now but we all seemed to manage. Someone likened us to "The Waltons" on TV but I did not feel we were quite like that family.

One Sunday evening we decided to take the family out for supper at the Country Kitchen in International Falls. While we were waiting until a table was available Dr. McIntosh and wife Carol arrived with their family of eight to fill the waiting area to capacity. Then I spied a teacher that I knew and said to Gale, "Oh, there's Vern." Gale's response was, "I hope he didn't bring his family."

FAMILY PICTURE-about 1975. Back L R: Liz, Ross, Lee, Jerry, Gale. Front L R: Mark, Guy, Rob Roy, Brian.

Gale had worked at a few different positions after the mining company left and was employed by Vernon Armstrong, then Elmer Norlund, always in a bookkeeping capacity. Earlier he had been a camp clerk in logging camps to the east. About 1970 he began to work for Earle Newman's Ford dealership and worked there until he retired in 1987. Although always employed away from home his first love was the farm and as I had been raised on a farm, I was very content to have our children grow up this way and they seemed to thrive. I might not recommend having eight children but I would change nothing, and a country setting was ideal for us.

We had cattle and poultry to look after as well as gardens and haying to do in the summers. Gale usually planted oats or alfalfa and had thrashing or combining to do. Although we did not have as much equipment as needed we often worked with some kind of arrangement with Dick Norris. Dick and Kate were wonderful friends and neighbours, and I know that the children have fond memories of them both. It was so exciting when Dick would come to bale the hay and would be there for meals. He had endless stories, was full of good humour and paid attention to each child. Dick was the barber for our boys and drove their school bus for years.

Other close neighbours and friends were the Mattsons, Hank and Lillian Van Drunen, Earl and Yvonne Hyatt, Harry and Vivian Beck, John and Della Sollen, Eddy and Marg Nelson, Roy and Edith Norris, Tom and Shirley Morrish, George and Denise Meyers, Archie, Mabel and Walter Topham and Morrison, Bessie and Bill Birrell. There were many changes in neighbours over the years. The original Norris farm across the road from us was sold about 1975 to John and Liz Bloetjes, a young couple from down east. Three children Mathew, Adam and Christine were born and they were our neighbours until they sold to Karel and Donna Vos with daughters Kari, Heidi and Krista.

There were many moments amusement, of absolute joy and amazement at the ability and resourcefulness of our children and it would be easy to look back and idealize a life style such as ours, saying it was no problem raising eight children. A person does forget and I can gloss over some of it but certainly not all. There were days when everything went wrong and I felt bogged down, incapable and overwhelmed by the sheer volume of jackets, hats, shoes, boots, lunch kits, socks, blue jeans, mittens, books and toys, cooking and laundry. It was best at these times to just leave everything and go outside.

I tried to keep organized and not let things pile up but they did and I lost my temper and was cross with the children. One day I was upset about the condition of the bedrooms and was holding forth about the mess, and vowed that if I ever came into their rooms and they were tidy, I swore I would faint! Ross spoke up and said, "That's why we don't do it, Mom. We don't want you fainting when you're home here alone." What could I do but laugh?

We ran a fairly organized household. The kids all had chores and were quite reliable but squabbles broke out and sometimes instead of hearing sides, I made them write out their complaints and then would deal with them. If two of them found it impossible to be together without fighting I would separate them and send them to different places, with the orders they were not to speak or have any contact whatsoever. It was usually no time until they were sneaking to be back together again. No one dared say they were bored, knowing that I had many things they could do. Having a large family meant that there was always someone to play with, someone to read a story to or amuse a younger one, someone to play a game with. They entertained each other and generally were on good terms with each other. Often there were friends or cousins that came to play ball or at the creek or the beaver pond.

They invented their own games and activities and were very creative in this department. One day a neighbour, Lil Van Drunen, said she liked driving by our place as the children were always doing such interesting things. This was when they were having a golf tournament with the two opponents in the foremost followed by the cheering "crowd," all arrayed in undershirts and hats, waving flags.

They spent hours "haying" in the summer, clipping the grass with my scissors and tying it into bales to store in the little barn that Ross built. One time they built a giant catapult from just the right willow shape and it was capable of firing quite large rocks. Even Gale's visiting cousins, Morris Donaldson and Elmer Gehrig, were impressed by this.

Endless hours were spent at the creek. Jerry described their activities there much better than I could and shortly after the death of his brother Mark he sent me the following:

Last night I dreamed of the creek, the creek of my childhood, of times spent with brothers and friends, doing the thing that boys will do if they have a creek available.

Our creek was not the crystal clear water, babbling brook of story books. Our creek didn't babble and for the most part it was quiet except when the winter snows melted, gathered and ran off to the south; or when the July thunder storms came with rains so heavy you could almost see the creek rise, overflowing the fields.

Our waters weren't crystal clear, they were dark and earthy, but that didn't bother us. It was a good creek.

The creek was a great source of education and recreation. We fished for mud minnows with bent pins and pieces of bread from the old wooden bridge. We made forts and played hide and seek among the willows and the bull rush flats. In the spring we would rush to see who could find the first pussy willows and marsh marigolds. When conditions were right our Dad would cut a willow branch and transform it into a whistle.

We swam in the muddy waters and when the July floods occurred we would try to ride a stray hay bale down the swollen channel to see who could stay on the longest. We picked our way across the rotting timbers of a bridge built by a previous generation, just to see who could get across without falling in.

In the fall there were partridge to hunt and weasels, mink, muskrat and beaver to be harvested to earn some spending money. If conditions were perfect in the fall, the creek would freeze hard before the snows came and we could explore for miles on boots or skates. I remember one such time and we built a fire by the old bridge and toasted cheddar cheese sandwiches and baked apples in the embers. It's hard to imagine anything could taste better.

The creek has changed over the years. The beavers have taken over and their dams and ponds have dramatically changed the landscape. But the old swimming hole is still where it was, maybe a little smaller and shallower than I remember. It's been over thirty years since I entered those murky waters. I think next summer I'm going to do it again- just for old time's sake and I hope to not swim alone.

We always seemed to think of the family as the older ones and the younger ones, with Jerry being the dividing line as there were three years between him and twins. There are family stories of Jerry bearing the brunt of the actions of the first three, such as when he would hide for Hide and Go Seek-and no one would look for him, but he has borne the scars of childhood, literally and figuratively, quite well. Jerry was the first musician in the family and the others all followed in his steps. It seemed as if there was always a guitar or two, or a piano playing somewhere in the background in our house. One time the noise of the drum set in the garage caused the neighbour's cattle to stampede. Emily and Ross as the eldest seemed to feel responsible for the younger ones and exerted their influence in various ways, generally diplomatic. I would only smile when teachers remarked on Lee's quiet nature.

It was Lee who invented the game of hand hockey, played on hands and knees on the basement floor with an old sock rolled tightly together with rubber bands as a puck. This was played by all, including visiting friends or cousins and I would hear the thumping and bumping going on and know they were having another game. I was unofficial referee from upstairs and they knew I would call the game if necessary. As the nature of the game changed with influence of TV, I would hear them singing the National Anthem, then the game would start with cheers and roars. They had a tape deck and interviews of players were conducted between periods, some with distinct Russian accents. This game resulted in many jeans with worn out knees for Grandma Anderson to patch.

Although we often spoke of "the twins" they were two distinct personalities. They were the first of the family to attend Kindergarten and Guy was just slightly less enthusiastic than Mark about that. When Guy was about five we found that he suffered from allergies and he and I travelled to Winnipeg to be tested where it was found that one of his main allergies was dandelions. He had a few bad experiences and went to the Emo Clinic for allergy shots for years.

Brian was very active and adventurous, and when he began to walk it was hard to keep track of him as our yard was large. Besides this, we had a large, overly friendly and ill mannered hound dog that, when the children would come out to play, could make one joyous turn around the yard knocking everyone flat. This annoyed me greatly and Gale decided to make a big pen outside that Brian could play safely in with his toys, and often Grandpa Jasper would sit out to watch and entertain him. The other children would climb over the bars much to Brian's delight but soon the dog found a spot where he could squeeze himself under the bottom rail to join the crowd.

One day I heard cries of distress and found that Mark had crawled into the dog house and then the dog, happy to have company, followed and refused to move and let Mark out. When Gale found someone that was interested in getting a hound dog, he wondered if I would agree to let the dog go. Would I? I was so glad the day I saw that dog, happily licking the face of his new owner, being driven away.

Brian's kindergarten teacher Colin Paulson said he had not heard Brian volunteer a word until one day he announced, "I can sing O Canada." and did. Brian was one of those unfortunate children who stuck his tongue on the metal railing on the school steps and was rescued by capable substitute teacher Ella Carruthers. Ella also rescued Jerry one day when he climbed up the backstop and got impaled on a loose wire.

Rob Roy did not arrive quite when expected and every day the children would get on the bus announcing. "Not yet," to driver Rosella Galbraith. When he finally was born, Lee rolled up paper cigars and passed them out on the bus. Rob Roy was a very placid baby who did not cry and seemed satisfied with his world. Rob Roy was of the generation that watched Sesame Street. He and I returned from Fort Frances one day to find that, even though we never locked the back door, that day it <u>was</u> locked and the keys were in the house. After a moment of panic I took him to a basement window and removed the screen and was able to push the window open. Then I lowered him in and let him drop, to land on a bed, with instructions to go upstairs and open the door. He met me at the door and said in his best Big Bird imitation, "Now, that's co-operation!"

Over the years we had many visits from my sister Marion and family from Thunder Bay. She and Ralph had three boys Paul, Allen and Neil, whose ages coincided with some of our boys and when the ten boys and one girl got together it was like an explosion of energy. Paul had an incredible imagination and was always involved in new activities ranging from hypnotism to origami. They played baseball, foot ball, hockey on our small rink and swam at Lake Wasaw with equal fervour. One year when it was very wet, mud football was the name of the game, horrible to watch envisioning the laundry. They played hide and seek, waiting until after dark and Rob Roy was so happy the year that Paul declared he was old enough to join in.

DONALDSON-POUTANEN COUSINS-1972. Back L R: Allen Poutanen, Paul Poutanen, Emily Donaldson. Front L R: Lee Donaldson, Neil Poutanen, Mark Donaldson, Brian with Ross Donaldson, Jerry Donaldson (missing Guy and Rob Roy Donaldson).

We all recall those visits with great pleasure, when Marion and I spent our time cooking, washing dishes and doing laundry. We always ran the well dry and then would have to travel to neighbours for containers of drinking water until water was restored. The city boys loved the novelty of this. One year my brother Eric and his three children Nathan, Guy and Joan came at the same time as Marion, and along with our brother Alan and his family, my mother and Uncle Tom Anderson we had a wonderful reunion at our farm.

We had various vehicles which Gale drove until he began to work at Ford Motors and he then drove a demonstrator model. The old white Chev became a part of our lives. The children were becoming drivers as soon as they were old enough and drove this Chev until we purchased a large dark blue Ford station wagon that accommodated the family a little better. We never travelled much but did make trips to Saskatchewan and Alberta to visit relatives. One time we tented in Alberta, six of us in an old tent that we set up nearing dark one night. In the morning we were told, "Nobody tents in Alberta," because of bears they said. I remembered something sniffing around the tent and hoped it was a dog.

Gale won a trip to San Francisco through Ford, with 200 Canadian Ford reps, for a week in California in August 1976. We met up with a friendly couple from Saskatchewan to join forces with. The death of Elvis Presley was announced while we were there and there were ladies in tears on the bus that day

Time seemed to have gone by so rapidly, bringing so many changes to us and one day I said to myself, "Where have all my little boys gone?" Some of the children were in high school, driving and becoming more independent and developing other interests. Things were changing in the education field and there were some drastic things to become accustomed to such as the new math, the open concept, consultants, Kindergarten in rural schools and new reading methods. The schools were encouraging volunteers and I enjoyed being one of those volunteers. At one point we had children in four schools.

In 1975 there was a very large kindergarten class enrolled at Burriss School and I was hired as teacher's aide and worked with Dorothy Weir for a number of years after this. I loved this part time job and being back in a school situation. It was a great change in routine and inspired me to jot down a poem entitled "Part Time Job."

> *Today I washed and ironed, and swept the kitchen floor,*
> *Made a batch of muffins, wiped hand marks from a door.*
> *I mended several pair of jeans, made a special stew,*
> *Tidied up the bathrooms, and made a bed or two.*
> *I picked up groceries at the store, had a neighbour in for tea,*
> *Helped a child with home work, not much time for me.*
> *Today has been so busy, there was no time to shirk*
> *But I look forward to tomorrow, for then I go to WORK.*

Changes occurred in our family as well, and Emily and Tom Mosbeck of Emo were married in 1976. When their son Scott was born, our status changed to grandparents, and Emily and Tom's brothers became uncles. When Scott was born the status of many people changed and he had two great grandfathers, four great grandmothers, two sets of grandparents, eight uncles and many great aunts and uncles.

Our niece Dianne McLeod had graduated as a teacher and when a substitute teacher was needed for the month of June 1976 at Burriss School she was hired and continued as the grade two teacher that September. She came to live with us and stayed for three years, fitting into our family and the community very well. One memorable time Gale was annoyed at something, and one of the children who was not listening to his tirade, made an off topic remark that made us all laugh uncontrollably. Gale sternly told the children to go their rooms, and when Dianne was unable to stifle her amusement she also was sent to her room. It's all in the family.

I worked with Dorothy Weir in the kindergarten for several years until a Speech and Language program headed by Janet Asplund was begun in the schools. I had done some supply work in this, (I worked three days a week in Kindergarten) and when the position was advertised I was hired. This was also fascinating work and I learned a great deal while working as a communications assistant. Janet Asplund was completely dedicated to her job and I considered it a real privilege to work with her and was deeply saddened when she died at an early age.

In 1980 I joined the local TOPS chapter and over the years have made many good friends there. I may not be the best role model for TOPS but it has become part of my life and, though over the years there have been changes, our chapter remains one of the most active in the area. Some long term friends are: Joan Hughes, Lois Shine, Freeda Carmody, Trudy Badiuk, Neila Booth, Marie Saunders, Rose Mose, Maureen Hanson, Josette Vargas, Jacqui Hunsperger, Gail Kelly, Lois Caul, Marie Major, Diana Mayes and Beth Brown and there are many others. Some, including George and Bev Hyatt, Pat Toop, Irene Bragg, Verv Galusha, Fern Robson, Heather Smith and Jeannine Shine, are now deceased. My brother Alan was a member until his sudden death in 2005 and was greatly missed. The support, companionship and good will encountered at TOPS is second to none. I have travelled to Spokane, Washington and St. Paul, Minnesota, as well as to many TOPS functions from Sault Ste. Marie, Thunder Bay, Dryden and Kenora with fellow members.

Liz Donaldson and Alan Anderson. TOPS Function about 2002

There were three weddings to attend within six months in 1984-'85. Jerry and Nancy McTavish were married August 25. 1984, Lee and Leanne Graham on October 20, 1984 and Ross and Denise Morrish on February 14, 1985. Grandchildren followed and we were so glad to be able to take part in their lives. I was still employed at Burriss School when Nathalie, Logan and Jason were students. Nathalie always referred to me as Mrs. Donaldson even though many of the students called me Grandma.

SLEEPOVER at GRANDMA'S HOUSE-about 1993. L R: Mallory Donaldson, Jason Donaldson, Eric Mosbeck, Justin Donaldson, Jay Mosbeck, David Donaldson, Logan Donaldson, Nathalie Donaldson.

Marking the end of an era, the school bus stopped at our gate for the last time in almost thirty years when Rob Roy went off to Lakehead University in 1991.

The next wedding took place on June 1, 1996 when Guy and Kelly Spicer were wed. Rob Roy and Heather Campbell were married August 20. 1999. Due to an unfortunate accident Heather was on crutches. Mira was born to Guy and Kelly and Rowan to Rob Roy and Heather. All the things I heard about the joys of being grandparents were true.

Life with teenagers when they went further afield for entertainment was different but we still enjoyed family occasions and excursions and this continued even after they were married with families. One thing we liked on Mother's Day was a jaunt to a big outcrop of rock north of our home, which we would climb to explore and enjoy the scenery and have a picnic. We carried in food, water, babies and blankets and, as it was usually just when the leaves were coming out, it seemed a lovely way to celebrate.

MOTHER'S DAY ON THE ROCK-about 1990. Back L R: Liz Donaldson, Denise Donaldson with David, Lee Donaldson, Leanne Donaldson. Middle L-R : Rob Roy Donaldson, Scott Mosbeck, Eric Mosbeck, Mallory Donaldson, Justin Donaldson with Ross, Emily Mosbeck. Front L R: Guy Donaldson, Jason Donaldson, Logan Donaldson, Nathalie Donaldson, Jerry Donaldson.

One fall we had set up an old tent back in the woods and decided to have Thanksgiving dinner there. It took some preparation but it did not really seem like work transporting folding tables, chairs, cushions and dishes beforehand. Trucks travelled back and forth all morning with supplies while the food cooked at home, and at the last minute the hot food was whisked up to the campsite. Coffee was boiled over a camp fire and young and old had a great time. This kind of thing has appealed to me since childhood and the children and I often went for a cook out at lunch time.

We have had many great times at Clearwater Lake at the Mosbeck cabins. Gale really enjoyed going there as the Donaldson family had had a summer home there in the 1930's. Sometimes he and I went for a weekend with Tom, Emily and the boys and we have nearly always had at least one family day there. The summer of 2011 we had an especially good family weekend there, with some of the overflow sleeping in tents.

SCENE AT DOCK—CLEARWATER LAKE-July 2011.

Does everyone look back over their lives as being in certain stages? Mine seemed to be divided with childhood and education, marriage and childrearing, then returning to work until my retirement. Those past years were full of graduations, weddings, births, funerals, trips, anniversaries, reunions and all those things that go to make up a life. Gale retired in 1987 and had a first heart attack a few years later, one of those major life changing events. He had always been extremely proud of his heritage and that the Donaldson farm had remained in the family for close to 100 years but now we did begin to think that changes would have to be made. A Donaldson/Norris centennial was held in July 1998 marking 100 years since those families moved here from Ohio. Doris Donaldson, wife of Jasper, at 96 was the oldest person there.

DONALDSON-NORRIS CENTENNIAL-4th Generation-1998. Back L R: standing Ross Donaldson, Rob Roy Donaldson, Lee Donaldson, Dianne Debenedet, Emily Mosbeck, Heather Miller. L R:seated Donnie Manty, Guy Donaldson, Jerry Donaldson, Mark Donaldson, Kenny Manty, Grandmother Doris Donaldson, Maureen Ricard.

Never noted for doing things quickly, we did talk about changes and decided when we moved, that Emo would be our choice. It grew more difficult to keep things up and the family often helped out at such things as cutting the wood to stoke the furnace and for snow removal. We had a large garage sale and donated some things of historical value such as the big sauerkraut cutter to Wayne Salchert for his unique Mud Lake City.

Finally in 2002 we were in the final stages of preparations to move into a house in Emo in September. Gale had been diagnosed with Parkinson's Disease a few years before this and the distressing symptoms of this were increasing, making everything more difficult for him. Lee and Leanne had decided to buy the farm which made us happy to know family members would continue to own the homestead. So things were progressing well, but then came the flood in June! One of the worst storms on record hit the area and soon every ditch, creek and the LaVallee River were overflowing their banks. The district was declared a disaster area. Lee and Leanne's house was among others that were damaged by the torrents. They had moved some things out and stored them at our place but they had to move in with Leanne's mother Joyce Graham with their two boys Jason and Justin.

Meanwhile in Emo the house that we were moving into was being renovated and everything speeded up to facilitate our moving which did happen in June, 2002 and Lee and family soon were settled into the place in Burriss. We were quite happy to move, even though it was a bit sooner than we had thought. I had had qualms about leaving the home where I had lived for nearly fifty years but I found that once our possessions were moved and my books and familiar things and my cat were with me I was fine.

By then I was working on the history book CONNECTIONS and that took much of my time. Gale always liked to have a project and began to grow grapes. They did quite well and the crop yielded very well and I made grape jelly as well as the juice to toast an anniversary. Gale and I celebrated our 50th wedding anniversary in 2006 with all our family, marking fifty years of marriage and all that happened in those past years.

We were fortunate indeed that most of the family chose to stay in the Rainy River District and that we have close contact with them, enjoying the society of the grandchildren. After all, what matters more than family?

Gale and Liz Donaldson –2004

Grandchildren

Chickens, Geese, Turkeys And Quail

I sometimes told Gale that he should have been a pioneer as he had such sincere admiration for their resourcefulness and ingenuity. If possible Gale would try the "old way" and would spend hours straightening old nails, trying to fix an old tool or piece of machinery that had obviously outlived its usefulness, rather than buy something new. I admired the pioneers also but only to a point. Gale enjoyed telling of the things his grandmother had done like quilting and plucking geese. I recall my Swedish grandmother spinning her own yarn to knit, but did not want to do that myself.

I practiced things I learned from my mother and grandmothers such as canning and pickling, making sauerkraut, drying corn and knitting. He liked the idea of trying things that the original settlers had done and he tried his hand at blacksmithing and growing things like peanuts and sweet potatoes or chicory to grind the roots to mix with coffee. Although Gale would have approved of me making soap and candles and spinning I drew the line at certain activities.

We did however agree to raise some poultry and Gale thought it would be good to have geese as the older Donaldson generation had. Every Christmas I listened to how the Donaldson Christmas dinner consisted of four geese and all the plucking and preparation by the women that went into it. Feathers were saved for pillows and a goose wing was kept as handy tool for cleaning the stairs.

The creek was close and he thought geese would be happy to be near the water. We got six geese and though I had unhappy visions of plucking geese for Christmas dinner, they were quite lovely. We quickly found out that domestic geese do not care to be near water, much preferring to sit on the doorstep or outside the windows leaving large deposits behind. They ate the gardens and flowers, honked annoyingly loudly very early in the morning, were cranky and the children and dogs and cats were nervous around them. We heard sounds of a terrific commotion one time and saw one of the ganders engaged in a fight with a fox. The fox did want not to give in but the goose put up a real battle and escaped.

The geese roamed around the yard, messy and noisy, but started to wander a bit and ventured across the road into the yard of Edith and Roy Norris, our neighbours. Edith would never complain but Roy was a bit testy and did not like the intrusion or the messes. We did our best to keep them away from Roy's place, but one day Edith called and said that Roy was chasing the geese home. I went out to see Roy running behind the geese, brandishing a broom and yelling at them. As they got closer I was amazed to see one of them take off in flight. I didn`t think they were meant to fly but this huge bird came hurtling in like a torpedo. It did not attain much height and crashed with a loud reverberating noise, wires twanging, right into the power line that came into the house from the hydro pole and then dropped straight down. Roy came rushing up and said, "He broke his neck!" The goose got up, honked, shook himself indignantly and waddled off. We laughed and laughed. When a hydro worker came to tighten the wires he did not believe me when I told him a goose had flown into them. We eventually sold the geese after an eventful summer with them.

We had given up raising cattle and the resulting wild cattle chases and went into raising more poultry. The chicken house that Gale and the boys built was like the old one that had burned in the fire and was a two storey structure. The upper story could be reached by inside stairs or by stairs from the outside. Gale always liked to do things just a little differently. When I used the inside stairs I always wore a hat because when the trap door was pushed open, it dislodged straw and other unknown things that fell on my head. The building was wired for electricity and this was a good thing for lighting and for the use of heat lamps. We were able to hatch a batch or two of chicks, praying electrical power would not be disrupted.

Our first poultry, though, was some year old hens bought from Harold Austin from Emo who was noted for his chicken raising. We kept these for a while and they laid an egg or two if they were in the mood, then we slaughtered them and I canned most of them. Canned chicken is delicious and useful to have on hand, as it can be used in a variety of ways. Then we started to buy baby chicks from the hatcheries near Steinbach and they usually seem to arrive at the coldest, wettest times imaginable. Sometimes even heat lamps were not enough and the baby chicks were nurtured in the house for a day or two. Although cute they are also noisy, smelly and crowded each other and some of them would keel over and die for no reason that we could see. Like the author of "The Egg and I," I suggested perhaps chicken pox or "eggzema" but Gale was not amused.

Generally though, they are much tougher than the baby turkeys which we also started to buy. We would order a dozen turkeys and would get them later than the chicks in hopes that the weather was better and warmer. It rarely seemed to be, and turkeys are so especially susceptible to cold and dampness that it seemed if they got one drop of water on them attempts to save them were futile. Mark tenderly nursed one that had got damp and we all felt bad when it died.

I rather liked the turkeys. As they got older and feathered out they seemed so gentle, dignified and thoughtful and I liked the way they would put their heads over to one side, look at you and say, "Prrrttt?" One Sunday morning I awakened to the sound of a dog barking and squawking from turkeys. We were looking after Jerry's dog and somehow the turkeys had got out of their pen, and by the time I got out I could see the dog running and barking and there seemed to be turkeys lying all over the yard. My heart sank and I thought they were all done for. Gale came out and we collared the dog and then assessed the damage. I went up to the first motionless bird and in a rather teary voice said, "Poor turkey." He lifted his head, looked up at me and said, "Prrrttt?" We were amazed and figured they had just collapsed from fright, sort of like those fainting goats do. The dog had done some damage but they all survived. In the fall when they were full grown Guy would stand outside their pen and shout, "Thanksgiving, Thanksgiving," and they would respond by gobbling excitedly.

One time Gale and I had been away for a day or two leaving the children, some of them in their teens, to take care of things. One of the turkeys had been sick and they told us when we got home that 'Harold' had died. Later I took a film to be developed and found some very odd pictures. When I showed them to Gale he exclaimed, "That's my suit!" and here was one of the boys dressed for the occasion (Harold's funeral they said), standing in front of the other turkeys and children.

One shot was of just the turkeys, and was told that these were the mourners. A eulogy and tribute booklet had been composed as well. They probably also served lunch.

The chickens were so excitable and when you went in they all flew up in the air, squawking, feathers and dust flying. They rushed at you when you came in carrying two pails of food and water and would try to get into the pail, when you put one down. I was used to chickens from my childhood and knew how to reach under a hen on the nest to get eggs without being bitten on the arm as chickens have a way of grabbing and twisting the flesh. Chickens can be vicious and will peck at each other until the blood comes and then that poor hen is fair game for everyone and the phrase "pecking order" is illustrated at its most elemental. We would put pine tar on a victim to try to stop the ravages. Once I stitched and bandaged the neck of a chicken that had been hurt and it healed nicely.

The turkey pen was separate but the baby chicks had to be tended to in the upstairs and the older hens were downstairs. The time would come when the hens had to be moved around, involving catching and carrying the squawking, resisting birds by squeamish and reluctant help. The ultimate fall activity was chicken killing weekend with the catching, killing scalding, plucking, gutting, washing and cleaning, picking pin feathers and final processing for freezing or canning. Working as an assembly line we would often process thirty or more birds at a time. The turkeys were done separately and were frozen ready for special occasions.

CHICKEN BUTCHERING WEEKEND-1979. Everyone helped. Gale always wore a long white butcher's apron.

We raised Red Sussex chickens for the eggs and raised white Cornish giants as meat birds that grew very quickly into 8 to 10 pound birds. Our Red Sussex chickens laid brown eggs and when we begin to sell eggs to the Cloverleaf Grocery we found they were in demand. These eggs had to be washed, candled and graded for size and we ended up with the slightly cracked and the ones with double yolks. We were somewhat like a neighbour who was selling eggs and thought he was doing well financially until he took an accounting course and found with the cost of feed and other things he was actually losing money. The brown eggs were nice and we stashed our egg money in a pint jar to buy more feed.

Next Gale got interested in quail and ordered 100 mixed sex chicks from somewhere to the east. I know we had to go to Thunder Bay to pick them up. They were tiny but seemed very hardy and they cheeped and peeped all the way on the four hour trip home. We got them settled in the upstairs part of the chicken house with heat lamps, water and special food. They were very active and quite cute with little brown stripes on their heads. When feathered out they were brown and tan and still had the striped heads. Small and neat, they scurried and scuttled, darting here and there sometimes flying straight up in the air. Gale liked the novelty of them and had plans to make them profitable. They began to lay eggs and were quite prolific but different from the chickens that laid their eggs in nests. These little creatures dropped their eggs all over the floor and gathering them was rather touchy as I did not like the squish they made if stepped on.

The eggs were speckled like birds' eggs and about one quarter the size of a hen's eggs. I used them for cooking and baking and would use 4 or 5 in place of one regular egg but the shells were much harder than a hen's egg. If a recipe called for three eggs it was quite a chore breaking all those little eggs open.

Gale thought that pickled eggs to sell might be a good venture, so masses of eggs were boiled and shelled, Gale helping, and packed into quart jars and the brine poured over them. Sixty five eggs filled one quart jar and they were very tasty. People were eager to try them and if someone liked them Gale would insist they take a jar home. (along with the profit) We gave pails of eggs away to anyone that would take them and displayed some at the Emo Fair.

Not all the eggs were used for pickling, baking or the frying pan as Gale decided to hatch some of the eggs as we had hatched baby chicks.. The eggs had to be kept at an even temperature, sprinkled with water and given a quarter turn every day. Gale had amazing patience to do this kind of thing. We had an incubator and did all the necessary preliminaries and in due time were rewarded with a healthy batch of baby quail. This crowded the quail quarters and they had to be moved around. One of the boys suggested that the older ones could be outside and this was a great idea, as a predator got most of them the first night out.

HATCHING QUAIL. Quail chicks, un-hatched eggs and hen's eggs to show size.

Gale decided that we should eat some of them. A restaurant we had been in served steak and quail and I found recipes for delicacies such as "Quail on Toast." I came home from work one day to find Gale looking grim with several pathetic little carcasses displayed. He said that he could process twenty chickens in the time it took to do these three or four quail as they were so tiny and hard to work with. I did cook some, but not properly I guess, as they were tough and stringy and too much like eating a robin's tiny drumsticks for my liking.

The novelty was wearing off for me. I was definitely tired of cracking those little shells and after a time Gale's enthusiasm began to wane also, as they were a great deal of work and they ate a lot. I am not really sure now but I think that he found someone that would buy them and we gradually gave up all the poultry after years of caring for them.

There were advantages to having the poultry and it was good to be raising something on our farm. Having plenty of eggs was a bonus and we all enjoyed the canned or fried chicken and the roasted turkey at holiday times. Some of the grandchildren liked seeing the chickens and I recall taking Scott with me to gather eggs. I held the chicken so he could reach under her for the egg. His look of amazement at the feel of the warm egg was priceless and I was able to talk him out of carrying it in his pocket.

After we gave up the chickens we used the cleaned chicken house for storage, for a greenhouse to harden plants and for sorting harvested vegetables in fall. Since it was beginning to show its age, Lee has renewed the foundation, repaired windows and doors, re sided and painted it to restore it into a useful building again, but so far not for poultry.

Post Script: There are now baby chicks in the renovated chicken house. Lee and Leanne ordered 25 mixed Columbia Plymouth Rock Cross Red chicks that are thriving in their new environment.

Raising Cattle In Burriss

When Gale and I were first married, he had cattle and what was to be the last flock of sheep on the Donaldson farm. There was a special barn with lambing pens built for them north of the house and other buildings. After shearing some of the fleeces were sent away to woollen mills in Manitoba and blankets and heavy socks were made from them. There were still a few fleeces with their distinctive raw wool smell as a reminder of the sheep flock in an outside shed. Many farmers in Burriss raised sheep as well as cattle but wolves were becoming a real problem and caused many farmers to give up the sheep.

Gale was working away from home by day, but although his father had had a stroke he was able to do some of the work. There were young cattle and also milk cows kept in the barn east of the house. This entailed milking, separating and other chores. One winter I had to water and feed the cattle in the morning while Grandpa watched the children. We had dairy cattle until about 1960 when Gale decided to try another way of raising livestock.

When the Stratton Cattle sale started Gale began buying about twenty five calves in the fall, wintering them over to sell the next fall. They were sheltered in the old sheep barn and watered at the trough at the well house or at the creek. The boys took part in the chores as soon as they were old enough and I helped at times. Fencing was always a concern and often Gale would take a boy or two and walk through the pasture and check on fences or the cattle if they had not been seen for a day or two. At that time the bush was well pastured and open, with the cattle trails inches deep where they had walked single file.

The chores in the winter were the hardest for the children, as Gale always worked away from home. The hay was not kept in a barn but had to be dug out, often from snowy, icy stacks. They hauled the round bales on the toboggan to the feeding area, taking care to close the gates behind them and always removing twine. This may have been forgotten on the most bitterly cold days. One time there had been an ice storm making it nearly impossible to loosen the bales. The older boys had gone on the high school bus, and though I hated to do it, I kept Mark home from school. After everyone had got away, I went out with him and we chopped out bales to feed the cattle.

On most days the cattle knew when to start out and would set off in single file to the water trough. If there was heavy snow the trails would drift in and the boys had to break trail with the calves following. We had a large metal watering trough and Gale had installed an electric pump that had to be primed but sometimes froze up.

Chores were never completed as quickly any other day of the year as on Christmas morning. It was my rule that they could open their stockings, but then the cattle were fed and watered, the wood box filled, a big breakfast cooked and consumed and dishes done before a single present was opened. Jobs were done in record time on that day.

All the children will recall times when the cattle seemed out of control. There were wild chases with a small boy standing and waving his arms, feebly trying to follow instructions to "Turn them!" or even worse "Stop them," while the herd galloped full speed straight at him. These are my least favourite memories of cattle raising, but most people raised on the farm will remember similar experiences.

A new herd in the fall meant various tasks including shots, dehorning, ear tags, and castration, if we had young bulls This involved getting the calves into the cattle squeeze where they were locked in by the neck and given their treatments with various instruments. Then they were released into the outside feed lot for the first time to recover from their indignities.

I think that Gale had commissioned Nick Rogoza from the Devlin Garage to build the cattle squeeze. It made handling the cattle much easier and neighbouring farmers often borrowed it. The children developed a fine game in the cattle squeeze when it was not in use, with some playing the parts of the unruly animals and others trying to control them.

Haying was a high point of the summer. Gale and Ross or Lee would cut and rake, and as we did not have our own baler, Dick Norris would come and bale. Usually at least one boy would be watching for Dick to come down the hill and then run to report the news. Some of the boys liked to follow the baler and walked round and round the field. The bales were hauled and stacked by whoever was working for us at that time.

Before the boys were old enough to be of much help, Gale hired Paul Donaldson and then his brother Steven who came and helped with the haying and spent some of the summer. These teen aged boys, the sons of Morris and Laura Donaldson, had been well trained to do household duties and they helped me and played with the children when they were not working in the fields. We loved having them with us. Steven was there the summer after the twins were born and pitched right in with their care.

Later Gale had local boys Ian Booth and Mike Clark who came by the day. One summer Roddy Cyr and his son Buddy from Northwest Bay were hired. They stayed several days and hauled and stacked the bales. It was wonderful when all went well with the haying. Sometimes, Gale would take his holidays, planning to get the hay crop in and it would rain most of the time. We often had visitors during haying time.

Cousins-about 1972. Back-On step: Dianne McLeod, Heather Manty. Ross with Rob Roy in stroller, Donnie Manty, Kenny Manty in corner.

We had a small Ford 8-N tractor and a fairly ancient Farmall tractor, both of which seemed to require work and repairs to keep running. About 1974 Gale bought an Allis Chalmers baler that did not work well at first. The belts kept slipping off until a technique was developed for keeping them on. The automatic twine cutter did not always work and someone had to follow the baler to cut the twine manually. Jerry was the most successful at operating it. Someone was always working on the tractors or machinery to keep it all running. I often told Gale that If I ever won a lottery I would buy him a brand new tractor. Meanwhile, we had cattle that had to be fed, so Gale and the boys kept working away at repairing and driving the old tractors.

At times some of the fields would be plowed, cultivated, fertilized and crops such as oats planted. Then he would have to hire someone to combine. One year Gale had a very good yield of alfalfa seed. He and the boys had built two good granaries and it was nice to see the bins and sacks full of oats or seed.

Since we bought only yearlings to sell the next year we did not have a cow/calf operation. The only calf that was born was to a young heifer that had somehow become impregnated. The vet said she was too young and small, so the calf was delivered by caesarean section. The operation was performed in the well house and her whole side was shaved, a large incision made and then nicely stitched up. One of the boys said she looked kind of like a baseball. The calf was healthy, cute and we named him Caesar for obvious reasons.

Another animal that we all remember was the one that went wild and escaped from the rest of the herd. It was in winter and it got spooked and just took off through fences and snow. It was chased and tracked for several days to no avail. Our neighbour Roy Norris was very interested and kept driving the roads searching and finally spotted it a few miles north of our farm. Feed was taken to it for the rest of the winter but it was wild and unapproachable. Toward spring Gale built a pen of poles and baited it with hay. Gradually it was lured in and trapped and we would go every day to feed and water him. When it was dry enough, Roy`s two wheeled wagon was brought up with the tractor, a pen built on it and the steer was captured and hauled triumphantly home in April.

BRINGING HOME THE WILD STEER-about 1972. Ross on bicycle, Gale on tractor, Guy and Lee in background.

Then there was the animal that we all began calling "Jerry's heifer." The summer that he was about ten he decided to try to ride one of the heifers. He just started to get on her back when she was lying down and she did not seem to mind. This started a summer of him riding on the back of an animal that seemed not at all bothered that he was there. He fashioned a sort of halter to slip over her head, but he had no control over her and where they went was her decision. I would look out and see the herd heading back to the bush with Jerry riding his heifer.

One day the herd got spooked when the lead animal apparently disturbed a hornet's nest in a swampy area and they all took off at a dead gallop. Jerry fell off, landing hard. Of course, I did not hear of this until much later, and incidents such as this increased my faith in guardian angels for children. Jerry rode miles that summer and the rope halter had to be removed before they were shipped in the fall.

Raising cattle as we did was probably not very profitable, but it was what we wanted to do and it was good to have some livestock. As the children grew up and left home, we gradually found it too difficult to continue farming to the extent that we had. Gale liked to keep the pasture growth down and rented the pasture lots out to neighbouring farmers, and neighbours also took off our hay crops. It was pleasant to see the cattle coming to water at the creek or to the salt lick and realize that we did not have to worry about them, unless they broke through a fence, as cattle love to do.

Since both Gale and I had come from rural and farming backgrounds, the way we raised our children seemed to just fall into place. I think we all loved country living, the bush, skiing, snowshoeing, the creek, walking country roads, roaming the fields, picking berries, the animals and birds, and growing things. The work involved and the satisfaction derived from that was part of it all, and looking back even on the times that were not the best, gives me a feeling of pleasure and satisfaction.

I enjoy driving and seeing the cows and calves out in the fields in the spring and often slow down to have a good look. I like checking out hay crops and seeing who has the first hay bales turned out. It is one of the pleasures of living in a rural area and it always reminds me of the cattle on our childhood farm and of our farm in Burriss.

Hockey

My great grandson received the puck, swooped down the ice and scored. The crowd in the stands cheered enthusiastically and the game proceeded. At intervals a buzzer sounded. All the players immediately skated to their respective benches and others skated out to take their turns. The players with matching uniforms, helmets, great looking skates and sticks, looked like a little army. My great grandson was five years old and he is the third generation of family hockey players I have watched.

The arena, even in the ice area, was comfortably warm. Spotless glass windows with nets above shielded the spectators from flying pucks. It was a lovely Saturday morning but my mind did not stay here but drifted back thirty or even more years and I could see the Donaldson boys outfitted for hockey.

The boys had sticks and batted pucks or balls around on any icy surface such as the driveway or a frozen pond in a field. I remember Mark going through the ice on a space we had cleared on the creek and all of us hurrying home.

We bought skates that came from Eaton's for Ross & Emily when they were small. They cost $4.99 a pair and buckled across the ankles. Second hand skates and equipment figured largely through the hockey years as our boys had very little that was new.

I am not sure when hockey was organized in our area but there was hockey played on the outdoor rink in Burriss. Other teams came and it was here that I first saw the Mosbeck boys from Emo, Tom and Chuck that we came to know well later on. The boys dressed in the rink shack and there was usually a good fire going. Some nights were very cold and I remember rubbing and warming the half frozen feet of a small boy while the others played. At first Gale took Ross to play. They did not all have the proper equipment and used to pass a helmet onto another boy when one came off the ice. Perhaps they had shin guards but none of the boys was anywhere near as well dressed as the hockey players are now.

Gale, with Tom Morrish, George Hyatt and others, was one of the parents that helped flood and maintain the rink at the school. Of course, after any snowstorm the ice would have to be cleared, the men sometimes turning out to help the boys when it was badly drifted, as it was all done by shoveling. If a thaw occurred there was no skating and the rink would have to be flooded again when it froze. Much hard work was entailed with the hauling of water, sometimes from the river, and later pumped with large borrowed hoses, from a pond at Angus Hyatt's place near the school.

We decided to make a little rink in our yard which involved dipping and hauling barrels of water from the creek on the transport box of the tractor. Our well would not support flooding a rink except for patching holes. It was cold messy work but the little rink provided hours of enjoyment and exercise for our children, visiting neighbours and cousins and the rink was in use for quite a few years. The twins, Brian and Rob Roy all learned to skate on "home ice".

OUR RINK IN BURRISS.LR: Jerry Donaldson, Mark Donaldson.

At some time in the 1970's the Emo & Devlin (Barwick joined later) municipalities joined together to erect a sports center in Emo. Compared to today it was a very basic building but it was under a roof. We stood at the ice edge at the boards as there were no seats. It was not artificial ice at first and it was a while until there was a Zamboni. Flooding was not done after each period, but each year some improvements were made.

The boys' hockey became a little more organized and we gradually acquired more equipment and clothing, much of it was second hand. Many times things did not fit well and you would see a boy in a sweater that came past his knees or in a pair of pants so tight he could barely move. Socks that did not match the sweater or each other were common. They took good care of their hockey sticks, though and taped them well when they cracked or broke. Hockey tape was always on the shopping list. We often gave hockey equipment as gifts at birthdays and Christmas. By the time Mark and Guy played, local organizations donated hockey sweaters for the teams. I did not like sewing the numbers on.

When I think of the "hockey years" a whole collage of pictures fills my mind. I see cheering mothers, crying children, endless car trips, broken hockey sticks, homemade hockey equipment bags, hastily prepared and eaten meals, helping boys dress and tightening skates as well as the actual game. I would take the younger boys and get them through the first two divisions and then Gale would bring the older boys. One year we had five boys playing in three divisions and often Gale and I would meet on the road. I hated driving when it was stormy or very cold, as all of the hockey trips were made in our old white Chev.

These were the formative years in hockey and there were many things that are different now. One of the best things is the mandatory change rule and now each child get ice time. Back then, some coaches bound for the glory of winning the game put their strongest players out for a huge percentage of the time. There were boys that sat hugging the bench and their hockey sticks waiting their chance to play a few minutes. It was not fair but it was hockey at that time.

I recall one such game. One of the boys who was a very good player belonged to the coach who kept him on the ice, depriving others of their turn. I hated this and at one time I roared out, just as there was one of those moments of silence that fall sometimes, "Take (name omitted) off." My voice echoed throughout the arena. Mark told me after that when someone asked who that woman was, he said he did not know. It was easy to get caught up in the game and I did also. A whole line of enthusiastic and often very vocal mothers lined the ice lined the ice, shouting encouragement and giving instructions. I recall one mother in desperation shouting, "Darcy, get the hell up the ice!"

Occasionally, some mothers with boys on opposing teams would clash with ridiculously intense results and even an actual altercation or two. Things would get out of hand with coaches and referees also. In the earliest days the rules were not strictly outlined or enforced. We saw some very bad behaviour on the part of parents that could not control their tempers when watching this child sports' activity. One night a coach leaped over the boards and punched the referee, knocking him down. Many nights I would not be able to get to sleep, thinking of actions I had seen at the local arena.

Both Gale and I tried to do our parts. We worked in the canteen, picked up other boys, and I served a term or two on the hockey executive as secretary. When on this executive it bothered me that no girls were allowed to play, and also that there was a banquet only for fathers and sons. In my estimation it seemed that there were far more mothers that lined the boards after bringing their boys to hockey, helping them dress, working in the canteen and just generally supporting minor hockey. The mothers were allowed to cook the food and decorate the hall, but not able to join in the meal and see their sons receive awards. I voiced some of my opinions and soon there was an annual family wind up meal with mothers present. It was not long also until there were some girls playing hockey especially in the younger divisions. This did not happen without opposition but it did happen. Perhaps I had a hand in this, I do not know, but I do recall one fellow that was very much against allowing girls to play hockey.

Our boys enjoyed hockey and it was very much a part of the winters. Although none of them were stars, Brian had the longest hockey "career." I think they were all good team players and they enjoyed it. There are a few memories that stand out and I remember one playoff game with the team Mark and Guy were on when they were about nine. In the final minutes of the game, the score was tied with play in our end. Mark got control of the puck. The crowd cheered, waiting for him to move down the ice, but by some fluke Mark scored on his own goal. There was complete silence and the whistle blew to end the game. Everyone was shocked and some uttered words of sympathy to me and some mothers had tears in their eyes. They were only little boys and it could have been anyone's child.

When I first wrote this Cameron was five and he is now eight and doing well. Three years later two more great grandsons Austin and Jack are playing beginners' hockey and my great granddaughter Teagan aged six has begun to play on an all-girl team. It is wonderful to see all these little girls decked out in pink or blue helmets and outfits swirling around the ice, as it seems that nearly as many girls as boys are registered for minor hockey. Minor hockey has come a long way.

Fire At Donaldsons March 31, 1973

The weather in March 2012 has been an ongoing topic of conversation with extremes of high temperatures causing all the snow to melt and growth to appear. Record were broken on many days, as we do not expect to reach temperatures in the high 70's F at this time of year. A younger friend asked me if I ever remembered a March like this one and I told her about the one I recalled one in 1973. The temperatures did not reach the heights of this year but it was very warm and dry.

Earlier one of the family had asked me about a fire at our farm and if I had written about it in my diary. I remembered it as a very frightening time and checked my old diaries for details. On Saturday, March 31, 1973 I recorded the following:

"Thank goodness this is a large page. What a day! Gale was burning back in the bush and Ross in the machine lot. Emily had a badly sprained ankle but went to 4-H. Ross and I lit a small fire around the garbage down by the creek The wind got up and the other fire jumped the creek and between the two it got out of control. We were frantic and called for help and the fire truck. We got cars and tractor and kids out to the road. The barn, old sheds, tool shed went up in flames, Gas tank was empty thank heaven. I was so afraid for the house as the door mat was smoldering and men were on the roof. So many came to help and we were thankful it ended like it did. Just exhausted and everyone looks the same, dirty and grim."

Like many others, we were burning as this was the last day before fire permits were required. It had been a very dry spring and the yard and fields were pretty well dried up by March 21. I looked back through the diary pages and Gale and many others had been burning the old stubble in the fields. We had been hauling the winter's accumulations of garbage and cleaning up the yard. The children had been flying homemade kites and we finally bought one that flew beautifully. Rob Roy was not quite two and had recently been moved down into the basement where all of his brothers slept. He was quite happy to join the gang. On March 30th Emily and Ross went to a dance in Emo and Emily sprained her ankle.

All these little events from my diary led up to the fire of March 31. It was a beautiful, warm, sunny spring day. Gale had gone to the back of our place to burn along some fence rows. Ross was burning a little in the machinery yard. I decided to burn up some trash down by the creek and Ross joined me. It had not been windy but suddenly we realized our fire was out of control and headed towards the buildings. Some of the children must have been in the house because I know that Rob Roy was in his crib in the basement for a nap and when we ran for the kids later, I found that this was the first time that he had ever climbed out of his crib and he met me at the top of the stairs. After the fire got going so badly Gale saw the smoke and ran for home.

By then I had called the fire truck and I was so rattled that I could not remember the numbers. At that time you did not ring 911 and we were to call Greensides Store and that number alerted the volunteer fireman. I got mixed up and first called the home of Phillip Bellamy who had a similar number. Mr. Bellamy was very deaf but I think that he did show up at the fire. By this time the cars and the tractor and the children were at the road and we just watched. There were men on the roof of the house putting out sparks and the doormat was smoldering. It was terrifying to watch.

Emily had sprained her ankle quite badly and someone brought her from 4-H and she came limping and crying up the road. Nonie Barker (I had also called their number by mistake) was always very efficient and knew what to do and told me that I should be making lunch for the firemen when they finished. By this time we knew the house was safe and so we went in and got the coffee on. I remember I had baloney and she started mashing it up to mix with other things to make a meat spread and I got out extra bread and cheese. We did have some sandwiches just made when suddenly the firemen all roared out of the yard. They were called to another fire. We were left with the smoldering remnants of the buildings and a few baloney sandwiches.

We did lose quite a few things in the fire and although I know that Gale was very upset he was not as harsh with me as he could've been. It was definitely my fault. We did not have cattle anymore but the old barn was nice for the children to play in and we had some things stored out there. One of them was an old cupboard or sideboard type of thing that one of the Donaldson men had made many years ago. It was made of very wide pine boards and though roughly made and not very beautiful, I was very fond of it for its rustic look, and we had used it right up until the time we moved upstairs in the house. There was a wooden rocking chair that had a broken runner that was going to be repaired some time and it too went up in smoke. The old sheds and chicken house contained pails of used oil and grease, old tools, rusty nails and that kind of thing. One time when Mark and Guy were about two and half they went in there and smeared each other with used black grease. It was very hard to get them clean again.

The tool shed contained the most valuable items and among them were several old trunks. Gale regretted the loss of these more than anything, as they contained old family papers and memorabilia that had belonged to his Grandmother Belle and Grandpa Jerry, as well as his Uncle Will. Every time he would mention these things I would feel so badly, although I wished that I had peeked into these trunks before they burned. Actually there could not have been too many valuable things as the Donaldson had had two houses burn in the near 75 years since they had come to Burriss.

The next day was April Fool's Day and we made a pact that I think everyone honored for no tricks. The sheds smoldered for quite a while and the yard was all sooty and so much of it seemed to track into the house. Then we had April snow and that was worse than ever for tracking. When the ashes were all cooled we picked through and Gale saved a few things like old tools and the old sheep and cow bells that I later spray painted for decorations.

The children lost bicycles that had been leaning against the sheds and of course they were upset to be without wheels. Imagine our surprise when George and Bev Hyatt brought over a load of bikes and would take nothing in return. It was so generous and typical of them as they had a large family also.

I felt very badly about this fire but new buildings were gradually erected and years later the area was plowed and now Lee & Leanne grow a wonderful garden there.

The Old White Chev

Most people have some sort of icon or object that they associate with their childhood. When I think of mine, the big barn, the cupboard that my father made or the Aladdin lamp are just a few things that come to mind. No doubt my siblings will recall other things.

My husband treasured the pewter spoon mold that had come from Ireland, and the White sewing machine that had been bought at the Chicago World's Fair by his grandparents. His mother had an incredibly ornate vase that her mother had brought from England.

Our children will also remember certain things, Gale's manual adding machine or the binoculars .Perhaps each one has a special memory, but I think they all will remember the "old white Chev."

Gale did not own a car when we were first married but he bought a huge old red van type of thing that was very uncomfortable and then we purchased the dark green car that had belonged to his brother Lyle who had died in 1958. This car that did not have an automatic gearshift was the car on which I learned to drive and took my driving test in Emo. Up to then I had driven my brothers' cars and the tractor. At some point Gale bought the vehicle that had belonged to Great West Mining and Smelting, the company engaged in mining exploration in the Emo area that he worked for. I don't recall ever driving this vehicle. Gale worked at various places and always had to take the car to work and all our family business was conducted on weekends. At that time most families were one car families.

In 1970 Gale began to work for Newman Ford Limited in Fort Frances and one of the provisions that he made was that he have with a demonstrator car to drive. He then always drove the latest model and the first one was a Cobra, followed by a Ford Galaxie. Shortly before this, we had purchased an off-white Chevrolet car from Bert Henry at Henry Motors and this was the beginning of the "old white Chev" years. It was not new, perhaps a 1967 model, and it was a family sedan type of car with brown upholstery. Now I had a car all through the day, and with a family of eight, Rob Roy being born in 1971, there many occasions on which it was a blessing.

We would never have survived in modern times when it is required that each child be fastened securely into a child seat. If I close my eyes I can see us in that old car. In the front seat Emily would be holding the baby and one other child would be in the middle. This child was never Ross as he insisted on standing on "the Hump." This gave him a clear view of the road ahead and a certain advantage over the other children. A child was set in each corner and told to stay there! Then Lee and Jerry stood on either side of Ross and we were off for perhaps a full day in Fort Frances for doctor or dental appointments, shopping and always a stop at both grandmothers. When Gale was driving that meant a shift of position and usually Emily and I each had a child on our laps.

Emily Donaldson Holding Orange cat Tom. In front of white Chev-1970.

    The car that we possessed did not seem to have the elegance or sleekness of those shown on the Internet now. Research showed that the price of a new 1966 Chevrolet Belair was $2531. Ours was not a Belair and $1100 is the price that seems to ring a bell that we paid. Our car was equipped with brown leatherette seats and not much else, no seat belts, no power door locks, no air conditioning, no power windows and maybe the biggest difference from today, NO RADIO. How did the children ever survive without a back seat DVD to watch or music to listen to? Driving that car was a far cry from today's vehicles and was much more of a physical workout. Imagine having to parallel park with no power steering and no power brakes. I still hate parallel parking and usually avoid it.

    In the summer of 1972 we took a little trip and travelled to Atikokan to stay overnight with my friend Byng Harrison. Ross had decided to not go with us and no amount of persuasion changed his mind, and Guy wanted to stay behind with Ross. I knew they would be fine as Grandma lived in the trailer beside our house. So off we went with the six children and stayed overnight in Atikokan and then with my sister`s family in Thunder Bay. The next day Gale wanted to go to Duluth so we set off along the north shore. It was very hot and we were all jammed in. Rob Roy wore only a diaper in the car, as of course we had no air conditioning and Gale did not drive with open windows. In Duluth we visited the zoo and I remember feeling so sorry for the animals that were in small concrete cages. Being packed in our car the way we were made me even more sympathetic to them than I normally might be.

On hot summer days we would see that all the chores were done, pack a lunch featuring mainly peanut butter or Cheez Whiz sandwiches, Kool-Aid, cucumbers and oranges to head back to Hope Lake. The children liked flying over Thrill Hill, anticipating the swim and picnic lunch. We would swim, eat our lunch and then swim again. On those hot summer days driving with open windows, we were probably just as hot and dirty by the time we got back home as when we started out, but that didn't seem to matter.

Gale did not like driving with the windows open and he favoured Lake Wasaw. Many a trip was made back there after supper. We trudged into the lake over a swampy trail, swatting mosquitoes, ready to swim in the shallow brown water with the muddy bottom which abounded in blood suckers and leeches. Gale liked this lake because this was where they had gone many times when they were children. They would travel by wagon and spend the whole day, fishing and swimming and picnicking. There was no road to the lovely lakes to the north then.

It was sometimes said that the old white Chev doubled as a truck as we often carried loads of grain, chicken feed, fertilizer, blocks of salt for the cattle, machinery parts, tractor oil, tons of groceries, baby chicks or just about anything that needed to be hauled. Sometimes Gale would call from work and instruct me to go to Emo to pick up six bags of fertilizer or to Badiuk's to pick up the mower blade. He did not want to get his demonstrator car dirty and I could see the reasoning in that.

We would drive through the back fields without worrying too much about damaging the car. I remember a few times when the field was full of hay bales, zooming around the field with the kids in the back and seeing how close I could come to the bales without actually hitting them. I would load all the children up with various pails and picking utensils and we would head off on berry picking expeditions to the back field. Parking the car in a shady spot the children roamed or could rest in the car while I picked berries. One time I was making a head count, and Guy was missing. I was nearly sick as a fear of mine was having a child lost in the bush. We called and searched and then one of the children said that he maybe had gone home, so into the car we jumped and, sure enough, there he was reclining on the couch at home eating his strawberries.

Driving in the winter with this car was no picnic, even though the car was very reliable as to starting in cold weather. When Diane was living with us there were mornings that her car did not start or would freeze up I would tell her to take the Chev. It was great at plowing through drifted roads also and I recall at least one drive when the snow was rolling up over the hood. Sometimes the heater was not working and the rides to hockey were almost unbearable. I would tell Gale the heater was not working in the Chev and he would tell me this and that to do with it but nothing was changed, until one time he drove the boys to hockey in the Chev. That night he came blustering in, hands and feet nearly frozen, wondering why I had not told him that the heater was not working. I did not even answer.

The Chev featured heavily in the hockey years. One year there were five boys in three divisions so it took some scheduling. We often had neighbour boys riding with us and in those years without seatbelts we could pack quite a few in, and the trunk held most of the smelly gear. If possible we came home via the Boundary Road and at just the right point we would see "The Flash." There was an old building on Arthur Mattson's property where Gale said that Larry and Marg Norris had lived when they were first married. Something in that house would catch the reflection of our head lights at a certain spot. This became a sort of ritual, as did our singing. We often would break into such old songs as "The Indian sits in his little Canoe." This was an old song that my mother said that her twin Barker uncles performed at concerts years ago. We sang, "They cut down the old Pine tree" and "Home on the Range", hymns, school songs and choruses learned at Sunday School from Mr. Hickey.

Gale did not like me driving onto the Ford lot with that old car. It did contrast quite sharply with the sleek new Ford cars displayed. There often was a child or two sticking his head out the window or someone was crying. Our car seemed to get more banged up and shabby looking every year and repairs were seldom done. There were holes in the hood from the prongs of a big fork that had come down on the car. The children told friends they were bullet holes and there were dents and scratches on the fenders. The brown vinyl on the seats had split and I resourcefully had covered the interior with MacTac adhesive.

When the gas gauge quit working Gale figured out how far we could go on a tank of gas and I kept track of mileage, hoping I was accurate. At one time some gear would stick and the car would move only in reverse. I learned how to lift the hood and make the necessary adjustment. Compared to nowadays there was next to nothing under that hood. Although quite dependable there always seemed to be something happening with that car and it was sort of an adventure to set out. My old diaries are full of references to flat tires, stalling, leaky radiator, run down battery, no heater, fuel pump, stuck gears, broken signal lights. If there were any major repairs I took the car to the garage at Devlin.

Emily, Ross, Lee and Jerry all learned to drive on that car and got their licenses on the first try. I am sure there are untold stories there and a few more scratches or dents were added. It was handy having another driver and sometimes it saved me from a hockey or 4 H trip, doctor's office for the allergy shot or any of the many other errands. It might entail some bargaining such as," If you take your brothers to hockey on Saturday you can use the car that evening."

Nothing lasts forever, even though it seemed as if that car would, after driving it for 12 years. It was replaced by a large dark blue Ford station wagon that did not have near the character of the old white Chev but was more spacious.

I was rather amazed when someone wanted to buy it and it was sold for $50.00. A slight connection to our family remained. Ross remembered: "Dad sold it to Willard Wilson of Emo and he used the motor in his skidder. That is the skidder that I now own but the motor has been changed. Willard was supposed to return the tires but he never did and Dad was always upset by that. I think Willard did the family a favour. We were never short of old tires."

Now I wonder why something that caused me such trouble and exasperation at times can now be remembered with a certain fondness.

My Mother

"There is no way to be a perfect mother and a million ways to be a good one."
J. Churchill

- Prairie River
- Rainycrest the Second Time Around
- Summer 1992
- My Mother's Hands
- Walking
- August 2000
- A Little Romance
- Homeless
- The Call

Prairie River

𝒫art One. (My sister Marion and I both wrote of this trip. The content was much the same but some of Marion's words are also included here.)

The name Prairie River, Saskatchewan has always been a part of our memories. My mother would sometimes mention the time she spent there and she received letters from Isabel Williams and Irene Rainbow, a name that I thought was lovely. Though not large, Prairie River was at one time a thriving lumber town in northern Saskatchewan where jack pine and poplar was plentiful.

We knew the story, his friend Ray Holmes offered my father a job to work in Lockhart's sawmill in Prairie River, Saskatchewan. It was just the start of the Depression and jobs were scarce. Our parents Axel Anderson and Ivah Strachan were married in April 1929 and after just a few days together he went there to find a place to live and to start work. He sent for Mom in early June and she packed up her possessions and travelled by train, the only way to reach Prairie River in those days.

Many years later Mom wrote of this time when I asked her to write the story of their marriage. She did not go into great detail but the description is quite poignant. They were newly married and pregnancy followed. As Marion explained, "We, as children knew of the baby who lived only three days and because the baby was born on Good Friday and died on Easter Sunday we believed this had some religious significance. We always included him in our family 'as the baby that died'." Our little brother was buried in what Mom called the Settlement and as she said, "I never saw his grave. I wish it had been marked in some way."

The mill later closed and they had to come back to Box Alder. Alan was born in April 1931, and though he would ease the pain of loss Mom never forgot her first baby buried so far away.

My sister wrote of her thoughts: "What an adventure it was, especially for my mother. She had lived her entire life in the beautiful, bountiful farming community of Box Alder in northern Ontario where her father had homesteaded the farm on which they lived. She was surrounded by the love and support of her father, sisters and brother and many aunts, uncles and cousins. The fact that her mother died when she was an infant would be a source of loss her entire life but was also instrumental into sculpting my mother into the warm and loving person she was. My father, the eldest son of Swedish immigrants had led a much different and worldlier life than my mother. He was born in Wisconsin where his father, my grandfather Abel, was an expert carpenter and millwright so the family traveled to many small towns in Wisconsin where my grandfather found work building sawmills. In 1918 when my father was 12 his family, which by this time including a younger brother and three sisters as well as an older half brother, moved to Fort Frances where my grandfather got work building more sawmills. They all became Canadian citizens. My grandfather died when he was 63 but not before buying a farm and building a house in the community of Box Alder, close to the farm on which my mother lived. They met, fell in love and married in April 1929 when they were both 23 years old. What a wonderful mixture of cultures. I marvel at things happening the way they do and the way things were meant to be. My mother was bought up in a close and a religious atmosphere of parents of British heritage and my father was from a Scandinavian, practical hardworking background. I am so proud of my heritage and so thankful what a merger of these two bloods has brought to my life."

I often thought of Prairie River when we visited in Saskatchewan and would suggest that we travel that way but it is farther north and the timing never seemed right. In 2001 our brother Eric heard a radio program about these "settlements" in Saskatchewan and was able to find out just where it was. He even obtained the birth and death certificates of little William Allen and it was an indescribable feeling to see them with my father's writing on them. Eric made all the arrangements and a small headstone was placed in St. Andrews Cemetery in the Soldiers Settlement in 2002. I was able to tell Mom that we had placed a marker at the grave of her baby that died. It was hard to tell if it meant much to her as her mind was not good but she did reply, "That's nice."

Marion wrote, "Of course, Eric who was instrumental in having the stone erected sent us pictures and our older brother Alan and his wife Inez visited the cemetery and the marker. Through circumstances and one thing and another Liz and I were deterred from making the trip, but finally decided we could wait no longer and we made our plans."

Part Two

It was not until 2005 that the time was right for us to go to Prairie River to see the stone and visit the little village where our parents had lived so many years ago. It was finally decided that Marion, my daughter Emily and I would leave on June 8. We were quite excited and had our journey mapped out on Mapquest down to the last detail, "estimated time of travel 13 hours, 47 minutes, 693.5 miles". I made other preparations and scanned copies of the old pictures, pictures from Eric, found the copy of Mom's book where she wrote about Prairie River and put these along with the maps and directions in my "Prairie River Folder."

Marion arrived from Thunder Bay the afternoon before and we set off in Emily's vehicle in wind and rain at 8 AM on June 8, destination Yorkton, Saskatchewan. Much of the conversation between Marion and me was about this long ago part of Mom's life. The realization that we were really on our way evoked emotions of nostalgia mixed with sadness. I was a little apprehensive and wondering about the wisdom of driving 12 hours in the rain to see a headstone in a cemetery. However, this is something I wanted to do, something I had to do and I recalled the disappointment when we first planned to go and could not. The three principals in this little drama are all gone; our baby brother died 75 years ago, our father 66 years and our mother three years ago. It was the time now for what is termed "closure" and to absorb this final bit of Mom's history.

We stayed at the Holiday Inn in Yorkton and in the morning, setting out on the next leg of our journey, we realized that before noon we would be seeing the grave of William Allen Anderson. I had never thought of Saskatchewan as timber country but as we drove we could see how the landscape was changing. It was beautiful but seemed remote and uninhabited. We saw plenty of abandoned buildings and log houses that told the story of the early pioneers. A mother moose and her tiny calf were a welcome sight in the more timbered area.

I began to think that it was just about this time of year that Mom had made her train trip. Grandpa had brought her to Winnipeg and put her on the train after staying the night with Grandma Strachan's brother and wife. He must have has some misgivings about seeing his youngest child set off in this manner. It would have been a long tedious trip with the steam-powered train chugging along and stopping at each tiny hamlet, but Mom always had a spirit of adventure and likely found many things and people to interest her. Waiting for her was her new husband and a new life in this place known as Prairie River. They were both excellent letter writers and the letters from him probably told her a great deal about the little town and what was in store for her.

Our road changed to # 47, a narrow but paved road. I saw a little graveyard close to the road with perhaps 6 or 7 gravestones on a farm that was inhabited and it would have been so interesting to find out the story behind those old stones. Then we turned on to a gravel road and we knew we were nearing our destination. We did have trouble finding the cemetery and Marion wrote "My sister became quite distraught and said she thought we might have to go home without finding what we came for." This was quite true.

We did some backtracking but at last a Good Samaritan came along and took us right to the spot. Here the little church and the plaque seemed familiar as Eric had sent pictures when the stone was erected. The site was attractive, serene and quiet set against a backdrop of the forest. Iron gates opened into the fenced in area of the graves. Some fir trees towered over the stones. Buried here were many of the early settlers and veterans of the First World War.

The day had turned pleasant. We found the stone that marked William Allen's place. So many years had passed since he came into this world. The connection, still there, was now complete in a way that it had not been before but there was no point to wish that things had been different. We took pictures and shed tears for the sheer emotion of the day. I was so glad that now the stone was there to mark the place the little boy lay.

In the lovely little church my imagination took over again. I knew from reading Mom's story that daddy had hired someone to bring the little casket out from Prairie River, by a horse drawn vehicle. The minister likely held a religious service for the very few people there. I wondered if somewhere there was a record of the baby's burial.

Marion wrote: "This was the year 1930 and the beginning of the horrendous depression. The saw mill where my father worked closed and they returned to the Rainy River District. They were not able to put up a stone for the little one and they never returned to this small community."

But now here we were. We signed our names in the book there and I wrote of the baby's burial in 1930. Here we met some people that had relatives in Emo. The woman, Eleanor, told us that she also had a baby buried in that cemetery. Somehow, that made me feel a little better, as they were such friendly salt-of- the-earth people.

We left the cemetery after a final look at the baby's grave and travelled on to Prairie River. In the time when my parents were there, there was no way in except by train and only municipal roads such as this one. At last we arrived in the quiet, sun-lit little village. A small, fast running stream flowed through the wooded area. Was this the Prairie River? It was no problem to find the railway station that had closed years ago and now was the museum. A beautiful old log house stood close by. Emily with her cell phone called the lady who took care of the museum. While we waited for her we strolled around the grounds and I walked the railroad tracks for a short way and imagined Mom arriving here.

The lady of the museum came and took us through the two stories of the old station. On the lower floor were the pictures of the old sawmills but none of the Lockhart Mill that I could see. The lady knew none of the names that I mentioned. Mom had said their little house that she loved was right on the bank of the river but we did not know where it would be.

Marion expressed it, "We saw the river but no big rock was visible in the area where we looked. The river was deep with heavy shrubs on either side and with evidence of old picnic spots and a broken diving board. It looked neglected but the river kept running along taking away all the secrets that the town once held." After spending the night in Swan River we drove home the next day. Our "pilgrimage" was over.

*P*ART THREE

I received an e-mail from Marion a few days after she went home. She had found a wonderful site on the Internet. There is a book called "Valley Echoes-Life along the Red Deer River Basin" and here we found information about Prairie River. The book contains nearly 700 pages and is presented to view page by page. We found the story of Mom's friend Isabel Williams and her husband Chris. There were pictures of them and Chris was a foreman or manager of Lockhart's Mill. Prairie River at that time was inhabited by over 100 families and was reached only by train. It was important, as it was the nearest point on the railroad to the Soldiers' Settlement. The arrival of the train each evening was a big event and people dressed up to go the station to see the latest arrivals. We found that Irene Rainbow was a young schoolteacher. There were many references to Lloyd Thompson's store that mom mentioned. Percy Sims was likely the husband of Marie that Mom wrote about.

The story of Thomas and Gertrude Bassett in this book written by their daughter Ivy gives a very good account of life in Prairie River of the little town itself. Mrs. Bassett was the woman who was sometimes called on to assist the doctor with deliveries and then looked after the new mother in the home. Mom said that Daddy did not like her as she was bossy. Ivy did list some of the men that worked in the mill and it was exciting to see A. Anderson listed.

After returning from Prairie River I looked through Mom's battered old autograph album and found items from her days spent there. She made friends wherever she went.

"Dear Ivah, March 11, 1930

From the time when first we start, Each in life to play his part,

Till we reach that perfect peace, Where all toil and care shall cease,

Fate can nothing better send, Than a true and loving friend.

Lovingly, Irene Rainbow"

We had seen and found out more about Prairie River and the area then we ever thought we would. Some may ask, "What does it matter after all these years?" It matters because it was our mother and father and our little brother and so it was a part of our history. Some may ask, "Why did you wait so long to go there?" That question is much harder to answer and one that I asked myself. However, there is a time for everything and maybe now was the right time.

Soon after arriving home Marion also wrote her account of our pilgrimage and of the importance of doing the things that your heart tells you to do. It was closure for us but also the realization of the value of family and love and caring.

Rainycrest- The Second Time Around

When my mother entered Rainycrest in April 1988 we never thought that she would be there for 14 and a half years. After all, she was 82 at the time and had some pre-existing medical problems. The worst thing was her shakiness and the trembling of her legs that, was at times of stress, almost uncontrollable. She told us that she first felt this shakiness at her retirement party when she was being presented with her gifts. Her legs began to tremble and she had to sit down.

This malady was really strange and Marion and I often discussed it. As it progressed she was not able to stand still or her legs would begin to tremble, yet she could walk and kept up her daily walks for many years. If she met someone she would just say, "I have to keep moving." If we were taking her to a funeral or wedding someone invariably would want to talk. Then I could feel her extreme tension and her body would become almost rigid until we could move on.

Twice she traveled to Thunder Bay to see specialists. They agreed that she had Parkinson's like symptoms and although she did not have Parkinson's Disease, the doctor prescribed L-dopa, which is used to treat that malady. Since "nerves" seemed to play a part in this condition the doctor also prescribed a tranquilizer. She took a blood pressure pill and other medications also, as Dr. Black seemed to be a doctor that believed in medicating. I know there were times when she got some of these pills mixed up. One time when Mom told me she just lay on the couch all day and "couldn't quite wake up," I was sure that she had made a mistake with her medications.

Mom was happy in her apartment at Green Manor, but there were other problems and times when she reported crawling to the bathroom. Another time she was unable to get out of the bathtub for a long time and the water had turned cold. We were glad when the time came that she decided to make the move to Rainycrest.

Christmas 1987 she had spent with us in Burriss. Christmas morning something happened to her right leg and she was virtually unable to walk at all. Ross and Gale carried her to and from the table and to her room and she never really walked unassisted again.

IVAH ANDERSON-1988.

Her doctor did several different tests. One time he took her foot and told her to press against his hand as hard as she could. Mom pushed and he nearly fell off his chair. "Why, you're strong as an ox," he said. She was quite pleased at this and strong though she might be she still could walk very little and only if supported. She was terrified of falling. He prescribed a wheelchair for her and an old one was found for her to use until the custom built one was ready. It was also arranged through Home Care for her to be taken in the Handi-Van to Rainycrest to use the whirlpool bath. The first time she went I waited nervously at her apartment. When I met her, she threw open her arms dramatically and exclaimed, "I feel like a new woman."

Sometime in January Mom decided to apply for Rainycrest. She invited Fred Whitehead, administrator, to her apartment and requested that Gale and I be there also. She was very much in command and since Fred knew of her twenty years as cook they had much to talk about. All the necessary arrangements were made for her admittance to Rainycrest and now we had to wait until there was a room

It was worrisome to think of her alone but her neighbours were very kind and cousins Percy and Eileen Barker were right across the hall from her. Eric came from Saskatchewan to be with her for a week, Marion and Alan both stayed with her at different times and I spent a few nights there and she loved having the company.

At this point, although unable to walk very well, Mom was able to do many things for herself and could dress and do her personal care. Sitting, she could prepare food and used the stove with care. She was still independent and loved her books and kept up her scrapbooks and daily writing. Visiting with her was a joy because of her spirit and wonderful sense of humour. She looked on Rainy Crest with a little dread and would say," Well, this will be my last move" but it was also an adventure and something new.

The call came from Tucky Polenske on a Tuesday in April and Mom was to be admitted to Rainycrest that Friday. We had just celebrated Easter and her 82nd birthday at Emily's. As Mom said, April seemed to be her month for doing things, born in April, married in April, had two sons born and one die in April-and now she was beginning a new phase of her life in April.

I was able to leave work, telling them I would not be back until Monday, went home and packed a little bag ready to stay with Mom. When I arrived she was half-laughing and half crying but she was pleased that the call had come so soon. I made that never fail panacea, a good cup of tea, and we discussed our plan of action. The first thing was to call everyone to tell them the news. Many people from her apartment building dropped in for tea and to cheer her.

The next few days were a blur as we packed and decided what to take and what to leave. Mom could not believe that all services would be attended to and wanted to take her Dust Buster. On the advice of a friend we took things to her new room, hung pictures, placed cushions and afghans, set out ornaments and her beloved books in her bookcase to make the room look a little familiar when she first entered it. We found this to be good advice.

Friday arrived and Marion was to come to help with the transition but she had been detained somewhere. Inez and I waited for her as long as we could but finally had to make the move. Just as we got to the door at Rainycrest, Marion flew up in her car and burst into tears. It was so hard for her to see this move take place and she had no idea what state of mind Mom was in. In my best big sister fashion I told her sternly to get control or we would all be howling. Mom had a few treasures in her lap and the three of us, all near tears, came behind. Once in the doors she spied the familiar face of Mr. Grennier and called a greeting to him. On her way down the hall she held her head high in the way I recognized, with a regal wave of the hand to the right or the left. I thought of a queen making her triumphal entry into new territory.

My mother entered Rainycrest with some trepidation but with dignity, faith for the future and with her own brand of confidence. As she said, "They won't put me to bed at 7 o'clock."

I have written about my mother in quite a few of my articles as she was such a major part of my life. She was a strong, self confident and resourceful woman and I valued her down to earth common sense and good sense of humour.

When due to health concerns she entered Rainycrest, she still retained many of these qualities until TIA's or "little strokes" began to rob her of her old spirit. Often after visiting her I would write a bit about the changes that were becoming more and more evident. It seemed to help keep things in perspective.

I include some of that writing here. Others with an aging parent may recognize similar experiences as you watch the physical and sometimes mental decline of the person that once nurtured you. My mother had some very good years in Rainycrest, and after a visit with one of us, she always was glad to be "home" again. After the advent of the little strokes she became increasingly disoriented and often did not recognize her family members or any place as home. This is stressful but we learned to deal with whatever mood she was in that day. When nothing else reached her I could always depend on singing with her, as she never forgot the old songs and hymns and she could sing all the verses of the hymns.

One day she sat with her head down and would respond to nothing that I said, so I began to sing. I sang and sang but she did not join in as she usually did. I tried all her favourites like "Blue Skies" and "Blessed Assurance" and many others with no response. Finally I sang "Down in the Valley" with that line "send it in care of the Birmingham Jail." Then, half in desperation to get some response, I said, " Mom have you ever been in jail?" At that she raised her head, looked at me, and said, "Good Heavens, no!" I just never knew how she would be and she often took me by surprise. There were other times when she would respond to nothing I said, but when I put one of her Johnny Cash tapes on, it was no time until she was tapping to the rhythm or humming along to "Ring Of Fire."

My mother did not have Alzheimer's Disease and right to the end she still showed surprising flashes of her personality. She had dementia or senility, or degeneration from the TIA's, but the label does not matter much when you are losing your loved one to this cruel fact of life. When she first entered Rainycrest there were many programs and activities and she took part in everything and one year was president of the Resident's Council. One activity that she really loved, and I often accompanied her to, was the weekly sing song. This was led by nurse Joyce Woodland and many of the old favourite songs were sung. They always ended with that popular one with the message of living "One Day at a Time" and it was termed the Rainycrest theme song.

It seemed like a good way to look at life in Rainycrest, as in later years there every day brought a different mood to my mother.

Summer--July 1992

The last few days have been filled with activity. Marion and Ralph came from Thunder Bay and we brought Mom down to the farm for a visit. It is much harder for her here but with some changes we managed.

Ross built a type of ramp at the front door. It is too hard now for her to go up the steps now and even worse trying to help her down. She gets so nervous and then her legs and muscles just seem to seize up so the ramp helped a great deal. It was quite steep and we had to fasten a rope onto the back of her chair and have one person pull back while another guided the chair down. I cannot manage her alone any more. We were able to borrow a commode chair from the CP&T that was very useful also. The cat loved to curl up on it when it was not in use. My mother always loved cats so that was fine with her. When all these things were in place we brought Mom down to stay for several days.

Mom enjoyed it all so much. She loves the constant attention of her two "girls." Actually she can be quite demanding but we are always able to temper things with a good dose of humour. We could always make her laugh and we would tuck her in at night after many preparations.

In the afternoons we went outside to find a spot without too much sun or breeze, with sweaters and afghans ready to drape around her shoulders or her across knees. She is very susceptible to temperature changes now and cannot stand a breath of cool air on her body. The weather was pleasant for the visit and Mom would throw back her head, inhale deeply and exclaim, "Ah, smell that air!" Sometimes, afternoon tea was served outside and she liked that also. Mom loves to watch the clouds and remarked on the lovely blue of the sky.

Naps are very important and necessary both before and after being outside. Mom enjoys the cold, hard well water and there was always a jug in the fridge for her. Grandsons were useful to bring drinks of water for her. Marion attended to her wants and entertained her while I prepared meals and kept the household running. It seemed to require many hands to look after one person but everyone was ready to see to the smallest detail of her care.

Mom enjoyed it all so much, especially the feeling of being pampered, and that made it all well worth the effort of ramps, commodes and changes in the household. With Marion there it was all "a piece of cake," as my mother said

My Mother's Hands—Summer 1989.

*M*om was in the hospital for some minor surgery, although my sister says no surgery is minor. She was 83 and not able to get around without her wheelchair and I hoped that this will not set her back or that it will not be the start of something more sinister.

I know that she worried too but she showed such courage and cheerfulness, as she faced what she termed merely an inconvenience. We went to see her settled in and found her sitting quite regally in her wheelchair. She was chatting with the neighbouring patient's visitors, almost as if entertaining them and was at her most charming.

Mom kept saying that we did not need to come and stressed that I did not need to come the next day. Knowing my mother as I do, she would like me to be there all the time but she was in control of the situation. Mom was looking forward to ordering her meals and was laughing and cheerful. The blue hospital gown looked quite nice on her with her snowy hair, blue eyes and fresh pink complexion. When I left she again told me, "Don't bother coming tomorrow."

She was sleeping when I arrived the next day and stayed dozing, rousing only to speak softly, throughout our visit. Mom had had a busy day with x-rays, blood tests, blood pressure checks, and vowed, "This place is worse than Rainycrest for activity." Only she could not quite remember and said, "Where is it I live?"

Mom reached for my hand from time to time. Her hand are so soft now and we talked about how her hands used to be. She had worked hard on the farm with shovels and pitchforks and at the base of each finger she used to have a hard, yellowed callous. Her fingernails were short and blunt, trimmed from time to time with her enormous scissors. No prissy nail files or emery boards for my mother. The scissors had been a wedding present and she had them yet in her drawer at Rainycrest. As children we dreaded nail cutting time.

Mom's hands were often cracked and chapped to the point of bleeding from working out in the cold weather or from scrubbing with lye water. There were always small cuts, burns and blemishes to examine. They were the hands of a hard working woman and she rarely, if ever, wore gloves.

Now her hands seemed small and so papery soft. She held her hands up and marvelled at how old they looked and that now she could see the veins. I showed her my few brown "age spots" but she scoffed at them as minor and insignificant, mere freckles to her. Maybe she does not want me to grow old either.

August, 2000

Saturday afternoon we visited Rainycrest. Mom was in bed all covered up and sleeping. I sat quietly and when she wakened such a look of joy came over her face when she saw me. I know that she was not seeing me as her daughter, but rather someone from her past that meant a great deal to her. Was it her sister, her grandmother, her mother?

What did it matter? I did not ask her.

I sat close beside her and she held my hand tightly. Once she said," I love lying here holding your hand." Her voice was so soft and low with almost a childlike, little girl quality. From time to time she squeezed my hand gently.

She laughed merrily when I asked her if she had been behaving herself and declared it was more fun not doing that. That hint of mischief has always been there and we had heard of her sometimes being naughty or saucy as a child. I loved that spark.

Mom was just so sweet that day and her mood continued when we went for tea and a muffin. Everything we did seemed to bring her so much pleasure. Compared to some of the visits prior to this one the change was so apparent and so welcome. We sat off by ourselves, as Mom never likes to share me with anyone else at Rainycrest. We sang the old songs and talked of her uncles, Rob, Dave and Charlie. She seemed to remember them clearly and could tell some little story about each. Aunt Annie was always a little snooty Mom said, and sadly that is the impression I had of Great-aunt Annie also. Probably elegant or refined would be a better way to describe this lady.

At supper I fed her a few bites, then gave her the spoon to eat by herself. This was such a change, as sometimes she would eat only if she were fed. Often food would have to be wiped from her chin or would fall in her lap. This evening she ate with relish, said the food was good and ate it all.

Only after supper was over did she say she was tired and she became a bit querulous and upset. She wanted to go home, she wanted to go to bed. I can no longer help her so we had to wait till the nurses came.

What a wonderful visit it had been. Of course not being able to leave it at that, I had to think it was good because Mom had been so easy to deal with and had not upset me. Feeling like that makes me feel so guilty.

Walking—1990

Today I watched my mother walk. She carefully positioned her wheelchair at the end of the parallel bars and made sure the brakes were on. She tested these several times. Several times also she pushed down on the arms of her chair as if to rise. Then her feet began to swing back and forth and she flexed them for the final effort.

My mother grasped the bars firmly and slowly rose from her chair to stand erect. Each foot was placed so carefully, and with deliberation, step by step, she walked the length of the bars. After pausing for a moment she slowly, planting each foot with caution, walked backward to her wheelchair.

The helper called encouragement, "That's good, Ivah. You are doing well," and to me she exclaimed, "See how well Ivah is doing." I too called encouragement and positive remarks across the room. My tone was much the same as I had used recently to a small grandson trying his first unsteady steps. I hated it when I sounded like this to my mother, but she was intent on her task did not comment on my condescending tone as once she might have done.

I was proud of my mother, as it was obviously a tremendous effort. Her face reddened slightly and she seemed almost to pant. After a few more lengths Mom sat down and announced with an air of satisfaction that was enough for the day.

Emotion flooded over me and I felt a sickness in the pit of my stomach. I had to turn away and pretend to be looking at something out the window. In my mind's eye I could see my mother in the days of my childhood walking effortlessly. She had walked everywhere, to school, to church, to meetings and to visit neighbours. With her, I walked miles searching for wild berries or going for the cows in the summer. She walked many miles when as a widow she ran the farm and her trips to the big barn, often carrying things, were endless.

In her later years when she visited us she would choose a grandchild to walk up and down the country roads with her. Walking was such a joy to her. Did Mom still feel this same joy as she paced carefully between parallel bars?

In those early days her leg never failed her. Sometimes at night after a bath she would sit relaxing and turn her foot this way and that, showing us the shapeliness of her ankle. This trimness she attributed to the walking she had done all her life.

Mom was always so strong and capable. That must be why it hurt so much to see her have to think and plan each movement this day, as I watched my mother walk.

A Little Romance

*E*veryone has some romance in his or her life even though for some it does not last. My mother had her share and I am glad of that and that my father courted my mother in the fashion of the day. Vehicles were few and they never owned one so my father devised means of his own. Mom told us how he said that she had caught his eye at a baseball game and he began to go to church so he could walk home with her.

Things progressed, in spite of a little parental disapproval, to the point where one day he said; "I don't suppose you would consider marrying a fellow like me." Indeed she did consider it and they were married. I am sure that they were very much in love as they both had a romantic, poetic side to their natures.

The marriage ended with the death of my father after 10 years and Mom went on alone. Mom once said that if you were a widow you were subject to certain jokes and behaviour from certain men. She did not elaborate on this. I cannot imagine that there was anyone in Box Alder that would interest her or if there would be anyone that Mom could not handle if the need arose. Mom had a dignified, no nonsense way about her.

Working at Rainycrest broadened her scope and she met many new people, fellow workers that she liked and joked with. There were at least two men that were attracted to her and that made advances to her. She liked them also and though she not could not help but be flattered by the attention, she "nipped things in the bud." She even had a marriage proposal from one of the residents who said he "would do anything to get out of Rainycrest." My mother found this very amusing and the elderly fellow remained in Rainycrest.

One is never too old for romance and after she entered Rainycrest a touch of romance entered my mother's life in the person of Alec S–. There were stories of him and his business deals that were not altogether savoury but when I met him I saw only a gentle old man, a little crippled, who shuffled along. He reminded Mom of John Lewis, that politician from the west that she admired. Her conversations began to be sprinkled with mention of Alec and meetings with him and being pushed in her wheelchair by him. This was enough to cause a stir as another Rainycrest romance developed. It was interesting to notice other couples that were obviously very caught up with each other.

Sometimes when I came the two of them would be having tea in the lobby sitting quite close and talking and laughing. Alec would chat with me for few moments, often making a reference to "two lovely ladies" in his courtly fashion and would then excuse himself. Mom would be animated and a little flushed. Sometimes Alec would be in her room visiting with her. He always seemed courteous and soft-spoken and Mom obviously enjoyed the masculine attention, so I saw no harm in the relationship. I do know that my mother would never have associated for very long with anyone that used coarse or suggestive language.

One day one of the staff said something to me, hinting that Alec was perhaps not the best companion. I said, "Don't worry, Mom can handle herself." As Mom was in a wheel chair but still strong and Alec seemed to have trouble getting around, I could not see anything too terrible happening. Mom had already chased one hapless old gentleman out of her room.

Others besides the Rainycrest staff were a little concerned. A cousin, Minnie Langtry talked to Mom and said that Alec was known as a "womanizer" and that Mom should be very careful.

When Mom told me of this she said, pulling herself up straight in her wheel chair," I am quite capable of handing myself and of choosing with whom I associate." Then she told me that Alec was a perfect gentleman and that they always kept the door open a little if he were in her room. "He kissed me only once, just on my forehead," she said, touching the spot.

These warnings added a little spice, a tiny element of danger that heightened the pleasure of the relationship. Love is not only for the young and beautiful. Mom at that time was still very perceptive and able to "see through" people. At any rate Mom continued to see Alec S– and the association gave her something to look forward to.

She wrote letters that he dictated to his granddaughter for him. Of course this was something she was extremely good at and that she enjoyed. She told me that they discussed money but in what context I do not know. Mom had little to worry about but Alec may have been pondering what to do with his savings. I do not think that Alec was interested in Mom's money. He obviously liked and respected her for what she was, a lady.

It became evident to me that Alec was not well. He had a sickly pallor and moved even more slowly, not able to push Mom in her wheelchair any more. One day Mom told me that he had cancer and was gone from Rainycrest to Thunder Bay. Before he left he gave Mom some of his old clothes that he thought some of her family could use. Mom was very pleased with this and thought the clothing was as good as new. A person that lived through the Depression never forgets!! We, of course, fell heir to the clothing, permanently marked with his name. I quietly disposed of it.

Alec died soon after and Mom in spite of the warnings about this elderly Lothario, enjoyed a little romantic interlude with him and kept her dignity and virtue intact. As I said, romance is not only for the young and beautiful

Homeless- February 2000

A thought keeps running through my mind. It was something I had heard or read about the heart losing its home and wandering aimlessly from then on. Is this what has happened to my mother? Has her heart lost its home? Usually when I have mentioned Box Alder a light of recognition would come over her face and she would say, "Ah yes, Box Alder."

This past week has been so hard as she constantly asks to go home. I question her and ask, "Does it seem you should be somewhere else?" and "When you say home where do you think it is?" Today I asked, "Which home do you mean?" and she said. "Do you mean I have lived in more than one place?" I named the five or six places that she had lived and she could recall none of them.

She has pictures on her wall of two of her homes but she looks blankly at them and I can tell they mean nothing to her. She had lived in Rainycrest nearly twelve years but it is not "home." They say that people in her condition revert back to thinking of the happiest time of their lives. If this is true she is back in Box Alder in her teen years, keeping house for her father, but now even mention of Box Alder brings no response.

We have brought Mom out to our place and we drive through Box Alder trying to bring back a memory, but she becomes disoriented and wants to start back. "Shouldn't we be leaving soon?" she will ask. It is painful to think that our aged mother feels homeless and that her heart has lost its home.

In Rainycrest now Mom roams endlessly in her wheel chair. I always have to look for her in the long halls and when I find her she is exhausted and distraught as she says, "Thank God you've come." She looks for her mother, or thinks it is time to go to school or church or to the store. She does remember that it is Uncle Dave Strachan's store in LaVallee. I can usually soothe her with the promise of a cup of tea and a cookie.

One day one of the nurses told me that when checking on Ivah late one night she found that her room was empty and the wheelchair was gone. A search found Mom down in the LaVallee Lounge looking for a baby. I was so touched and wondered if this was the little baby that died so many years ago in Prairie River. Mom always said she would never forget him and perhaps some dim memory from the past surfaced again.

The staff members are kind and thoughtful but are now so pressed for time that Mom is alone so much. They say they cannot stop her from roaming unless they restrain her. Some of them have said they love looking after Ivah, another pronounced her a "sweetie" and Mom would have snorted at that. One said Ivah has an answer for everything and she does. Even though she cannot remember she is still enough of an actress that she can pretend. Sometimes a visitor will come and I will say, "Mom, you remember Mrs.–." She will rise to the occasion and say, "Of course I do," but I know full well that she has no recollection of that person.

You would think that after twelve years that something would seem familiar or homelike. Sometimes she will say how glad she is to see her bed but any bed would be the same to her. One afternoon I went to see her and she was nowhere to be found. I walked all the halls both east and west and checked the hairdresser and every place I could think of. I kept asking the staff but no one had seen her and did not seem unduly alarmed. At I last went to the desk and said that I had been looking for my mother for forty five minutes and did not know where else to look and that I would sit in Mom's room until they found her and that I hoped it was soon.

It was not too long until they brought Mom to me in her room. I could tell she was upset. They apparently had found her sound asleep in Mr. Booth's bed, covers pulled up over her head. They must have said something to her that did not sit well with her. She was at her most haughty and regal and said in icy tones, "If I have caused anyone any trouble I am very sorry." I thought good for you, Mom and thought that they might possibly have done a little checking a little sooner. The mention of a cup of tea drove everything else from her mind and after being tidied up and made ready by the nurses we set off.

When she looks at me so anxiously and says for the tenth or the twentieth time, "Shouldn't we be leaving for home?" or when she says, "Please, please take me home," it is so hard to bear when I realize that she will probably forever feel homeless.

The Call–January 2001

We went to Rainycrest that afternoon, Gale to see his mother on the west side, and I to my mother's room on the east wing. Mom looked so peaceful in bed covered up warmly. She slept for a while and when she wakened I went to sit by her, and she was so happy to see me. I am never sure who she thinks I am on any particular day, as she never calls me by name now.

This day she wanted me to get into bed beside her, but as it was a single bed I made a joke about there not being room for us both. She replied that there was plenty of room for three. I recalled that we often slept three in a bed, she. my sister and I, when we were young, so I thought that was what she meant.

Then she asked about her father and said that he had always been so good to them. "Is he still living?" she asked and I had to say that he had died many years ago.

"I know he is in Heaven and sometimes I go there to talk to him," she said softly and smiled as if she knew a happy secret. As she talked she kept glancing to either side of her in the bed. When I asked if she remembered her father's name, of course she did, it was George Strachan.

Then as she looked to the side again she once more said there was room for three in the bed, and she said that it was so nice lying there between her mother and father. At this I was quite astounded. Her mother had died when Mom was about one and a half years old. Did she have a fleeting childhood memory of being in bed between her mother and father? If so, it was a wonderfully happy memory to her. Or was this a premonition of the joining of them all together again? Mom mourned the loss of her mother all her life, so it was quite wonderful see her so happy now and for her to have these few moments of joy.

When I asked her mother's name with no hesitation she replied, "Elizabeth Harriet Barker. "The expression on her face was one of such bliss, and then from something she said I knew she thought it was her mother sitting beside her. She kept looking from side to side and she said drowsily that it was so lovely in bed and that she would like to stay there forever. Then she said her mother was in heaven, but in the next moment it seemed her mother was there beside her. Added to this was the idea that I was her mother sitting there talking to her. It was quite a revelation and confusing for me, but she was obviously in some kind of contact, real or imagined, with her mother.

"This is it," I thought. "This is the end of Mom's life, but she is so happy to be joining her parents so we cannot be sad." I was sure that night that I would be receiving that dreaded phone call.

"I miss my father," she said, "but my father is in Heaven. I am happy for him but I am not happy for me."

The nurses swept in ready to get Ivah up and changed and I took her for tea with Gale's mother. The mood was gone, but the thoughts of those moments with her when she was obviously somewhere else stayed with me. I phoned Marion as soon as I got home. Marion, the nurse, said, 'She is being pulled and wants to go." I thought that was a lovely way to look at the inevitable.

No call came that night or the next day. When I next went to see my mother she was back to her "normal" self. The joy, the utter happiness was gone and she could not remember the name of either parent. I was glad that I was there that day to see her in such a blissful state. Mom lived for nearly a year and a half after this but I often wondered about that afternoon, and what she was seeing, and the strange ways the mind can work.

Selected Poetry

*"There is not a particle of life which does
not bear poetry within it."*
Gustave Flaubert

*W*hile still living on the farm I had the opportunity to join a poetry group in Emo. I enjoyed the social aspect of this group very much and was very impressed by some of the writing that was presented. I had written bits of poetry off and on all my life and am thankful that not too much of my early efforts have survived. I have written many poems for birthdays, anniversaries and special occasions. Once I was actually offered money to write a poem for a going away gathering. I was so shocked that I declined the offer but wrote the poem.

Being part of the group in Emo did make me less reluctant about sharing my work and so I present some of my thoughts here, most in free verse. My sister described some of my poems as "dark", so I have included none of those, as well as certain others, in this small collection.

My husband Gale liked poetry that rhymed so the first one is dedicated to him.

Poems

The Millionaire-If You Could Know-Violets-First Snowshoe-LaVallee Lounge-The Wanderer-Chores-My Crooked Eye-Late Spring-Lines For Today-Memory-November Promise-If Wishes Came True-Things My Mother Taught Me-The Sisters-Swimming--4-H Calf-Lessons-The Gift- Cosmetic Surgery-Treasures-The Morning After-The Tamaracks-Weeds-I Remember

•

The Millionaire

Who wants to be a millionaire? You probably will agree
That of all the things to wish for, this is the thing to be.
You'd have no more worries with all that money rolling in,
You could change your lifestyle and a new life you'd begin.

But on more reflection, I'm already in that state,
A millionaire already, but not with riches great.
Each night I can gaze at a million stars that shine for me,
And a million diamonds sparkle on each glittering winter tree.

I tread on the softest carpet of a million blades of grass,
And watch the ever changing sky where a million clouds will pass.
Wild flowers bloom around me and I watch them come and go,
Soon to see the falling leaves, and then a million flakes of snow.
Rich am I in many ways, though not with jewels rare,
But I lack for nothing—I am a millionaire!

2001

If You Could Know

If you could know that you would count this day

As one of the happiest days of your life,

Would you take more note of the world around you?

Then the glory of this day

Could be etched in your memory,

And taken out now and then

To warm your heart.

Would you revel more in the clearness

Of that brilliant blue sky?

Would you marvel again at the first tender green

That thrusts itself through the cold bosom of the earth?

Would you feel more expectancy?

Or could you possibly feel

More alive and more welcoming

Of spring than you do right now?

2006

Violets

Shrinking violet? Shy and timid flower?

Don't you believe it.

These little harbingers of spring

Are the first to announce

The parade of the wild flowers.

They push their way quite boldly

Through the still cold, tough old earth,

To mass into carpets, saying,

"Look at me, I'm here already.

Let the others follow if they will."

1999

First Snowshoe

The woods encircle me

With familiar and welcoming arms.

This is my domain and I look back

At my broad tracks with satisfaction.

I am not the first to leave a mark on the forest's winter face.

Rabbit tracks are splattered across the snow in abandon.

Can't you see them dancing the minuet in the moonlight?

A fox zigzagged over the pond on dainty paws,

His trail criss-crossed

By a slinking coyote.

A great bird has swooped down

And left imprints of wing feathers etched deep.

A crimson drop of blood and a tuft of soft fur,

Tell the story here.

This year's sewing circle has begun.

Is it not appropriate that a bird leaves

Such exquisite featherstitching

On these snowy linens?

The tiny precise seams of the mice

Sew quilt patches on the snow.

2002

Lavallee Lounge

Large windows look out on the wide stretch of grass.
Positioned to get the best view
Of a scene that might stir memories of other days,
We watch the long freight trains rush by.
Flocks of seagulls flutter and swirl
Landing to search for food,
Then whirling up again with white brilliance,
Flashing against the blue.

We are not alone.
Another grey haired old lady, sits staring out,
Wheelchair by the big windows,
Other frail old hands are folded on knees,
Neatly wrapped in a bright afghan,
She sits transfixed, just staring out,
Alone with her thoughts, at last she speaks,
"I wonder if there are any mothers and daughters,
Out there in the birds."
A tear glistens on the soft old cheek.

2009

The Wanderer

She roams aimlessly, endlessly,

Searching for some touchstone

Something that will give her boundaries,

Some familiar face or scene.

Her own face is a mask of despair

For none appears.

"Is this my home? Is this where I live?

Her constant queries tear me apart.

There is no way to reassure, no way

To relieve that constant uncertainty.

How sad it is when the heart

Has lost its home,

And the wanderer remains homeless forever.

2000

The Tower

Heights terrify me, but one day I climbed a tower.

Things were good that day.

Up I went, exhilarating in this new-found freedom,

And no old fears haunted me that day

At the very top I looked down at him,

A mere ant on the ground.

"Get back, don't go near the edge," he shouted,

But I stood there

There was no danger.

It was wonderful to be on the edge of something.

1999

Chores

Dear me, it is time to tidy the earth again,

Although I seem often to be at this task.

The trees have this habit of dropping their leaves just anywhere,

Without a thought, except to blanket the earth.

An exquisite red maple leaf catches my eye,

As I crunch through piles of gold and brown,

Wishing, that like the wind, I could swoop them up

And let them drop somewhere else.

I watch a single leaf swirling, dipping, falling

Glorious in its path, and I marvel at its grace.

Summer trash is cleared away

And gardens put to sleep lay black and barefaced as a lie.

Now the trees go about their massive cover-up.

The leaves do their best but soon will come the final blanket,

Sent special express by winter.

Why do I feel I have to tidy up such an efficient system?

2007

(Nature does not hurry, yet everything is accomplished–Lao Tzu)

My Crooked Eye

I have a crooked eye and my picture frames

Are all slightly atilt.

The offending frame is straightened

With a triumphant, "There!"

I blame it on my crooked eye.

My words, however brilliant, end up aslant,

Leaving odd spaces at one corner of my page.

"Can't you write straight?" they say,

Not knowing I have a crooked eye.

I cannot walk in a straight line.

Some peculiar force pulls me to one side.

"What is the matter with you?" they ask.

How does one explain a crooked eye?

Sometimes I see little things that are just not right,

Changes in expression, a shrug, a toss of the head,

Subtle ways of showing displeasure.

Words have that little twist to them,

Just a little off centre.

A crooked eye has ways of noting things like that.

2002

Late Spring

The ragged, barren shores hold fast,

Reluctant to let go their layers of ice.

Drab, beaten grass shows through the snow,

Like stains on a carpet.

Tulips that thrust their brave swords upward,

Now stand still, drooping in the cruel wind.

Trees stand somber and sullen,

Not sure if they dare to herald spring or not.

Leaden skies show no promise

Of warmth or sunlight.

The earth, not ready to give up its treasures,

Is like stone, until that happens.

But—today there is something in the air!

2007

Lines For To Day

Today it was risky to travel in the skies.
Cruel men plotted mass destruction of innocent people.
The giant planes plummeted from the air
Like broken and wounded birds.

Today it was not safe to be in the streets
Of some far away cities,
Where bombs exploded leaving smoke,
And mangled bits of buildings and bodies
To lie like rags in the streets.

Today it was not safe to be in my backyard.
My cat killed the tiny chipmunk
That I had grown used to seeing.
I welcomed his presence on the deck,
Carrying seeds and kernels to hide
In his secret chipmunk places.
I could make no excuses for my cat.

These events made me sad and wonder about life.

I seem to do that often.

God sees the little sparrow fall.

November Promise

No snow, no ice, no rain,

But the wind has rearranged the fallen leaves.

They linger, coloured like bits of calico,

Heaped in ditches and caught like tiny flags

To brighten the forbidding fences.

Trees shiver in their nakedness,

Clutching their barren arms around them,

Their colours faded into a tired dryness,

They await the blankets that will come to them

From the white skies of winter.

The snow, the ice, the rain will come,

And we shiver like the barren trees.

(words from Sybil) 2007

Memory

I once saw the flash of a blue jay's wing

Against the spruce-dark wood,

It rivaled the brilliance of the gem

That was the October sky.

I once saw the season's first wild rose, alone,

But with budded promise of many more.

In morning dew its exquisite scent

Was lovelier then any bottled fragrance.

I once saw water rippling over mossy stones

In a deep shaded wood full of ancient secrets.

The drops fell from my fingers like angel's tears

Glistening in the dappled sunlight.

I once held a newborn babe next to my heart,

Marveling at the artistry of shell-like ears,

And tiny crumpled hands opening like flowers,

Amazed at the perfection of this little being.

Once, just once, I saw these things?

Oh no, not in such fleeting fashion.

But each time these miracles come to my eye,

It is like the first, new and filled with wonder.

2000

If Wishes Came True

I wish that I had nothing to do,

No pressure to be up and doing,

No guilt that I was accomplishing little

In spite of daily tasks not done.

Perhaps if I just sit in my deck chair

Pretending that nothing awaits my attention,

Nothing more important than picking

That dried leaf from my red geranium,

Than I could feel that there was nothing to do.

The past is shut up in tight smooth compartments,

Locked up forever.

Funny how one key can open any door,

Letting out the torrent of memories to be mulled over.

But for today I sit in my wooden deck chair

With nothing to do but contemplate the future

Filled with picking dead leaves from my red geranium.

2006

The Sisters

They roamed knee deep in buttercups and daisies,

Enchanted by the array of beauty.

They cupped the blossoms in their hands

Gazing into the flowery faces with delight.

Then the older one gathered them,

And deftly, swiftly with her slender fingers

Wove daisies into a crown, a tiara fit for any princess,

And placed it proudly on her auburn hair.

The little one tried to imitate her sister.

But could not twist the wiry stems into a circlet to wear.

In disgust she threw them from her,

And began to roam again, knee deep in summer

2002

Things My Mother Taught Me

There is joy in small things, a good book to read,
The first spring violet, fresh wind on my cheek,
A cat on my lap, good coffee, an afternoon nap.
My mother taught me that life is full of small pleasures.

I learned how to make bread with my mother,
To get the feel of it, to know when to add more essentials,
And to know when to just let it be, and trust in the outcome.
Life is like making bread.

She showed me how to find humour in situations.
It is there, even in darkest times, if you will look.
My mother taught me to laugh, and to let the tears well up
Even behind the laughter.
Is life not meant to be full of laughter and tears?

Elizabeth Donaldson

She taught me not to fret over things that can't be changed.

"After all," she would say, "It will all be the same

One hundred years from now."

I hear those phrases come from my lips now: "A way will open,

It will get better, You'll rue the day, Life goes on, Time never stops.'

"It is as it is," she used to say.

From her I learned to think of the endless rolling of time,

And how quickly the years slip away.

I learned of the fierceness of a mother's love that comes full circle,

When I became the mother,

Wanting to protect her as she always protected me.

2001

Swimming

Gliding through crystal water, feeling the pull but no pain,
My arms stretch and muscles tighten.
No feeling but glorious freedom and lightness
Beneath the exquisitely cool blanket of water.

I dream of swimming and when I awaken I smile,
Remembering, and thinking of how I slipped
Effortlessly through the water
Carrying no burden of weight or time.

Like a winged creature I flew,
Swiftly, cleanly, my arms cutting the water
With no splash or sound.
I swim so fast and so joyously.

It is a favourite dream.
Do you wonder I smile when I awaken?

2008

LESSONS

My grandmother wore a suit of white linen to church.

Shading her face was a broad-brimmed lacy black hat.

Gloves removed so slowly, smoothed from her fingers,

Just before she played the old pump organ.

"A lady always wears gloves, Elizabeth."

Her white china plates had rims of cobalt blue.

She taught me to rub the pointed silver spoons until they gleamed.

Grandmother made sandwiches of thin brown bread.

"Always trim the crusts, Elizabeth."

Testing the flat-iron quickly near her dusky cheek,

She taught me to press the snowy damask linens.

"Iron into the corners, Elizabeth."

My grandmother was teaching me to be a lady.

"A lady does not spit, Elizabeth."

A lady does not laugh loudly.

A lady keeps certain thoughts to herself.

Oh, Grandmother, you should not have died

The year that I was twelve.

1996

TO A 4H CALF

Bounded by blue steel bars and white board fences,

No open gate to rush through,

Strange sights and sounds on every side,

Staring eyes riveted on them, they are captive

Do they want to be here?

Do they think of escape to green pastures,

Standing knee deep in clover, or belly deep in some dark pool,

Dipping the head to fling

Delicious wetness over a sun warmed back?

Some stand calm and docile,

Submitting to prodding and petting and combing,

As if knowing they must look their very best.

Others resist, tossing their heads and tugging at restraints,

Even though their efforts are to no avail.

Do they look on their trainers as gods,

To be worshipped and obeyed,

Or just as another annoying kind of insect

Buzzing ceaselessly,

To be flicked away with a toss of the head

Or the swish of the long plumed tail?

For Julianna–2010

The Gift

No one really listens to anyone else.

We are too busy plotting out what we will say

When comes a lull in the conversation.

Will they never be done speaking?

I have important words to say,

Nuggets of gold to fall from my lips.

We hear but we do not listen?

We listen but we do not hear?

What does it matter?

If you truly listen you will hear

The unvoiced cry for understanding,

The hopelessness behind the brave façade,

The subtle nuances of despair,

That are all coming from

The secret places in the heart.

Give the gift that really matters.

Listen and hear the echoes

Beyond the frivolous words,

Then you may understand and forgive.

Elizabeth Donaldson

Cosmetic Surgery

I've noticed certain things of late
As I view my pots of creams and lotions,
A person must keep up to date
While knowing there are no magic potions.

I've tried "up lifting" and "age defying"
And even have "Rejuvenation."
Someone out there must be lying,
This I note with resignation.

"Retroactive" –what a laugh!
At even those with added brightener.
There is one thing I know for sure
They definitely are a wallet lightener.

1999

Treasures

Before they married he gave to her
A cut glass bottle of perfume, lily of the valley it was.
For years you could see the silvery label
With spikes of green leaves on it.
We would open the dresser drawer.
The little glass bottle, empty now, was tucked away
With pressed flowers, a tattered autograph book,
An old brooch, unstrung pearl beads and other bits of memory.
The bottle had that lovely familiar scent.

We put all her bits of memory,
With old letters, yellowed and brittle in a little box.
A lacy handkerchief wrapped the little bottle,
The lovely scent of lily of the valley was still there.

I cleared away tattered books and bits of cracked china,
Cards and letters, tarnished beads,
And keys that fit unknown locks.
With the flotsam and jetsam of years tangling around me,
Is my mother's box of treasures.
The bottle is there—does it still have a faint elusive scent?
Or do I just want the fragrance to be there?

Elizabeth Donaldson

The Morning After

Random flakes fell, as the sky, leaden with low slung clouds,
Waited to give up its burden.
Then came fine ribbons of snow
Slanting through the light,
Some great white feathers floated by the window,
Like chunks bitten from white foam and spat out to drift down.
The roof tops wore ridiculous, puffy white hats.
Each bare branch, coated with snow,
Stood out in stark relief against the evergreens
Drooping to the ground with their burden.
The snow fell all day.

In the morning sunshine glittered on the laden trees,
Shrubs like molds of frozen desserts,
And fences draped with snowy linen.
Such beauty surely was meant to last,
Until our senses were sated with the intricate patterns
That the shadows created on this brilliance.

But then came the big yellow machines,

Relentlessly pushing and cutting,

And tossing the snow aside

Into amazingly neat and tidy piles,

And soon no paths were obstructed.

But the restless wind whirled powdery sheets from the roof tops,

And strove to repair the damage inflicted by monster machines.

It did its best to undress the trees, but some were too modest

To stand bare again after such elegant attire.

2009

The Tamaracks

A lone tree lights the brown barren field
Like a flaming torch of radiant symmetry.
Then our senses are assailed by the massed glory
And ethereal golden splendor of the tamaracks in autumn.
Surely some mysterious candle illuminates them from within.
Are we to believe that this glowing brilliancy is a natural state?
Golden spears push their way through dark and somber firs,
And stand in graceful relief against trees
Clutching last leaves to near naked breasts.

Standing in serene elegance, not flaunting their beauty,
Gracious and self confident,
Seemingly unaware of the sheer glory of their presence,
They will soon stand bare and stark,
Etched against the autumn sunset,
Or bowing with the grace of a dancer
In the gusts of winter winds.

2009

Weeds

The weeds are there, but sometimes,

They are allowed to grow,

So I can see what a nuisance,

Full blown, looks like.

The pleasure of removing a great noxious plant

Is much greater than destroying

An innocent-looking tender green shoot.

I am not good at knowing

When to nip things in the bud.

2007

I Remember –

Tall sinister cedar trees hiding unknown terrors

That grew beside the road,

Made me pant with fear as I rushed through them

On my way to school.

I remember this.

The smell of dusty old books,

Of onion sandwiches and rubber boots,

And wood smoke and chalk seemed to float

Just above my head.

These things I remember.

There are tales often-told

Of bygone days and history past,

Of hard times in times of old,

These are the memories that seem to last.

First loves and moonlight nights we walked in,
Summer sun when we picked the purple berries
That stained our fingers and our lips.
These, and the echo of children laughing,
Are etched with the sharp finger of memory.

Memories of missing dear ones,
Swirl around me as dreams unfold.
I remember laughter and tears, grief and joy,
But I don't remember growing old.

2009

Time's Passages And Thoughts

"We do not remember days, we remember moments." Anonymous.

- The Remnants
- Food, Not Just for Thought
- Burriss School Destroyed
- None So Deaf
- Making Connections
- One Day at a Time
- Closing

The Remnants

Tompkins Hardware acquired a large amount of remnants that had come from a fabric store in Minnesota. They were going to be taken to the garbage dump but through some arrangement could be brought back to this store. There were many large boxes packed solidly with goods. When I heard of this it evoked no special interest, as I am not really a devoted seamstress.

One day I was in the store and began to examine the contents of a box. The first piece I pulled out was a beautiful dark blue upholstery type of material with tiny gold stars woven in it. Another blue background had gorgeous Indian elephants woven into the material. I was hooked. I began to search through the boxes and found piece after piece with beautiful patterns and colours, all made of high quality fabric. When another customer came to browse I jealously guarded the lovely pieces that had attracted me and I clutched them closely for fear of losing them. The material was sold by the pound and I went home with quite an amount, rather amazed at how heavy the materials were.

At home I inspected them again and I pressed and carefully folded each piece, exulting in the vibrant colours and patterns and the feel of them. Vague stirrings of a long forgotten dream began to possess me. I had suppressed these longings but the sight of these bits of cloth brought it all rushing back. I was going to make a QUILT.

For several years the vague notion of making a quilt had been in my mind. After all, I was in my sixties and time was running out. I had the feeling that nearly every woman should make a quilt at some time in her life. I did not want an ordinary "flowers in a basket" type; rather I envisioned a brilliant coloured silk, satin, velvet or brocade covering. I could see it in my mind's eye. Alas, in the past I have seen many things in my mind's eye, but I do not have the true artist's eye that is able to transfer images from the mind to the canvas or other medium, but I was determined.

Each time I went to the store, and I seemed to go quite often, the big boxes would draw me like a magnet. The pieces were packed tightly and I would reach down and pull them out to smooth and examine. I would bring home a few more to add to my growing collection. Of course, I told family members of this treasure trove and as we had Emily as an inside source, one Sunday morning a group consisting of Emily, my sister Marion, two daughters-in-law Kelly and Nancy went to the store to examine the treasures. Jerry was also there, We pawed and picked and pulled out pieces that were sometimes yards long, exclaiming at our finds. They were usually about eighteen inches wide and were cut in odd ways and to my mind certainly were never saving of the material. When I took Home Ec in High School we were taught to lay out the pattern to utilise the material but that did not seem to be taken into account here. Many cuts were curved and there were also a great many triangular pieces.

We chatted and visited as we selected. I often have flights of fancy and the thought of merchants from the far-east travelling to a bazaar came to my mind. We were gathering in the market to buy or trade the rich satins and brocades that would later grace some sultan's couches or provide draperies for his harem. At some point we would load our camels with our riches and trudge off across the desert stopping at an oasis to nibble dates and drink water from a spring. I am subject to fantasies like this.

All the while that I was collecting the rich colours and fabrics, I studied library books and borrowed quilting books. Nothing in current magazines caught my imagination. I made cushion covers and covered a footstool and a larger ottoman and sewed curtains for the basement windows. A lady from Emo was making gorgeous purses and vests from the brocades. Mennonite ladies were buying material and making quilts. The possibilities of these wonderful remnants began to obsess me and I still kept collecting, pressing, folding, and sorting the pieces. I bought big plastic Rubbermaid containers to keep them safely. My cat Miz often slept blissfully on a pile of them and loved them warm from the iron.

One day, browsing at the magazine rack, an image popped out at me. There was my quilt ! It had the brilliant colours, the shapes and the look that I could see in my mind. I could hardly wait to get home to study my pattern. The name of it was "Rainbow Ribbons" and the squares were a version of the "Ohio Star" and were done in different values of red, orange, green, blue, purple and yellow. I knew that there were many names for the patterns that women had been stitching for generations. I had helped my mother "tie" quilts that were made from old materials whose main quality was warmth. For a wedding present my great aunt had given me a quilt with blue backing in the "Dresden Plate" pattern.

When I was married there were many examples of quilting that Gale's grandmother Belle had done, all by hand stitching. Most of these were of the "Log Cabin" pattern. I marvelled at the tiny exact stitches and noted how the beginning piece was one inch square and then strips of graduating length were added on to make a square block. She also made many of the "Flower Basket" design. Some of these quilts are still in the possession of family members. Perhaps I too would make an heirloom.

Now that I had found my pattern all the remnants had to be sorted again and arranged by colours and shades and types of material. I read the instructions and studied diagrams but must confess I did this quickly as I was in such a hurry to begin the project. Then the cutting began. The pieces were 5 inches square and then were cut diagonally to form triangles. It seemed so easy and I cut and slashed away to make pieces for a trial square in shades of blue. It was not as easy as it looked, as each piece had to be the exact same size and the seam allowances ¼ inch. If they were not done properly the points would not come together. I fitted, I sewed, I examined and I ripped out seams. At first I would be impatient and annoyed when I had to rip out, but then I realized that I would be doing plenty of ripping out, so I might as well accept what had to be done gracefully. This attitude helped immensely, as did the purchase of a new deluxe seam ripper. I worked and worked to get the points to come together properly. Emily gave me a cutting wheel and board for Christmas and this helped with the measuring and having exact cuts.

The pieces were cut, then sewed back together with a dark and a light side, then the squares were sewed to make the pattern with one dark square in the centre. There were 16 little squares in each quilt block, so by the time I finished one block I had sewn 64 little pieces together. I worked and worked at my "trial block" and as Gale approved of quilting and was interested in my efforts and problems, one day he asked, "Have you got a keeper yet?" By then some of the pieces were so mangled that I had to cut new ones. At last I had picked up enough expertise and confidence to actually start a whole block.

I found as I was working that I would not have enough of a certain colour and back to the store I would go to paw through the boxes looking for reds or greens to finish a block. The most difficult to find were shades of yellow and purple. I went to Nancy to look through her collection of remnants to beg a few. I worked through the winter accumulating more remnants as my pile of finished blocks grew. I bought another plastic keeper to hold the remnants and baskets to hold the cut pieces. I was very thankful that I had a basement room in which to work, for sometimes when I left the floor would be littered with scraps and threads, and often I got on my knees with a magnet to gather up the dropped pins. I spent every available bit of time in the basement in the "sewing room."

The Rainbow Ribbons quilt although not full sized was finished with a saw tooth edge on a dark green background. It was quite pretty when it was new and I was gratified one day when showing it to Denise and family. I spread it out on the floor and after a few moments Nicholas, aged about four, said, "I want to feel it." He lay down spread-eagled on the quilt with a look of satisfaction, obviously liking it.

When I finished my Rainbow Ribbons quilt I did several other projects, including quilts for grandsons. The pattern called "Rail Fence" was not so complex and was done in 4 inch strips. I made several smaller sampler type projects and from a number of Gale's old blue-toned dress shirts I made a baby quilt for a great grandson that was quite attractive. I liked the idea of making something new from something old, as I could feel an affinity for those pioneer women who used every scrap of material.

So I worked away. I got a quilting book from the library and found the perfect quote to express my feelings as I worked and dreamed: "QUILTS–Some are traditional in the finest sense. Others, both antique and modern break all the rules but in doing so reach another visual level and transcend the simple materials from which they are made. Some quilts are for show and are highly decorative, while others convey a much deeper purpose and meaning and seem to awaken more primitive responses," Michelle Walker from the <u>Complete Book of Quilting</u>.

This expressed perfectly what I was doing in this time, when there were other parts of my life beyond my control. I did not feel quite so bad when my work did not the reach the levels of perfection for which I strove. This book also told about the experienced Mennonite and Amish lady quilters that left a "humility block" with a mistake to show that no one except God is perfect. That concept suited me to a tee and heaven knows it was a humbling experience for me, as it showed me anew what an imperfect workman I am.

Perhaps I should think of my quilt as one huge humility block.

I doubt that any of my quilting efforts will be handed down through the generations. I do not think that any descendant will hold up my quilt and say, "Imagine, great-grandmother made this in her little room in the cellar on the farm with only the light of a sixty watt bulb."

What has become of my Rainbow Ribbons quilt? It is on the bed and I use it often when I pull it over me for an afternoon nap. It gives me a feeling of comfort.

Food

PART ONE:

One of the things I brought to my marriage was a hard cover book entitled The Meta Given Cook Book, c.1942 that I bought through my book club. I never found out much about Meta Given but her book was a good basic book without exotic ingredients and did not call for fancy equipment. In fact it was so basic that there was a recipe for bologna sandwiches: (ten slices of bread, 5 slices of bologna, butter, mustard etc). I consulted with Meta for many years and certain dog-eared pages indicating my favourite recipes were spotted with grease, globules of egg or sticky with bits of molasses or jam.

Meta did not use microwaves or mix masters, electric fry pans or kettles or things like that. Meta used no cooking spray for pans and she beat eggs with a rotary egg beater. She did not call for pasta other than macaroni, noodles or spaghetti. No ingredients such as artichoke hearts, yogurt, soy sauce, jicama, jalapeno peppers, mozzarella, coconut milk, pesto, cilantro, balsamic vinegar, Hoisin sauce or Neufchatel cheese were listed. Gradually I collected other cook books (as some wit once said 'more cook books than cooking') and finally got rid of Meta Given after tearing out two pages, one with the recipe for Old Fashioned Baked Beans and the other for Pumpkin Pie, that still are favourites.

Neither my sister Marion nor I can remember our mother having a cook book although she may have had one of those old Blue Ribbon or Five Roses books. Mom knew the rudiments of cooking and then cooked by feel or instinct or whatever you want to call it. Her measuring was done with a cracked cup that stayed in the flour bin and she used just teaspoons or dessert spoons for measuring. She knew when the cake batter had enough flour by the feel, she knew when the cookie dough was just right to drop or roll out. Preparing bread dough was done by feel also. If you asked her she would say "just add flour till it feels right." She came from the "butter the size of an egg" or the "scant cup of milk" era of cooking.

Mom may have used a recipe for something important like the Christmas cake or bread and butter pickles. I remember things written down just on loose pieces of paper or the backs of old envelopes and kept in the buffet drawer and Marion recalls handwritten recipes also. My mother was an excellent cook and when she went to Rainycrest to cook she changed her methods only slightly and was praised as a cook there, cooking good basic food, for twenty years. She had a Rainycrest cook book though, for things like pumpkin pie, 8 cans of pumpkin, 12 cans evap. milk etc.

Since the times I remember in the 1930's and '40's, changes in food availability and preparation have been tremendous. In those days there were no mixes, nothing 'instant,' and everything was made from scratch. Shopping was a simple matter. If you needed a can of tomatoes you did not have to choose from the bewildering varieties of diced, whole, pureed, sauce, crushed, Italian, stewed, salt free, seasoned etc., that you find on the shelves now, you just bought a can of tomatoes. It was the same with many other products.

Mom used yeast cakes that had to be broken up and set in warm water and sugar. I recall being sent on the path across the field to borrow a Royal yeast cake from my Grandmother Anderson. She wrapped it and put it inside my hat for safe keeping on the walk home. Bread was set to rise overnight, often covered with a clean old blanket on the open oven door.

With no refrigerators or freezers meat was frozen outside in the winter and pieces sawed off as needed. Pork was often salted or cured to eat in the summer. A product called Habacure was rubbed into the meat to preserve it. Mom canned meat also and at times there was wild meat and occasionally fish. We had chickens so usually had eggs. Mom knew which hens were laying and would pick one that was not doing its duty for Sunday supper. She made her selection, chopped off its head, de-feathered and cleaned it, stuffed and roasted it. I have plucked many chickens but have never, ever cleaned one.

We ate only what was in season, never thinking of strawberries or radishes in winter but Mom bought oranges for us and apples in the fall. The rural grocery stores were limited in fresh produce. We had potatoes, carrots, turnips, cabbage and onions that were grown and stored for winter. In the summer lettuce, green beans, peas, corn and tomatoes abounded. There was no lack of root vegetables in winter but none of the leafy green ones that are recommended daily now. Later when Grandma Anderson came in a taxi from Fort Frances in the winter she would bring the wondrous treat of a head of lettuce and a loaf of dark rye bread in its white waxed-paper wrapping with red and green writing. Those lettuce sandwiches were wonderful in the dead of winter.

Jars of green beans, especially prone to botulism, were canned in a long, hot, laborious process. The beans fresh from the garden were cut and precooked, then packed and sealed in quart jars. The copper wash boiler was full of hot water on the stove, the jars placed in this hot water bath, the water brought to boiling and processed like this for up to four hours. Tomatoes, beet and other pickles, raspberries, strawberries blueberries, rhubarb, plums and wild fruit were preserved in season but not in the hot water bath.

Sauerkraut was made in large crocks in the late fall. The cabbage was finely shredded with a sharp kitchen knife and put in layers in the crock, each layer sprinkled with a little coarse salt. Then the cabbage had to be carefully tamped and crushed until the juices ran freely. It took a lot of pounding or tamping with a wooden pounder and we all took turns. The amount of salt was crucial, for if there was not enough the cabbage would spoil or rot and too much salt made a bitter product. Everyone tasted and tested and pounded. In a day or two it would start to bubble and you could smell it and know it was "working". It took about ten days to two weeks for a batch to ferment, depending on how warm the weather was.

Mom loved making jelly and jam and was thrilled with the new product powdered Certo that came out. Her one problem with canning fruits was being able to afford the sugar that was needed. Mom liked wild plums but no amount of sugar could ever quite disguise that bitter tang they had. Blue berries and rhubarb could be canned by a special sugarless process. I remember two quart jars of rhubarb with its peculiar greenish brown colour.

Our food was plain, well cooked and usually plentiful. My mother made wonderful soups and stews, good bread, homemade butter, plain cakes and cookies. In baking or cooking she used only salt, pepper, sage, cinnamon, vanilla and nutmeg for seasoning. Mom cooked with butter and lard or chicken fat rendered in the oven. Rendering was done by placing fat from chickens, beef or pigs in a shallow pan and put in the oven at very low heat. It took hours but the finished product was a clear oil with all the bits you did not want at the bottom. It was strained into containers where it solidified when cool. Beef tallow was used to grease our boots. Probably the most exotic thing we ate was macaroni and tomatoes and I tasted spaghetti for the first time at the home of a friend. Oatmeal porridge or the dry puffed or shredded wheat were the cereals of choice.

We were taught to never complain about food and if we did, we were admonished, "Eat it and say nothing." This applied to food we did not like, that was burned a bit or anything else. If it was impossible that we eat the food, we were told to, "Quietly put it to one side." I consider these excellent rules. My mother told me that when they were young they were encouraged to eat a slice of bread and butter along with their dessert and that seems strange now in these calorie watching days.

In retrospect I cooked much the same as my mother had in her growing up years. These were the years before electricity and how it changed the face of food preparation. Think of cooking without electric stoves and ovens, mixers, coffee makers, microwaves, toasters, deep fryers, slow cookers, electric fry pans and griddles, tea kettles or pressure cookers and things like George Foreman grills and other gadgets and appliances. Think of your home without a refrigerator or freezer to store food. Imagine having no running water and then think of how people cooked and prepared food in rural areas 60 or 70 years ago. It was all done with much more hard work involved than now and much more time involved, but wonderful meals were prepared in vast amounts for threshing or wood cutting crews or for special company. One of the first things my mother bought when we got the hydro power in 1949 was a hot plate with two burners on which she could cook a simple meal or boil a kettle on a sweltering summer day.

Part Two:

I do not want to give the impression that I did not know how to cook when I was first married. Both my sister and I learned by doing and could put a simple meal on the table by the time we were ten. I had taken four years of Home Economics in high school and knew the basic methods of mixing cake, muffins, and making oatmeal and cocoa and white sauce. I knew the principles of egg and cheese cookery and learned never to beat an egg on a saucer with an egg beater ! In spite of some messes and lots of laughs I still often use what I had been taught in Miss Yakimischak's class. We were taught to cook from "scratch" and used no mixes or short cuts.

I cooked for myself for two years when I taught at Burriss School and lived with Melta Farmer. She drove a school bus and did many other things and did not want to be tied down cooking. We ate quite differently and she did much of her cooking in a lovely little three legged cast iron pot with a round bottom. Chunks of beef cooked slowly in this were wonderfully tender. We shared some meals and she always ate with an old fashioned three tined fork with a wooden handle. I had grown up on Mom's homemade soup and found canned soups a real treat. I ate Campbell's Vegetable Soup nearly every day for about three months until I suddenly became very sick of it and went back to homemade.

Hydro electrical power had come to the rural areas a few years before I was married but most places still had no indoor plumbing facilities or running water. After marriage we lived at first with my in laws and cooked on the woodstove and carried all the water. Living with my mother in law I was not really able to try out my culinary skills or use my wedding presents like the toaster or electric kettle. Doris Donaldson was also a very good cook and unlike my mother, always used recipes, loving to try new cakes or cookies. Now margarine was coloured instead of the white that you had to mix the colour in and was often used in baking instead of butter. Chocolate chips became popular.

I wanted to try everything but it was hard in someone else's kitchen so I helped rather than cooking much. I knew the rudiments of making bread and by now we used yeast granules so one fall day when the older Donaldsons were away I decided to make bread. I made just a small amount and set my little batch to rise. It was a cool fall day and no matter how often I looked at the dough, there was no change. It just did not rise. I did not know what to do with the wretched thing, so finally thought I will get rid of it. I took it out behind the barn and threw it, a miserable looking white lump, on the manure pile and returned to the house.

After a few hours I thought I should look at it, hoping that maybe something had dragged it away. The day had improved and the sun was hitting the manure pile and to my horror I saw that my bread had raised into quite a big puffy ball. I was so afraid that someone would see it, so I grabbed a hay fork and pounded it down and scratched some manure over it and returned to the house. It worried me so that after an hour back to the scene I returned to find the dough triumphantly rising with clumps of manure adorning it. I had to get rid of it so I found a good hollow in the pile, smashed the bread down, hauled and forked about fifty pounds of manure over it. When I checked later there was no sign of the offending dough ball. I learned from that experience to not be in hurry for your bread dough to rise.

I was not an adventurous cook like my sister who was always trying new recipes. I clipped them out but rarely tried them and continued to cook in the way my mother had taught me. The food industry began to change, slowly at first, then with amazing speed in the 60's and 70's. I remember when Cheez Whiz first hit the markets in about 1953. Bisquik had been out for some time as well as Aunt Jemima Pancake Mix. I never used these, preferring to work from scratch. Many convenience foods followed, all designed to make life easier. I still stuck to basic cooking especially as the family increased. I did not really approve of convenience food, except for Kraft Dinner and Lipton's Chicken Noodle soup which the children loved.

In the 1960's ethnic food began to be popular. We never had anything such as this at home and I remember first tasting chili at the school cafeteria when I was sixteen. Chili was added to my cooking repertoire. I began making spaghetti sauce using a 'Sure Fire Spaghetti Sauce' recipe given to me by a friend at a shower and spaghetti became a regular.

All of a sudden I found myself cooking regularly for a family of ten and there were often more at our table. It was not as hard as it sounds, as I was able to draw on my experience of making things do from my mother. By then we had a fridge, a freezer, a toaster, an electric fry pan and other small appliances. Cooking for a big family seemed to be a matter of having large cooking pots and serving bowls. I cooked, and still do, with a cast iron Dutch oven and iron fry pans.

Potatoes were a standby and often I would put on a pot of potatoes and plan the rest of the meal. "Oven Potatoes" cooked in the big yellow Pyrex bowl were a real favourite. Baked potatoes were easy and popular with meat loaf. Mashed potatoes also filled the yellow bowl as did fried potatoes. Scalloped potatoes were not as universally liked. Soups, stews, ground beef mixtures, dumplings, meat pies were all things that could be easily extended. Sometimes we had our own beef, but one time we bought half a beef from someone and it was just terribly tough. I used every method to tenderize it but it seemed to be tough even when it was ground up. Later we raised chickens and turkeys and this helped add variety to the menu. The jars of home canned vegetables, pickles and fruit were always available.

Everyone had their favourites and I tried to cater to all tastes just a bit. Sunday nights when we often had visitors we always had a full meal of roast beef, chicken or turkey, gravy and mashed potatoes, two vegetables, salad, pickles and always dessert. Dessert was my least favourite thing to make but I made pies, cakes, cookies, doughnuts, puddings, fruit cobblers and crisps as Gale was known for his sweet tooth. Bavarian might be a better name but the kids all enjoyed "Fluff", which was Jello, usually red, beaten with Dream Whip when it was set. Ice cream was a special treat.

I encouraged the children to help in the kitchen and to cook simple things. Emily at a young age wrote her own recipe for cake which called for a cup of everything plus "a slab of butter." One day I overheard Mark aged eight telling his brother how to make scrambled eggs, "You just put butter in the black frying pan and let it melt. Then you crack the egg on the edge and put it in the pan. Then you stick your thumb in the yolk."

A certain amount of ingenuity was called for and I did plan meals around what was on hand or on sale. My repertoire expanded somewhat when Emily began 4H and then some ethnic dishes such as pizza and lasagna appeared on the table. More and more new items were available in the stores. I found them expensive and did not like the idea of chemicals and preservatives.

Over the years my cooking has changed. We enjoyed food with an ethnic flavour and Gale was especially fond of oriental stir fries. I have never learned to like shellfish. There are many more fruits and vegetables available now and we eat kiwi, mango, pineapple and sometimes pomegranates that are supposed to be so good for you but I still favour apples, pears oranges and bananas. I know there are scores more to sample. Although I really enjoy Greek foods, curry, pizza and Chinese food, I still cook very plainly. My cupboard holds herbs and spices like rosemary, basil, oregano, cilantro, cumin, coriander, chili powder and I use a variety of sauces including hot sauce. Salsa has become a staple food.

Shopping now is rather bewildering with the vast amounts of convenience foods and snack foods galore. There are so many choices for any ordinary item that you buy. M & M is convenient for serving sized portions of fish and chicken. I find packaged coleslaw and salad mixes handy now, though I would never have considered doing that when cooking for the family.

Part Three:

My love/hate relationship with food being too much of a good thing at times, maybe started in childhood when I seemed to equate food with being safe and secure. We would come home from school knowing that a bad storm was beginning. There was a feeling of urgency as we rushed to water the cattle and horses that seemed to drink so much. Milk the cows, give the horses their oats, feed the chicken, hurry, get it all done. It would be dark and snowing hard by the time we finished and it was hard to see the path to carry the milk to the house to separate. We walked in the circle of light from the lantern not sure what was beyond the light. No doubt my mother, a widow with four young children, did feel a terrific sense of responsibility that would be heightened by the imminent storm.

Nearly always Mom would have a pot of soup simmering and other good wholesome food and some treat for us. Some nights we would make candy. When I was raising the family I would get that old sense of waiting for the children to get off the bus on a stormy night and getting the chores done up early. I still get that feeling of anxiety as dark approaches on a stormy night and I want to make soup and bread and see if everyone arrived home safely. Most people have a comfort food or soul food that often stems from childhood associations and it is usually hearty, substantial food. When I need something like this I never crave lettuce or celery!

Food rationing was used in the 1940's during WW11 and continued for a few years after. We each had a ration book with coupons that were torn out and were allowed just so much. Sugar, butter and meat were the main things that affected us being rationed. In the morning we were each given brown sugar for our cereal. Eric would eat his cereal without sugar and save his in a little jar. When he had enough he would make some fudge which he did not share. Living on the farm we made our own butter and sometimes Mom would trade butter coupons for sugar with town people.

My bread was still not great until one day when Mom was there we went through the process step by step. She gave me many pointers and I found I was not beating the sponge thoroughly enough and mixing in too much flour. Once I learned how to make good bread I loved doing it. Don't be in a hurry, take time for each step. Give your yeast time to grow. I still preferred the slower kind. Give your batter a good mixing until it is smooth as silk, then begin to mix in the flour. When it cannot be stirred anymore turn it out on the floured counter top to begin the kneading. With the rhythm to it, lifting and turning, kneading a large batch takes from fifteen to twenty minutes. At some point the dough will "squeak" as the air bubbles break.

I found making bread a type of therapy and sometimes worked out some anger or anxiety while punching down a mass of dough. A person can be quite aggressive while kneading and the bread doesn't mind a bit. Kneading was absolutely therapeutic.

At the library I found a series of around the world cookbooks and read the bread sections of countries Italy, Spain, Russia, Morocco, British Isles, Germany etc., trying many of them and experimenting with different grains and flours. Jerry gave me a bread cook book that told how to collect yeast cells from the air. It was called poolish. You just set out a little bowl with a mix of flour and a bit of sugar with water and soon bubbles would be forming and it was quite exciting to watch as the yeast grew. It was a slow process but resulted in lovely dense, dark European breads depending on the grains and flours used. I would haunt the bulk food stores for varieties of flour.

I loved making bread and began to enter the Emo Fair competitions. One year I won first place in all categories, white and whole wheat, loaves and rolls, reaching a high point in my life. However, just to keep me humble, I was never able to win at baking powder biscuits. Bread is such an elemental part of life and turning out a baking of eight big loaves, two pans of buns and some cinnamon rolls could be a most satisfying experience. When the children came off the bus I would hear the first one in call out, "She baked!"

Soup was always a favourite part of my cooking and I have continued that, while I have not made bread since I left the farm. I make soup of some type at least once a week.

While on the farm I also enjoyed canning and preserving and canned hundreds of jars of vegetables, fruit, jams and jellies, pickles, beef, fish and chicken. The pressure canner instead of the boiling water bath method that my mother used cut the time by at least three quarters. Tomatoes are so versatile and in peak years I tried different things such as green tomato mincemeat, tomato soup, chili sauce, pickled green tomatoes, ketchup and spaghetti sauce along with plain canned tomatoes. Salsa came a little later. I even canned Swiss chard and baked beans and jars of diced carrots and vegetable soup. Canning was one thing that you did where you had something to show for a day's work. Gale built the canning shelves to store the jars that were a testimony to a great deal of hard and time consuming work. Lee and Leanne on the family farm carry on that tradition.

Canning Shelves on a Good Year.

All my children are good cooks and my sons enjoy time in the kitchen. I think they have all made bread and continue to turn out excellent products. Guy has built a beautiful outdoor oven on their island on Rainy Lake and makes good bread as well as many other things. Our family gatherings always feature something new that someone has tried, as well as the old favourites.

When I started this I meant to just jot down a few thoughts about food and cooking but it seemed to evolve into a treatise and I have to think how to end it. Perhaps it should have ended sooner but even as I write more thoughts come to me about this very important and elemental part of our lives. The food industry has changed so much that, according to surveys hardly anything is safe to eat because of additives and preservatives, but I still agree with George Bernard Shaw in some ways when he wrote, "There is no love greater than the love of good food."

Burriss School Destroyed By Fire

An old landmark in Burriss Township disappeared in the early hours of the morning of July 29, 2010 in a dramatic fire. The burning of this historic school seemed to release a torrent of recollections and emotions throughout the area as people shared their feelings about the loss of the school that was "always there." I admit that I shed tears when my son called me with this news and others also reported being deeply affected.

Many have fond memories of this fine old building and of attending school there, as people have a way of remembering the first school they attended. Burriss School was built in 1923 after the Consolidated School Act was enacted in 1914 and replaced two log schools in east and west Burriss. There was bitter opposition to building the school and a vote was held. Many of the residents of Burriss were originally from the United States and several young men took out their naturalization papers to be able to vote in a Canadian election. The decision for the building of the new school passed with the majority of two votes.

John Herrem, whose brick work was second to none, built the school in 1923 on 10 acres of land donated by Dan McCormick. With its two front entrances, it was a beautiful structure with three large classrooms, a library and a teacher's room on the first floor. Hard wood floors, dark wainscoting and transoms above the doors, gave it a look of elegance. Cloakrooms were behind the classrooms and there were little storage rooms off these. Before the installation of electrical power it was lighted with brass hanging gas lamps, and in a day when most schools used outdoor bathroom facilities, Burriss featured indoor toilets that emptied into cesspools. Drinking water was carried in and kept in large crockery urns with little spouts. The poor water supply at Burriss School was perhaps its one drawback.

Students at first were transported to school by horse drawn vans in summer and sleighs in the winter, one of them even being an old fashioned stagecoach. The only stipulation was that the vehicle had to be covered. There was a barn built to stable the horses, as some of the drivers just stayed at the school during the winter days playing cribbage in the kitchen and keeping the fires going in the wood furnaces. The earliest students had many tales to tell about riding in these vans that were heated with small stoves in the winter. There were not nearly as many rules and regulations regarding student safety as there are now, but many of those students speak of that experience with real fondness.

The school also served as a community hall and down the dark wooden stairs steps was the auditorium with a good hardwood dance floor and a stage for concerts and plays. To each side of the stage was a dressing room so it was quite an up to date building. On the south side of the building was the kitchen or domestic science room and to the north was the manual training room. At one time both shop and home economics were taught and agricultural short courses were held there. Behind each of these two rooms were the furnace and wood rooms. Many social events such as wedding receptions, teas, card parties, plays and dances took place in the spacious hall.

The first renovations took place about 1956 after electricity had been installed and major changes were made to the Community Hall. Thereafter, many changes took place over the years to make a more modern school and bring it up safety standards, but the same atmosphere was retained. Burriss and Cornerbrook Schools later operated as one campus and about 1966 the children from the Northwest Bay Indian Reserve began to be bused to these two schools. Burriss continued as the primary school and Freeda Carmody as teacher and then principal for many years.

Perhaps it was because of the design that people often mentioned the warm, comfortable and welcoming feeling that was sensed on entering. Hundreds of children passed through the doors to receive their elementary education. Dozens of teachers taught and guided those children. It is thought that Helen (Angus) Hyre was the teacher/principal of the longest standing at the Burriss School, remembered by former students and fellow teachers alike as an outstanding influence, as well as for the excellent Christmas concerts that she directed and her superb piano playing.

After the school closed in 1996 it was bought by Danny Rea and stood vacant and boarded up looking rather forlorn and deserted but still a familiar landmark viewed with affection. These words from the history book "Connections" might sum up the feelings of local residents. "It was once the hub of the community, echoing to happy cries of children at recess or the sound of lively dance music in the evening as people celebrated the wedding of a local couple. Suppers and teas, meetings and courses, concerts and plays, school inspections and parents' days were all held under this roof."

Even though it stood vacant since 1996 I liked seeing it when I drove by and it evoked a good feeling. I have been asked if I had any special memories of the time I spent at Burriss School.. That is a hard question as it seems that all my memories are special and dear to me. My husband Gale attended school there, all our children were students there and later some of our grandchildren. My aunt Grace Loney had taught there soon after it opened and had enjoyed her time there. It was my first school as a young teacher and I recall the first students that I taught there in 1953-55 with great fondness and can even remember the dates of some of their birthdays. Those children were not nearly as sophisticated as the ones that I encountered when I returned to Burriss School in 1975. In those twenty years television had greatly broadened their scope and influenced even the youngest child.

A real closeness developed among the teachers and support staff. We all knew so much about each other and shared good and bad days. We had the sorrow of losing Colin Paulson, Ardeth Gardner and Robert Smith. We celebrated births in families and mourned with each other in deaths, as we were all united in doing our very best for the students and school and community. It was our school and it was a grand old school.

The building may be gone but never the memories.

Making Connections

*M*any of the local municipalities were celebrating centennials around the turn of the century. LaVallee Township was no exception and plans were underway for a big event in 2004. Council woman Freeda Carmody called me to see if I would consider joining the planning group. Late in 2000 I went to the first meeting of this committee, most of whom I knew. Ken McKinnon, Reeve and chairman, was leading the agenda with talk of ball games, pot luck suppers, concerts and parades. At the second meeting I finally spoke up and said that I was in the wrong place, as all I was really interested in was the history part.

The woman next to me quickly turned and said, "Then you can write the book." This was Joyce Witherspoon who I came to know, admire and rely on through the next years. It was true that I was interested in local history and had contemplated doing more research. I was the great granddaughter of original settlers in Devlin Township and after my marriage I had learned more about Burriss where my husband was raised. When Joyce mentioned a history book I envisioned a photocopied booklet of perhaps fifty pages, neatly done with spiral binding. Our deadline was February 2004 and after talking to others that had done this kind of thing and finding it took about five years, there was a big job ahead of us.

There were several people on the book committee: I was editor, Joyce was the financial expert and dealt with the publisher Friesens of Altona Manitoba, Maxine Hayes worked on research and with pictures and documents, and Freeda Carmody was the liaison with the Council and helped gather stories and interviews. There were many others that helped with research, typing, proof reading and doing whatever was needed at the time, as well on working on the centennial committee as a whole.

At first we were involved with generating interest and sending out requests for family stories and pictures. Several things impacted my work:

(1) I found I knew very little of the history of the municipality.
(2) Joyce envisioned a much more ambitious book than I did.
(3) I knew nothing about putting a book together.
(4) The expense involved was high.
(5) I did not type and resisted getting a computer.
(6) I really loved doing this.

As material started to come in I soon found that my beforehand knowledge just scratched the surface as I jotted down topics to explore. Joyce brought a book called <u>Evergreen</u> that became our ideal of the type of book we might put together. It was a large 9 by 11 inch, beautifully bound hardcover book and was a far cry from the fifty page booklet of my first thoughts. We had instructions that seemed overwhelming from Friesens, the printer, to guide us in the mechanics of putting a book together. Estimates were studied and the large amount of money needed to print the 1000 or more books was to be paid in three installments. An application for a Trillium grant was prepared and we held our breath waiting for an answer.

All my writing was done in long hand as I had no typing skills. Some family histories came in quickly so I spent hours compiling. Research on the historical aspects such as the steam boats on the river, transportation, roads, schools, churches etc of all four townships had to be done. Maxine Hayes was a wonderful researcher, combing old issues of the Fort Frances Times and finding information on the "old timers." She sent everything on to me.

This book should have been done by the generation before us and since so much valuable information had already been lost, it became important to get a history book out before more of the old lore was forgotten. We all realized that we should have listened more and asked more questions of the older generation. On the other hand, I was amazed at how much information was out there to be found with a little digging. Pictures that were excellent in helping tell the story of our past, and documents, even one signed by Abraham Lincoln, were offered and catalogued.

I became excited over small pieces of information such as a date, and my sister once remarked on "how happy Liz was when she found a good obituary." Cemeteries and tombstones, always fascinating to me, had new meaning with the stories they told and I carried my notebook everywhere to record details of interesting interviews with people. I sent out scores of letters and made phone calls. I kept writing and re-writing and the pages began to pile up. Many people dropped in with a story and pictures and we had some wonderful visits over coffee or tea as they shared their family history.

I spent hours every day at this but one's life had to go on and attention given to other duties and family. There were appointments to be kept, a household to run and a family of which to think. My husband Gale had been diagnosed with progressive Parkinson's disease. My mother-in-law Doris died in February 2001, a granddaughter Mira was born in August 2001 to add to our twelve grandchildren, and many other changes and events were to follow in the next years.

June 2002 was the year of the heavy rains and floods that made Rainy River District a disaster area. Our son Lee and family were flooded out by the LaVallee River and moved temporarily. We had been planning to sell the family farm to Lee and Leanne and move to Emo in September. The flood changed that plan and we moved to Emo on June 30 and Lee and Leanne took over the farm.

Through all these changes I kept working and even found there had been a flood of similar proportions in July 1919.

Moving from the family farm where we had lived so long and where Gale had been raised was a major change in our lives. The death of a brother in law Glenn Manty occurred in July 2002 and in October of that year my mother Ivah Anderson, aged 96, died. At times I found working on the book and keeping focused on the task at hand was almost a solace and I knew my mother would approve of what I was doing.

My pages of longhand writing were increasing and I had to get them typed. Gale decided I needed a computer and after conferring with Emily and Rob Roy had ordered one, unknown to me, from Geoff Pearce just before my mother died. Our house in Emo had a small room that I had already chosen as an office and soon after the funeral the computer was installed there. I sat and stared at the screen and the confusing tangle of wires and cables. I was worse than unskilled as I was afraid of the thing.

There were resource people available, mainly family members, and many were the calls for help that went out after I learned to email. I started right in and even though it was a mess I bravely sent out my first document to the committee for proof reading. It came back to me almost completely covered with red marks and arrows and circles. I still have that page and keep it as a humility sheet, but as someone had written "good story" among all the red marks I felt there was hope. It is surprising what one can do when one has to and though I was slow my efforts improved. There is no way I could ever thank all the people that helped me. It was mostly family, but Geoff Pearce was incredibly kind and helpful when I got bogged down. One of the worst errors I made was that no one told me I was supposed to close and exit and I ended up with dozens of programs running.

We realized that the book was going to be far bigger than originally planned and when we heard that we would receive a Trillium grant some of the pressure was off. Money was secondary in my thoughts as I was overrun with documents and research papers. Many people handed in stories and gave me free rein to edit as I saw fit. I would try to make sure that the story flowed and that the dates or information did not conflict. If drastic changes were made the person was notified. Sometimes only a list of names, dates and events was given me and I would endeavour to piece it all together. Others handed over their writing and wanted no changes at all made.

I learned anew the power of language when I made one small change in a story, changing 'was' to 'is'. This involved a relationship and fortunately this error was caught before publication. I was careful not to impose my thoughts or comments, although at times I was tempted.

As editor, I stressed that I would not write anything that would hurt or disparage anyone. Part of one woman's story involved her father who had put their family through real hardships. She wanted this part of her story told but did not want to make her father sound like a terrible person, as he thought he was doing what was best. Her words of praise for what I wrote meant a great deal to me.

The whole process was incredibly fascinating and engrossing and I became totally immersed in the work. It was like a giant puzzle with many pieces, and bit by bit they began to fit together as I found the various connections. Certain characters became so familiar that they were like old friends. I could almost see them in my mind and some even inhabited my dreams. The stories of hardships suffered, deaths of children and spouses, poverty, raw courage and incredibly hard work obsessed me. Pioneer life was harder on a woman than a man, it seemed to me, and I sorrowed over many of the stories.

Gale was great in bringing me back to reality if I got too carried away by the stories of the pioneers, as he was of a more prosaic temperament. Through the years he gave me constant support and was able to give advice and information as he obviously had listened more attentively to his elders. He was an invaluable source of information about the surveying of the townships and could always tell me where certain people lived, and if I gave a location description he was able to tell me who had lived there since it was first surveyed. Gale was very tolerant of my absorption in this project and in how it affected our home life, and he was ready to make any allowances necessary. More changes occurred in his health and there were the increasing demands of local and medical appointments in Winnipeg but we managed.

When I look back now sometimes it is with amazement at how we did manage it all. Six more babies, (two grandchildren, Rowan and Teddy, and four great grandchildren, Cameron, Teagan, Austin and Jack), were born from 2003 to 2007. We had the sorrow of losing another brother in law Lawrence McLeod in 2003 and my brother Alan Anderson died suddenly in December 2005. I tried to keep things in perspective and continued working every available minute.

In choosing a cover design and name, the name took a little longer but realizing how many times we used the word connections and discovering how many of the families were associated with each other, CONNECTIONS became the obvious choice. Proof reading was never ending as a book with no typing errors was the goal. Did we attain this goal? No.

Over seven hundred pictures and documents were handed in. Maxine Hayes was in charge of the huge task to caption and catalogue and there were meetings to choose the 400 pictures that we had estimated would be in the book. Another goal was that each picture submitted would be returned safely to the owner. Did we attain this goal? Yes.

One weekend we went to Altona, Manitoba to meet with the publisher and printer Freisens, a memorable and fascinating experience. A tour showed us the enormous presses and scanners and something of the process our book would go through. We worked one fourteen hour day and six hours the next day, going over every aspect and marking where pictures were to be placed. It was intense work guided by our efficient representative Lynda Hiebert.

At last the final proof was approved and then all we had to do was wait for the book to be printed and shipped, and prepare for the book launch on February 28, 2004. Elegant invitations had been made for dignitaries and the Devlin Hall was full to capacity at the wine and cheese event. No one had seen the books until the first copy off the press was auctioned off by Rod Salchert. It narrowed down to two bidders and the winners were family members Guy Donaldson and Kelly Spicer. The books were beautiful and the pleasure of actually holding mine in my hands was beyond description.

Some responses were very touching and often tears were shed when the book was first seen. I delivered a book to Ella Jewell, an elderly lady that I had conferred with often, and she sat just holding it, not opening it, and as she ran her hands over the cover she said softly, "The book, our book." Then she opened the inside cover to find the location of her father's homestead on the municipal map. It was so touching and responses such as these more than made up for anything I had done in bringing the book to completion. I wished again that my mother might have seen it.

Another person told how her father in-law held the book with tears streaming as he said, "I wish the old timers could have seen this." It was gratifying and moving to receive letters and emails from across the country and to see that many, my brother among them, mentioned being touched to the point of tears.

There was still a nagging feeling with me, a feeling of being unfinished. After the deadline was past there was still material that we could not use as we had reached the quota. A lady approached me and wondered why their story was not in the book. When I asked if she had sent it in she said, "No, I thought Aunt Myrtle did." There were other remarks similar to this. Some material was incomplete and there were stories of others that we had not had time to pursue. I was sorry that we had not been able to include anything about Dance Township. Dance and Burriss townships were very closely associated in the past days of logging and timbering. There was the tragic Dance Fire of 1938 and I wanted to know more about that.

A great deal of information about Dance Township had been written by Lillian LaBelle Kellar and printed in the Fort Frances Times. Maxine Hayes kept sending material about Dance and other families that we had missed and it was impossible to just stop writing. I loved the way the pieces fit together and I realized again how we all were connected in our close knit area.

The documents kept accumulating and one day I printed everything and realized I had to either stop or go further. In March 2006 I called a meeting of the committee and laid out some possibilities. By the end of the evening we decided to go for another book to include more of what we missed in CONNECTIONS plus the history of Dance Township. A possible date was October 2008 as this was the 70th anniversary of the historic and tragic Dance Fire.

The history of Dance was fascinating and finding the whole story of the Dance Fire in the old newspapers was overwhelming, as I had always heard of the fire but never really knew the details. I had tremendous admiration for Lillian Kellar and what she had written. This seemed like an ideal way to include her writing and have it all in one place. So much credit goes to her for the work that she did.

There were several examples of what I called "mystery men" in Dance, often well educated and talented, and one had to wonder just how or why they ended up and stayed in remote and isolated places like Dance Township. I must admit that I did use my imagination more in writing about some of these men such as Billie Bear.

The previous experience helped somewhat but new problems were encountered so we worked away at overcoming the obstacles. The new book would be smaller in content but would contain many pictures and it seemed logical to call it FURTHER CONNECTIONS. It was intended to be a companion volume for CONNECTIONS.

One thing was different since starting this project in 2000 and that was the use of computers. At first Maxine was sending packages to me by various methods and we had a kind of a network but as time went on the email system proved to be much more efficient. I could send out an article for approval or to be proofread and receive a reply soon after. The dealings with Friesens were conducted this way and I could send a picture or corrected article so easily. Joyce had even acquired a new computer so hers was compatible with mine and some days the emails were just flying. By the time we were finished the computer was used almost exclusively.

Neil McQuarrie had been commissioned by the LaBelle family to write the story of the Dance Fire in this anniversary year and a large memorial was being erected to remember the seventeen victims. Harl Dalstrom, retired professor of history from Omaha, Nebraska, was also working on a project about the many fires that took place in the fall of 1938 on both sides of the border. That book was called *We Were not Worried at Dinner Time*. None of the three publications did coincide with the actual date October 10, 2008 but they were not far behind.

We did not reach our original deadline of October but we did want our book printed before the end of the year, so Joyce, Maxine and I made the trip to Friesens in Altona, Manitoba. We found that plans were being made to move their printing presses into a larger building and that our printing might be delayed, but we were hoping to see our book arrive before Christmas. We were surprised and pleased when Lynda Hiebert told us that she had worked with many book committees, but that she had never seen the same committee return to work on a second book.

Things were not good on the home front and Gale's health was deteriorating to the point that I hated to leave him for very long. Joyce kept in touch with Friesens and though it was touch and go, our book was delivered to the Municipal Office December 17, in time for us to get the mail ordered books shipped out. The book went on sale right away and we were able to get the pictures sorted out and back to owners.

More than ten years after beginning the project two handsome books stand on my shelf. I have read that in every person's life there are certain defining moments and having the opportunity to help produce these books has been one of those moments for me. Learning so much about our local history and being able to share it in this way was a unique experience for me. Some of that experience has been involved in working with the computer and finding what an incredibly wonderful and useful tool for writing it is. I have always enjoyed jotting down thoughts and impressions but the computer is such a wonderful tool for writing and storing information.

Not many days go by that I do not do a little writing or some type of research. Since working on the books I have had calls asking for assistance in finding family history." Some were as a direct result of reading the book, others were the result of people calling the local museums, municipal office, libraries or the Fort Frances Times and being given my name. I had a request from the Simon Fraser University in BC from a group doing research on women authors as they were interested in Kate Ruttan, a local author from LaVallee in bygone years.

One person had plenty of prior information right up to the time their ancestor moved to this area and I was able to supply them with past activities here as well as dates of death and burial sites. Several times I have taken pictures of old memorial stones in local cemeteries and sent them on to the family. This research was an unexpected offshoot of working on local history and it was interesting and gratifying to be able to help someone fill in a few more spaces on their family tree. Making connections was and has continued to be a very good experience.

None So Deaf

Before I began to write this, I checked the Internet for quotations about the condition of being deaf and was surprised that there were things written by people ranging from Mark Twain, Leo Tolstoy, Helen Keller and also from Jewish and Italian proverbs. "No one is as deaf as the man who will not listen" these proverbs told me. I am willing to listen but often do not hear. It was a little comforting to know that I was in good company, for wasn't it Beethoven who was deaf?

Losing my hearing was not in my plan of things and I never gave it a thought as my hearing was excellent. I was tuned in to hear the first cry of a child in the night and Gale would often remark that the baby must have slept all night as he did not hear a sound. At night I would awaken thinking I heard a noise or a creak of a floor board and would wake him to go and see what was out there. He did not like this. but would appreciate it when I would hear a neighbour's cows in the garden eating our cabbage or if our cattle broke down a fence to escape. Chasing cows in the dark is no fun but at least I heard them.

My problems began approximately thirty years ago. We were at the lake, my son and I in a canoe, having great fun in the water trying to tip each other out and he won. I got water in my ears which resulted in an ear infection, the first that I had ever had. With antibiotics this cleared up but I noticed an intermittent and annoying ringing or buzzing in my left ear. Dr. O'Sullivan gave this its proper name of Tinnitus and said that very little could be done for it and that you learned to live with it. In all of the years of seeing specialists, tests and reading everything I could find on the subject, Dr. O'Sullivan's diagnosis has pretty well proved correct.

Soon after the noises in my head began, I experienced a terrifying attack of dizziness or vertigo as Dr. O'Sullivan called it. I bent to tie my shoe when the whole room turned upside down, and I fell across the bed unable to move a muscle without my whole world spinning in a sickening fashion. This lasted hours and left me unsteady and very careful how I moved. The doctor referred me to Dr. Robson, an ENT specialist in Winnipeg that I saw three times in all. I had tests and I was diagnosed with Méniere`s Disease, a condition which seems to be a collection of different symptoms, deafness, disturbances in balance, vertigo, and Tinnitus among them and I have experienced them all. I have learned to be very careful to not make sudden movements or turn quickly because of the vertigo.

At first the ringing in the ears was the worst problem. I know that many people have this and it is hard to explain to someone that does not. The noises ranged from incessant ringing, a high pitched tone, buzzing, whooshing like tidal waves, loud roaring and sometimes, the least disturbing, like music far off in the distance. At times the noise was so loud that I was sure that Gale would be able to hear it also, and it seemed to take over my whole life. If I had to describe my tinnitus visually, it would be like the pictures you see of a tornado with the dark vortex and then the whirling and spinning that grows or lessens in its width.

There were things suggested, like giving up coffee, cutting salt intake, and the use of what was called white noise. This was adding another noise like static on a radio, or a noisy fan that was supposed to override the offending noise. There is a machine especially for this but I have not used it. Medication produced undesirable side effects. Over time I learned to distract myself in some way and to try not to give in to the tendency to want to burrow in bed with a pillow over my head. I imagine everyone deals with it in his own way and although Dr. O`Sullivan was sympathetic, his advice of learning to live with it proved true. It has lessened over the years but that may be because I am virtually deaf in my left ear.

I began to realize that my hearing was changing quite rapidly, so back to Winnipeg I went to see specialists and audiologists. I had scans and x-rays, one that was taken through my open mouth to test for tumours. I remember one audiologist so keen on his work that he said he would put a hearing aid on a fence post, although I did not find the analogy comforting at the time. I was fitted for a small in the ear device through the Canadian Hearing Society, and found it did help me hear.

It was amazing to again hear paper crumpling or the TV from the next room. I still had trouble hearing certain voices and could not distinguish voices on the telephone but did find life easier with improved hearing. One day I was working with a student who often had ear infections and remarked to her that she seemed to be in a very good mood. "Yes, "she said, "this morning I could hear the tap dripping." I knew exactly what she meant and am still pleased the days I hear the wall clock ticking.

I retired from work sooner than I might have, as it did not seem fair to the children when I could not quite hear what they were saying in their soft little voices. By now I was wearing a more powerful over the ear type of hearing aid and also trying other devices to improve my hearing.

I found it was important to keep my sense of humour and to be ready to laugh at myself. One time one of the family seemed very surprised when I said there were fresh tomatoes he could use, as I thought he said he had said he was going have a salad. He actually had said he was he was going to have a bath. Most people were understanding, but some found it hard to realize that what they said was not always what I heard.

Like most other situations there are compensations or advantages. I do not hear that annoying whine of a mosquito just as I am dropping off to sleep or the piercingly loud whistle of a night train. I do not hear the barking of a dog at night and I have slept right through a bad storm.

I know it is frustrating for hearing people. I have said that the only thing worse than being deaf is living with someone that is deaf. This was driven home to me when Gale became very hard of hearing and was fitted with hearing aids. But as Gale said, "At least we did not spoil two families." His type of hearing loss was different from mine and he did not understand some of the annoying symptoms that I had. Although we both had difficulty hearing in a crowded situation, he found it terribly distressful and would get upset. He wanted to hear everything.

Over the years in situations like this I have learned to not try too hard and I just kind of retreat. Whether this is good or bad I am not sure but it is less stressful. At a funeral I once attended there was some kind of fan or motor running and I could not distinguish one word until I heard "green pastures" that told me I was at a funeral. In such cases it is not difficult for my mind to go off on a tangent and I think of other things and have composed letters or a bit of poetry in my head. I mean no disrespect but find it amazing where the mind will go at such time.

I am very thankful for the modern technology that has enabled me to hear as much as I do. There are many things available that I have tried. I have a telephone for hearing impaired people, but like it when people will tell me right away who is calling. I use closed captioning on my TV. It has never been recommended that I wear a hearing device in my left ear, but one time my audiologist suggested I try a device that would transfer sound waves from my left ear to my "good ear" somehow. As I am not always able to tell which direction a sound comes from this was helpful. However, this device was not totally compatible with the brand of my aid and kept breaking. Gale, as a veteran, dealt through the VLA for his aids and a Sennheiser was recommended for his TV use. This device was attached to the TV and there was a headphone with dials to adjust the sound. It worked very well for him while I use closed captioning.

There is good in any situation and it was fortunate that I was used to handling and caring for hearing aids. As symptoms of Parkinson's Disease worsened for Gale, he could not manage his aids easily. I made a little box with places for left and right and would often have to remove or place his aids in the boxes or in his ears for him. It was just as easy to clean two sets as one. Inserting the tiny batteries was also impossible for him so I was able to do these things as I was used to it, and could tell if there was any problem with them. As he liked to say, we did not spoil two families.

I bought another piece of equipment with a head piece and a speaker part you aimed at the sound source. It was expensive and I found it really did not help me as much as I had hoped. Gale used it far more than I did for conversations with his friend George Wegman. With anything like this back ground noise is a problem. Now I have something that seems to me very high tech. There is a receiver to wear around my neck that is tuned to my hearing aid and then a microphone that another person wears or that can be placed by a sound source such as TV. This is wonderful for watching a movie and since it has a range of about 30 feet I can go from one room to another. I have used it with a family group and found if I left the room I could hear what they were saying about me. It is also very good to use in the car, especially if one is the back seat. I used to say that the people in the front seat could plot my murder and I would not hear, but not now with my Phonak Device!

Another distressing thing is that music is distorted and I have what is called recruitment where noise builds up and is amplified; thus, the slamming of a door seems to go all through me and is actually painful. Violin music seems to pierce and vibrate and most music is only garbled noise to me. Wedding receptions are not enjoyable and I cannot stay long as it increases the Tinnitus. Fortunately, I can still enjoy some music and find that my car is the best place to listen to and sing along with tapes. Country western music is the best and easiest to listen to.

When we moved to Emo, Gale was worried that the ordinary smoke detector would not be enough for me. The special one that was installed should waken almost anyone with the noise and brilliant flashing lights. I have heard it when I was in the yard and my dinner on the stove set off the alarm. I hope it is never tested in any situation other than this. My door bell also is extra loud as I do not hear a knock. One time when I had a bad ear infection I could hear neither phone nor doorbell and the sense of isolation was very distressing.

Some may just skim through this as it does not apply but many are affected by age or noise related hearing loss. It is a much noisier world and the noise of machines in the work places such as the mill had caused hearing problems for many. The whole environment is filled with noises that cannot be avoided. I live very near the railway tracks and often find the whistles with their different tones startling or almost painful.

The music levels of the younger crowd, with or without headphones, is being warned against by professionals and it is predicted that there will be far more people wearing hearing devices. Some hearing loss is health related and can be helped with surgery or other treatment. It is extremely important to protect your ears if at all possible because it is no fun being deaf, and it is wise to seek professional care as soon as possible. There should be no stigma attached to wearing hearing aids.

I have found myself avoiding certain situations and I know that is probably not good but it is stressful to sit through a meeting or gathering, hearing only a word or phrase here and there. If there are a lot of visual aspects, that helps to piece information together as it is embarrassing to always be asking what was said. In a recent letter my cousin Sybil Johnson expressed it like this:" Deafness does make you live with questions. So often what I've heard isn't what was said. I find if everyone smiles, I smile too. If they look serious I look serious too. It's upsetting when they turn to you and ask, "What do you think?" I laughed when I read this but it is so true.

In an L. M. Montgomery book one of her illustrious characters says, "Nothing's so bad that it couldn't be worse" and that is how I include deafness in my life. I have learned to deal with it in my own way as I am sure most people do. I find it is best in most situations to tell people right away that I am hearing impaired and generally they will try to compensate for that. I am so thankful for the wonderful technology and resource people and can only hope there will always be something that will help me and others like me.

One Day At A Time.

William Shakespeare wrote many years ago that." All the world's a stage," and that every person will go through stages in his life. As one ages the truth of that is realized much more fully than when it was first read in a high school English class.

Sooner or later loss will be encountered and each person will learn to deal with the grief in his own way. Much has been written about the stages of grief and there are support groups and counseling opportunities for people who are experiencing this very taxing emotion that can involve and invade every aspect of your life. Over the years everyone suffers losses and there are people who seem to have had more than their share. You wonder as you grieve with them and for them, how they can deal with blow after blow.

I knew that my mother's mother had died when my mother was about 18 months old and that she and two siblings had been raised by loving grandparents and then later a stepmother who did her best to be a mother. As I grew older I realized that my mother grieved the loss of her mother all her life, to the extent that when she was an aged woman and her mind not clear, she would look at me and say, "Are you my mother?" I did not have the heart then to say, No I am not your mother". My mother also grieved the loss of her first born son.

When I was about eleven, three of my grandparents died in the space of about eight months. I loved them all and mourned their loss in my own childish way but I did yet not understand how the breaking of the continuity of generations affected a family.

My father had died when I was past four and I have only a few memories of him and truly did not miss him until I was an adult. Again, there were many things I did not understand about losing someone. It is good that very young children have that insulation I think. My older brothers found this loss harder, as they remembered more of him, while my younger sister remembered him not at all.

When loss becomes a reality to you it is hard to understand and you search for answers. One of these times was the death of our tiny granddaughter Sarah Emily Mosbeck, only ten days old, daughter of Tom and Emily. My grief, as well as my own sense of loss, was for my daughter and son-in-law and for their little boy Scott who would never know his sister. The loss of a child is one of the hardest things to bear and is never forgotten.

After Gale died July 9, 2009 I began to write of some my thoughts and emotions as a way of sorting things out in my mind. Perhaps I should have done that sooner and I might have been prepared, as in the space of eight years four close family members had died. My mother died in 2002 aged 96, my brother Alan in 2005, my husband Gale in 2009 and then my son Mark in 2010. I have been asked if it is harder to lose a husband than a son and other questions. I cannot say which is harder, just that each loss was different and each draws a different response. No one is quite prepared to lose their mother, no matter what the circumstances. I know how very fortunate I was to have my mother for so many years of my life but at the time of her death I thought to myself, "Already?" and when my brother Eric said that 'we were orphans now' I knew he was only half joking. There is that sense of losing the strongest tie to your whole being.

There are similar feelings on the death of a sibling and the family circle seems violated as the person that has always been there, is now missing. All the memories of childhood flooded back. My oldest brother Alan had protected me in childhood and as adults we spent happy times talking over the "good old days." When the death is sudden, such as his was, the shock leaves you bewildered and stunned, until some sense of the reality hits.

Gale had several health concerns as he had at least two severe heart attacks that were treated with medication before he was diagnosed with Parkinson's Disease. This is a progressive condition and though he did his best to cope with the cruel symptoms it took its toll. He did not give in and continued to keep up his interests such as growing grapes and walking as long as he possibly could and we all admired his perseverance and determination. He kept up with and was concerned with all family affairs and welcomed each new grandchild and great grandchild into the family with delight, while being amazed at, and so proud of the accomplishments of the older ones. Our family may be a bit unusual as there are thirty one years between Scott the eldest grandchild and Teddy the youngest and then Cameron our first great grandchild is four years older than Teddy.

Gale was hospitalized and then in Rainycrest for a few months before he died and others may agree that watching a person slowly lose vitality brings a form of grieving and it is almost like losing a person twice. One night we were called to the hospital to find Gale so unresponsive he could not squeeze my hand and another time he crumpled to the ground at a son's house. Each time we thought it was the end, so we were not unprepared, but even though you realize what is ahead, the shock of the final break is indescribable.

Gale was twelve years older than I and often stressed that I would be left a widow. It is hard to imagine that any wife likes to hear this but Gale was a very pragmatic person and he felt I should be prepared. I often turned a deaf ear to this, in later years in more ways than one. As time went on he increased his efforts to give me advice and to plan what time he had left and to think of every possible detail. He planned his funeral from start to finish. Even though my reason told me the end was imminent I could not think that he would be gone, for how can a living breathing person in the space of a heartbeat be gone? We had been together over fifty two years.

Later I learned, after the natural denial, that disbelief is one of the first stages of grief and as the days followed I kept thinking that I should be feeling more than this incredible numbness. The stress and worry of the past months were still with me and it seemed like I should be doing more, or taking some kind of action rather than just sitting and looking out the window at the same scene over and over, or walking to the river to watch the water flowing endlessly by. Nothing seemed real. During this time I was so tired and would sleep and sleep. If I sat down in my chair for more than five minutes I was asleep and I would wake and be astounded that I had slept for so long. Sleep has always been a bit of defense mechanism for me during times of emotional stress and I realized this, but I was shocked at how much I could sleep and still not feel rested or refreshed.

The support of family and friends cannot be overrated but basically it is up to you to find your way. Other family members are grieving also and finding their ways to deal with the loss. As Gale had been in hospital for over six months I had got used to coming home to an empty house and to being alone, but there was something that I truly missed and I found that it was terribly hard to have no one to tell things to. These were just little everyday things, like who I had met at the post office, a death in the community, the price of coffee, finding something that had been misplaced, new growth on his grapes, a new bird at the feeder or even a silly dream. A dozen times a day I would think, "I must tell Gale" and when I realized he was not there it was almost a physical pain. You do not realize how important this is until it is gone, but that is true of so many things in life, I guess.

As I looked back over the stages of grief I realized I had pretty well run the gamut of them from the numbness, extreme sadness, fatigue, anger, guilt, remorse, unreality, detachment and even a few obscure physical problems.

Guilt had surfaced when my mother was in Rainycrest and both my sister and I felt that we should be caring for my mother at home, even though Mom had decided on her own to go into this type of care. I felt extreme guilt and remorse with both Mom and Gale, and there was always the feeling that I could have done better. I wondered if I had done everything I possibly could have done. Maybe we are meant to feel guilty, maybe we are meant to feel remorse.

It is a common saying that the first year is the hardest as there are so many "firsts" – the first Christmas, the first anniversary or birthday. A year does help put things in perspective and to know that time does not totally heal, but it does lessen the acute and raw sense of loss.

The family and I were recovering and remembering and dealing with things as they arose and then we were faced with losing our son and brother Mark at the age of forty-four. We were totally unprepared for this and were so stunned and completely shaken up. My brother Alan had died suddenly like this and one often hears of someone that died in a similar manner but this could not be happening to us. Mark had complained of "indigestion" pains and had made a doctor appointment, but none of us had any idea that he was so ill. Losing a child is like losing a piece of yourself that can never be regained.

We had a great deal to think about as Mark had had a rather different adult life. He was a bright and happy child, twin to Guy, attended the local schools and did well, was a talented and well liked young man. After completing high school he took a year off and worked before enrolling at Carleton University in Ottawa. It was in his third year there that life changed for him and to some extent also for us.

When we began our family we thought of many things, measles and mumps, broken bones, tooth aches, bruises, cuts and scrapes and all manner of things like this but we never thought of mental illness. Mark called from Ottawa and said he had some problems and wanted to come home. Of course we thought he was just stressed out, too much pressure and that some rest and relaxation would fix things. That was not the case and it was the start of many difficult years. He made an effort to go back to school but could not handle the pressure. These years were filled with doctors, hospitalization, trying different medication, counseling, trial and error, soul searching and questions (always the questions) while Mark struggled with depression and many things that we will never know. There were times of utter despair and times when he chose to be estranged from his family. Doctors for some reason seem reluctant to diagnose early on in these cases and one doctor suggested that dissension in the home might be at the root of Mark's trouble. Gale and I looked at each other, wondering what we had done wrong but were ready to deal with anything that might help. Mark and I spent hours talking and analyzing his earlier years and trying to figure out why this was happening. Then talk did not bring any answers and medication took over.

Over the years it was established that Mark had bi-polar disorder, caused I believe by a chemical imbalance in the brain. He had been on many different medications, completely ineffectual for his problems and some causing other problems. Gradually, with the proper medication and being sure that he took it, he began to be able to cope better. Perhaps as he grew older the cruel symptoms lessened and his moods leveled out and life became more "normal." Mark, from the time he was a little boy, was very social and made friends easily and always had a circle of friends. Throughout the most difficult times he had some friends that supported and never gave up on him and through them he realized the meaning of true friendship.

In the last four or five years of his life we began to see the changes as he got more settled in the apartment building where he had made many new friends. We did not interfere in his life but made sure we were available if he needed us. Mark did not like being in crowded situations but he did begin to take part in family gatherings and other things again. He lived his own life in his own way and that was accepted by all that knew him. He often mentioned helping someone or driving someone to run errands and also drove people to medical appointments in Thunder Bay or Winnipeg. Often he was my chauffeur and Mark and I both enjoyed an afternoon at the casino in Thunder Bay.

The news of Mark's death of heart/respiratory causes was a shattering experience to family and friends but it was not long before we began to realize how many lives he had touched. It was amazing to hear of things that he had done for other people and of people with which he kept in touch. The Face Book tributes were incredible and so heart warming as they described his gentleness, his generosity, his kindness and his wonderful quirky sense of humour. Among other things, one of the memories I treasure is how Mark could always make me laugh.

GUY and MARK DONALDSON–August 2001.Mark is holding his niece Mira Donaldson.

Although grieving at the death of a loved one may be the ultimate, grief can also take other forms, such as grieving the loss of a relationship, an older person may grieve the loss of freedom and independence, another may mourn lost hopes and dreams and lost or wasted opportunities.

Often grief is tinged with "what if." There was grieving such as this for Mark, as he was never able to achieve what he might have been capable of. He was highly intelligent, possessed a friendly warm personality, was always aware of world events, was talented musically and able to express himself well in writing but was just not able to cope with things that other people take for granted like daily routines and the pressures of time constraints and a career. He had to live at his own pace, one of those people that "march to a different drummer." Acceptance was the key for us and above all for him, in accepting what life handed him.

Mark had gone through some very difficult, dark times but had come through this and was able to find his own place in life where he was comfortable with himself and others. No one knows why things happen as they do and there may be a reason, but I am more inclined to think they just happen. I do not like to question either the good or the bad. After the first unbelievable shock and pain there was consolation in thinking that when he died he was at a better place in his life than he had been for a long time. His life had become one of service and of helping others in ways that he could do, touching many lives and making a difference without a thought of how he could benefit from it.

I have found that many people really do not want to talk about and are uncomfortable in the face of someone else's grief. I understand this as I have felt this way also, not knowing what to do or say. It may be better to say something than nothing at all. There is comfort in the squeeze of a hand or just a simple "I'm sorry." I met a friend on the street and she turned and said, "I think you need a hug" and then went on, leaving me feeling the warmth of that gesture. There are times that you do want to talk and usually there are people that understand this need. William Shakespeare wrote. "Give sorrow words," adding that the grief that is not spoken of "bids the heart to break"; however, each must find his own way of dealing with the emotional pain. For me, the phrase, 'one day at a time 'is like a talisman but there are times when it might better be to say one hour a time, as ultimately we all have to live life one day at a time.

I am a lover and collector of good quotations, as no matter what you experience someone else has also experienced that and has written about it, thus you can delve into the wisdom of the ages. Recently I found some words by Don Juan, and while I have no idea of the context in which they were written, they really appealed to me: "You cannot prevent the birds of sorrow from flying around your head, but you can stop them from building a nest in your hair."

While most people will find themselves at some time dealing with a great loss there are ways to live through the stages and be able to let go, although always affected by that loss. The sad reality is that life goes on relentlessly and there are times when you might feel that you do not have the time to grieve properly, as other events unfold around you.

What I have written is from what I have experienced and thought about, fully realizing that my experience will not be the same as that of others. However, I do believe that there are certain stages in dealing with grief, and not all will go through them in the same order. Time does not fully heal but it makes the scars of raw grief a little easier to bear. Grief is the first heart wrenching, world stopping sense of loss that is felt. Then the grieving goes on to be handled the best way you know how—one day at a time.

Closing

$\mathcal{R}$ecently, I read that a true writer knows exactly how and when to end what he is writing. If that is so, I definitely am not in that class. It is also said that a true writer lets nothing stand in his way of writing every day, but again I have failed in that way. As I go through my day, though, I am often forming things in my mind, and that has been true in the past week or two, as I have tried to think about the ending words for this book.

In my Foreword I stated that I had always wanted to write a book, but the book that you have in your hand is quite different from the one that I visualized back in earlier days. Then I thought about just sitting down and starting to write with no interruptions and having the proper beginning, middle and ending and then just being finished with it. As someone wise once said, "Life is what happens when you are making other plans," and that may apply to what has happened to my early ambitions.

That is not at all how this came about, as I wrote in bits and pieces. The thought or memory of an experience would come into my mind and I wrote what I was thinking about at that time and not thinking about it in relation to anything else that I had written. Then I would put it away until another set of thoughts compelled me to sit down and write . The crazy quilt mentioned in the Foreword is a very good term for it, for without a proper beginning and a substantial middle, how can there be a definite ending?

It took a lot of thinking before I finally decided to edit and put my writing together as a book, as I have led a very ordinary life, have not travelled widely, had a limited but satisfying career, have raised a family, and have certainly not attained worldly acclaim. The recent books put out by local authors have my complete admiration and were an inspiration.

The books of those writers, Frank Maraj, Fran Shelfantook, Dave Loney, Elaine Wilson are all on my shelf along with those of Neil McQuarrie, Elizabeth Klug Adam, poetry by Margaret Jewel, Harl and Kay Dalstrom's WE WERE NOT WORRIED AT DINNER TIME and my mother's book OTHER DAYS AROUND ME. A favourite saying is that everyone has a story and with that in mind, and with reading the above books, I decided, "Why not add mine to that list? and so now all that is left is the ending.

It is ten years since Gale and I left the family farm in Burriss and moved to Emo. At that time we were all working together for our move, and also for Lee and Leanne and their boys, whose home had been damaged in the disastrous flood of June, 2002. We all experience life changing events, such as moving, illness, a death, injury or accident, a change of occupation ,a birth, natural disaster, divorce or end of relationship, or winning a lottery. The year 2002 held several of these major changes for us as this was the year of the enormous flood, and the year that we moved from the farm that Gale had lived on most of his life and where we raised our family. Gale had been diagnosed with Parkinson's Disease, another life changing event. In 2002 I was putting in hours every day working at the local history book CONNECTIONS. In October of that year my mother died at an advanced age. Added to these events was acquiring my first computer. One of the lessons we learn is that life goes on, no matter what.

Emo is a very good place to continue the walking that I did in Burriss, and no matter where I start, I usually end up down by the river. The Rainy River is beautiful in any season or mood and is one of the nicest of features of this town. The river walkway is unique with the park and facilities available. The wide main street with its lookouts and benches and stairs to the walkway is a very pleasant place, as well as being an international boundary. I am close to post office, drugstore, grocery store, library, church and clinic, so consider myself very fortunate.

When standing by the river on a morning in May sometimes I can almost see one of those old steam ships coming around the curve of the river with its load of settlers to disembark at the old docks. It must truly have been an exciting event when the first steam ships started coming again in the spring. The history of this town should never be allowed to be forgotten by the younger people.

One thing that I did not continue was the snowshoeing that I had done on the farm since the early1970's. I truly enjoyed this form of exercise and being able to go places and make trails all through our bush where it was not possible to go in summer. I ventured out in nearly any weather accompanied for some years by our Samoyed dog Kemo, sometimes family members or a friend or two but more often alone. The solitude in the woods on a clear crisp winter day, or even when snow was swirling, is a good memory.

Looking back over some of my writing I realize anew how very different my childhood was to my children's childhood, and how vastly different it was to that of my grandchildren and great grandchildren. My early life was not that different to the way my mother was raised, with no electrical power, limited modes of transportation and definitely limited methods of communication. Then the world began to change more rapidly and my children's childhood was quite different to mine.

It might be hard for a grandchild to realize just how Grandmother managed when she was young. Maybe reading this book they may realize why I am still so amazed at the wonders of email, and why it is so hard for me to adjust to the ever changing technological advances. Their Blackberries and IPhones are a far cry from the huge old wall telephone that I had to crank myself. Our big wooden radio that operated on three big batteries took up a small table top. I was in my twenties before I saw a television screen. It is easy now to be in touch with the students at university through email and Skype. I cannot help but compare that to the year I was in Teachers' College at North Bay when during that year my mother telephoned me one time, Gale called me once and sent me a telegram on Valentine's Day. The rest of the time we relied on letters which I would usually receive weekly. I do not like the term Snail Mail but it is descriptive.

The photography is another thing that is very different. Now there are pictures taken of babies when they are minutes old and then scores more follow every step of a child's progress. Our first child was born in October and the first picture of Emily was taken at Christmas that year. From the years that followed I have a small box of little black and white photos of the children, many off centre or of odd poses, as I am not a talented photographer. Both Gale and I had old cameras and mine was one of those where you bought the flash bulbs and put them in one at a time. He thought if we used both cameras and snapped them at the exact same time we would get a good picture. Need I say that we have no pictures from that effort?

Going further back, there are even fewer pictures of my siblings and me as there was limited money for photography in those Depression days. We thumb through the old pictures looking at faces and picking out things in the background. Each picture is familiar to us and now my sister and I have scanned some of them to send back and forth and reminisce about. I am sure there are not many more than a dozen.

Reviewing what I have written, I realize how much I have left out. Not everything that I have written will be of interest to every reader, but to me, in a book such as this, there is a very fine line between what is for the reader and what is for the writer. When my mother wrote she would often state that she could not go into detail or "it makes too long a story to write it all." I understand that a little better now and know that there are many gaps in my story.

We were always thankful that we were able to put our mother's book "Other Days Around Me" together. So many people since then have said that they wished their parents had written of their lives. With that in mind, my writing carries on with my experiences in different times and places. My children's memories will be quite different to mine and perhaps their memories will be recorded someday.

Now even my oldest grandchildren are speaking of the rapid changes just in the past few years making their children's lives different from their own childhoods. Maybe one of them will struggle with a new device, just as I struggled with my computer ten years ago.

Knowledge of these things may belong under the category of local or folk history. Stephen Leacock wrote," I never knew that there was history too, close at hand beside my very own home. I did not realize that the old grave that stood among the brambles at the foot of our farm was history." We are all part of what has gone before.

It takes a while before you realize that we are all living in history and adding to it, each in our own subtle ways. Let us hope that there will always be time enough to remember what has gone before and sometimes to ponder just a little about our own personal histories.